Antonio Mota Pizarro

Strategic Management of Profitability in Banking from an Asset-Liability View

The Moorad Choudhry Global Banking Series

Series Editor
Professor Moorad Choudhry

Antonio Mota Pizarro

Strategic Management of Profitability in Banking from an Asset-Liability View

Macroprudential, Microprudential, Stress Testing and Planning

DE GRUYTER

The views, thoughts and opinions expressed in this book represent those of the author in his individual private capacities, and should not in any way be attributed to any employing institution, or to the author as director, representative, officer, or employee of any affiliated institution. While every attempt is made to ensure accuracy, the author or the publisher will not accept any liability for any errors or omissions herein. This book does not constitute investment advice and its contents should not be construed as such. Any opinion expressed does not constitute a recommendation for action to any reader. The contents should not be considered as a recommendation to deal in any financial market or instrument and the author, the publisher, the editor, any named entity, affiliated body or academic institution will not accept liability for the impact of any actions arising from a reading of any material in this book.

ISSN 2627-8847
ISBN 978-3-11-132816-4
ISBN 978-3-11-132838-6 (PDF)
ISBN 978-3-11-132847-8 (EPUB)
DOI https://doi.org/10.1515/9783111328386

Library of Congress Control Number: 2026944510

Bibliographic information published by the Deutsche Nationalbibliothek
The Deutsche Nationalbibliothek lists this publication in the Deutsche Nationalbibliografie; detailed bibliographic data are available on the internet at http://dnb.dnb.de.

De Gruyter and Walter de Gruyter GmbH are part of De Gruyter Brill.
www.degruyterbrill.com

Questions about General Product Safety Regulation:
productsafety@degruyterbrill.com

Cover illustration: Nikada/E+/Getty Images

Contents

Acknowledgements

Books, even when they bear a single name on their cover, never belong entirely to the person who signs them. In every book, readings, conversations, inspirations, objections, examples and affections converge, without which no reflection would ever take definitive shape. Every work is, to some extent, the sedimentation of a shared time, of another's patience, and of a network of intellectual and personal loyalties that sustain it from places that are often invisible. This book is no exception, as it is indebted, in a profound sense, to those who accompanied me, encouraged me and challenged me during its slow maturation.

I wish to express, first and foremost, my most sincere gratitude to Moorad Choudhry, whose support for the idea of publishing this work provided a decisive stimulus at a particularly crucial stage of the project. Moorad is my 'intellectual father'; I owe my inspiration to him as a result of the practical application of his entire prolific body of work. His intellectual generosity, his willingness to listen and his confidence in the value of this work served, for me, as confirmation that an intuition honed over many years could aspire to become a contribution worthy of being shared. In the realm of specialised thought, where technical rigour often coexists with silent doubt, having the backing of a voice of such authority and prestige in the field was not only an honour, but also an additional reason to persevere. Moorad, you know you are my mentor! Simply thank you for encouraging me, supporting me and always believing in me.

I would also like to express, in a very special way, my gratitude to Juan Ayora Aleixandre, whose help has been, in the fullest sense of the word, invaluable. Few things are as valuable in intellectual work as finding someone capable of acting, with rigour and honesty, as a true critical interlocutor. Juan has been precisely that to me: not only a constant source of support, but also a source of ideas of extraordinary quality. In our conversations, often lengthy ones, my arguments have had to be better justified, my hypotheses have been put to the test, and my conclusions have been forced to gain in precision, consistency and soundness. If these pages now present a firmer argumentative structure and more robust conclusions, this is largely due to the intelligence of his observations, the timeliness of his objections and the intellectual integrity with which he has always known how to disagree. Some forms of support consist of simply being there; his, moreover, has consisted of strengthening.

To the publisher De Gruyter for their faith in the project. To Jaya Dalal, for your infinite patience. This book always seemed to stretch out on the calendar. Jaya, thank you for everything. You are incredible.

And finally, I come to those who occupy the most intimate and essential place in these acknowledgements: my wife, Alicia, and my daughters, Alicia and Irene.

Whilst any extensive work demands dedication, perseverance and sacrifice, those who truly know the human cost of that process are those who share it from a position of daily closeness. They have lived with this book for years, even before it existed as

 | https://doi.org/10.1515/9783111328386-203

such. They have accompanied me in the form of stolen hours, silences, worries, absences and that incomplete presence which so often accompanies long and absorbing work. They have accepted with immense generosity the space this work has come to occupy in our lives, and they have done so with an understanding whose value far exceeds anything I can express here.

To Alicia, the woman of my life, I wish to thank her for her patience, her understanding and her serene love, without which this book would scarcely have come to fruition. Only those who have sustained a prolonged endeavour from within know to what extent one's own effort rests, so often, upon the silent generosity of another. Thank you for always being there and for understanding even that which was not always easy to understand. For having accepted, with unparalleled nobility, the demands of a task that for too long claimed a part of me that also belonged to you. In your support I have found not only comfort in moments of weariness, but also the deep certainty that every effort is worthwhile when it is sustained by a true bond.

To my daughters, Alicia and Irene, I wish to express my gratitude with an emotion that these words can scarcely contain. They have been, even without realising it, the most accurate measure of the time that has passed whilst this book was being written. If at times this work took me away from moments that will never return, it is also true that it was my love for them, and the desire to honour, through this work, a form of personal and intellectual responsibility, that helped me persevere to the end.

To all three of you, I also owe an apology. I apologise for my absences, for so many moments put off, for the hours this book demanded and which, in all fairness, should have been yours. No work can fully make up for that cost, and that is precisely why I wish to acknowledge here, with all humility, that if these pages have seen the light of day, it is not solely due to my dedication, but, above all, to your understanding, your patience and your immense capacity to love without measure. You have supported this project in a way that is deeper than may ever be known, and that debt will remain with me forever.

And finally, Dad, Mum, Jesús, wherever you may be, I hope you feel proud.

Foreword

I've been employed in the City of London since 1989, and during that time have had the privilege to work with some supremely talented people, individuals who genuinely understood how finance works, how the banking system works. One might think that this is a surprising statement to make. Surely most people, if not everyone, who works in finance, particularly those who have achieved senior executive and board positions, should have a genuine understanding of finance?

Well, as they say – you'd be surprised. Finance is not an arena that demands absolute precision in any of its undertakings. In that respect it's quite unlike (say) astronomy, or real "rocket science". Launching satellites that are required to orbit another celestial body, or indeed simply fly by it, or to undertake a soft landing on another planet – these require pin-sharp precision. Or, I should say, absolutely precise mathematics. What we model has to turn out exactly as we modelled it. Otherwise we miss the planet by millions of miles or crash land on it and are destroyed.

Finance isn't like that. Finance is all about assumptions. Some assumptions appear to be realistic, while others are closer to mere finger-in-the-air conjecture. In banking, when I lend money to someone, I have a "probability of default" that may or may not turn out to be accurate, by some margin. When I use my customers' deposits to fund loans that have a much longer "expected life" (hah!) than the deposit base, the expected life of the deposits may turn out to be shorter – much shorter – than I had modelled, leading me into a potential liquidity crisis.

It's quite possible to reach senior exec level in a bank and still not really understand finance. I've worked with one or two of those as well. Of course, it's also possible to have a superb appreciation of how finance works and not reach a senior executive position! The one is not necessarily a pre-requisite of the other. And that's to be expected, because just like in every other industry that employs human beings, other qualities beyond mere technical expertise are also required in order to progress up the ladder.

But in a bank, technical understanding must not be merely a "nice to have", it needs to be an essential pre-requisite. Because unlike in other industries, when banks fail because of management incompetence, the negative impact reaches far beyond the collapsed firm's immediate stakeholders.

Which brings me to this book.

I have known Antonio Mota Pizarro for some years now, and it's evident to me that here is a person who genuinely "gets" finance and banking. Whether it is discussing the proper, and correct, way for a bank's asset-liability committee (ALCO) to be set up and run, or how credit risk, interest rate risk, liquidity risk and foreign exchange risk are not separate elements but all part of an integrated balance sheet risk, and should be managed as such, it's clear that Mr. Mota has realised, as a practitioner, that bank risk management can be merely "adequate", or it can, with some further thought, be "optimum".

 | https://doi.org/10.1515/9783111328386-204

That is why I commend this book to everyone who works in bank balance sheet management, from the Board down. It explains clearly asset-liability management (ALM) concepts that bank senior executives should understand, as well as recommending a specific approach to ALM, that of managing the "pricing gap" (a central tenet of the book), that is genuinely innovative and well worth a read.

But no need to take my word for it – simply take a look for yourself and decide. One of the many things I love about this text is how universal it is. Its concepts are applicable at any bank, in any country, in the world. So much of the financial markets literature out there is really only relevant for developed country markets, or for "G-SIFI" banks. This book is relevant to every bank. It's a refreshing, accessible treatise on what is arguably the most important topic in banking and always has been: how to manage the balance sheet well, and for long-term resilience. Or, as I'm fond of saying, "The balance sheet is everything!".

An excerpt from the author's introduction will suffice to close this account:

> *"In the aftermath of financial crises, regulatory responses have largely focused on strengthening capital requirements … . While their usefulness is not disputed, this book [challenges] the tendency to treat capital as a near-universal solution. Capital absorbs unexpected losses, but it does not correct poor pricing, flawed risk identification or weak balance sheet governance.*
>
> *"In other words, capital provides protection, but it cannot substitute [for] a sustainable business model or adequate governance."*

Spot on 100%.

Professor Moorad Choudhry FCSI FLIBF FRM FIoD
Surrey, England
30th August 2026

Introduction

There is a traditional way of understanding ALM. It is the one that places it, almost automatically, within the perimeter of treasury. It reflects a conventional approach focused on liquidity management, control of maturity transformation, balance sheet sensitivity to interest rates, hedging, and limit monitoring. This view is not only understandable, but for a long time it was also sufficient to explain a significant part of the ALM function. ALM emerged in response to the need to structure the institution's financial profile, ensure its funding capacity, and prudently manage the risks arising from maturity transformation.

However, the limitation of this perspective is that, when it becomes the only one, it ultimately reduces a discipline whose scope is in fact much broader. ALM is not merely about monitoring the balance sheet once it has been built. It is -or should also be- about participating in the decisions that shape it. That is where the real purpose of this book begins.

This book is grounded in the idea that ALM can no longer be interpreted solely as a technical extension of treasury. Its natural domain should be broader, more nuanced and, above all, more strategic. In its most mature form, ALM should cease to be a back-end control function and become a function of balance sheet architecture and optimization, helping determine what kind of balance sheet should be built, with what mix of assets and liabilities, under which liquidity assumptions, with what sensitivity to interest rates, and with what required level of profitability given the risks embedded in the business model.

This change in scale is critical. In practice, it means that ALM should not enter the conversation only when liquidity tensions arise, margins deteriorate, or duration mismatches become evident. It should be involved from the outset. The proposal included in this book is not simply for a more sophisticated ALM in terms of tools, but for a different positioning within the organization.

A key component of ALM is the FTP framework. The book presents FTP as far more than an internal allocation mechanism. A well-designed FTP framework assigns an internal price to funds flowing between the ALM/treasury function and business units, reflecting the marginal cost of liquidity and capital across maturities. However, this book introduces a particularly powerful conceptual shift in FTP and pricing, integrating and connecting the balance sheet, risk, profitability, liquidity, capital, and strategy within a single analytical framework.

In many instances, banking analysis rightly places significant emphasis on risk. However, this book challenges the idea that risk itself should be the core focus. Risk should not be seen on a standalone basis. Banks exist because they assume, transform, and distribute risk. The real issue is not the existence of risk, but the fact that it is not always properly remunerated.

This distinction is fundamental because it reframes the key question. The issue is no longer simply how much risk an institution carries, but whether the pricing of its

 | https://doi.org/10.1515/9783111328386-205

business adequately compensates for the risk structure embedded in its balance sheet. This shift in the ALM perspective proposed in this book is critical because it fundamentally changes the nature of the discussion. The focus moves beyond measuring exposures, setting limits or allocating capital. It becomes a question of whether the bank is building profitability that faithfully reflects the underlying risk structure of its business.

In other words, an institution may operate within prudent limits and still deteriorate the quality of its profitability if it grants credit at insufficient spreads, raises funding without properly internalizing its future cost, which must be reflected in asset pricing or engages in maturity transformation without adequate compensation. Risk alone does not destroy value; inadequate remuneration of risk does.

When this imbalance becomes persistent, problems begin to build, often silently. What appears to be growth may in fact be an accumulation of fragility. What appears to be margin may be a temporary income stream unable to absorb the true cost of the balance sheet. And what appears as profitability may ultimately prove to be conditional on a benign environment. Viewed in this way, the origins of many banking failures lie in accumulated imbalances between price and risk, rather than in sudden disruptions or external shocks. It is not risk per se that destabilizes banks, but its mispricing. This is the fault line that the book places at the center of its analysis.

Several factors such as competitive pressure or the accounting frameworks may contribute to these distortions. One chapter of this book is dedicated to explain these factors.

This book acknowledges the limitations of existing FTP systems and highlights the need for a concept of continuous or "permanent" FTP, applied throughout the life of the transaction rather than only at origination. If strategic ALM provides a coherent view of the balance sheet, and FTP translates that view into internal prices and profitability thresholds, one question remains: how can the gap between observed and risk-adjusted required profitability be measured in real time?. This book introduces the concept of Pricing Gap, which addresses precisely this issue. It is not a standalone metric, but the formal expression of the imbalance between observed and required risk-adjusted profitability.

The ambition of the book extends beyond internal management. Once established, this framework is applied to the analysis of banking crises, stress testing and strategic planning. Banking crises are interpreted as the outcome of accumulated imbalances between risk and remuneration. The Pricing Gap methodology presented in this books offers a tool to assess the sustainability of business models. Stress testing evolves from a purely capital-focused exercise into an assessment of the resilience of profitability under adverse conditions. Strategic planning, in turn, moves away from abstract growth targets toward a more demanding question: what level of profitability can the balance sheet realistically sustain?

Within the prudential framework, this book also introduces a nuanced perspective. In the aftermath of financial crises, regulatory responses have largely focused on strengthening capital requirements and buffers. While their usefulness is not disputed, this book questions the tendency to treat capital as a near-universal solution. Capital absorbs unexpected losses, but it does not correct poor pricing, flawed risk identification or weak balance sheet governance. In other words, capital provides protection, but it cannot substitute a sustainable business model or adequate governance.

In summary, this book proposes more than a new technique. It offers a different way of structuring the discussion about banking. Rather than presenting isolated tools, the book develops an integrated view of banking, one that is relevant for supervisors, regulators, financial institutions, rating agencies and investment banks alike.

The book is structured as a sequence of interrelated themes that progressively build its central argument.

In Chapter 1, the book opens with a description of the basic function of a commercial bank, namely to intermediate between those who save and those who require financing, by buying and selling money and complementing this activity with services remunerated through fees. However, this opening is not merely introductory. Its true purpose is to lay the groundwork for the development of a pricing methodology as the central thread of the book.

In Chapter 2, the book establishes a risk-based profitability model. Financial risks are production factors of the banking business. Credit risk, interest rate risk, liquidity risk and foreign exchange risk are not peripheral elements, but inseparable components of banking intermediation. From this perspective, capital assumes a clearly defined role: to absorb unexpected losses and sustain confidence, but not to replace sound pricing policies nor to compensate for a deficient profitability structure. The conclusion is clear: the problem is not the existence of risk, but its inadequate remuneration and management.

In Chapter 3, the book warns that observed profitability may be misleading. Competition, the accounting treatment of credit risk provisioning and the limitations of accounting information can temporarily mask the economic fragility of the business model. The message is less technical than it may seem: in banking, visible results do not always reflect the quality of underlying fundamentals. Therefore, it is not enough to measure margins or profits; it is necessary to understand whether those margins truly reflect adequate compensation for risk.

Chapter 4 represents the main turning point of the book. ALM ceases to be viewed as a technical function associated with treasury and is redefined as a strategic center of the balance sheet. It emphasizes the need to integrate ALM into daily operations, into new product committees, into ALCO, into Boards of Directors and into strategic planning.

In Chapter 5, after redefining the ALM function, the book focuses on the tool that translates this vision into concrete decisions namely, FTP. FTP is presented as a pricing, profit management, and risk management tool. The chapter also shows how profitability can be decomposed into asset commercial margin, liability commercial margin, and treasury margin derived from maturity transformation.

Chapter 6 is the conceptual core of the book. The Pricing Gap is introduced as a methodology designed to measure the gap between observed profitability and the profitability required to adequately compensate for the risks embedded in the balance sheet. The distinction between PGa and PGt (sustainable and viable banking business) broadens the scope of the analysis, but the most important contribution lies in the shift in perspective: it is no longer sufficient to know whether the bank is profitable, but whether that profitability is economically sustainable.

In Chapter 7, the book applies its analytical framework to the dynamics of crises. The Pricing Gap is therefore proposed as an early warning tool for detecting the economic deterioration of the business. This opens the debate on whether macroprudential policy should continue to rely primarily on capital buffers as currently designed, following the proposal of a novel automatic stabilization mechanism for the banking system based on the Pricing Gap methodology, which bridges macroprudential, microprudential and strategic perspectives within financial institutions.

In Chapter 8, the methodology is extended to the microprudential supervisory domain. The chapter first argues that supervision should place greater emphasis on the quality of profitability, rather than relying solely on formal compliance with capital requirements and buffers. The logic remains consistent with the rest of the book: the Pricing Gap may provide value from a supervisory perspective by enabling the internal assessment of business sustainability.

In Chapter 9, the Pricing Gap methodology is applied to stress testing exercises. The chapter suggests that a stress test should not be limited to measuring losses and capital consumption, but should also assess how the institution's ability to generate sufficient profitability deteriorates under adverse scenarios and in subsequent periods. Integrating the Pricing Gap into this framework makes it possible to link the prudential perspective with the economic deterioration of the business model within a single analytical structure, while also providing a traceable framework for determining appropriate levels of capital add-ons.

Chapter 10 concludes by bringing the framework into a strategic context. The central idea is that a strategic plan is only meaningful if it is grounded in a robust concept of sustainable profitability. It is not enough to grow, gain market share or improve short-term results; this must be supported by a balance sheet capable of sustaining such ambitions.

1 Banking business model: Main aspects

The aim of this chapter is to present some basic principles on banking business models, the main management tools, and a series of relevant business issues, not as a formal definition, but as an introductory basis for the presentation of a novel concept called "pricing gap", which is the cornerstone for strategic profitability management in a financial institution. This concept of pricing gap will be the common thread running through the different chapters of this manual and will be the cornerstone for strategic profitability management in a financial institution.

For a more detailed and comprehensive overview of the banking business model, excellent reference manuals such as Choudhry (2023) can be consulted. Accordingly, it is assumed that the reader has a basic understanding of financial institution management.

1.1 Introduction to the banking business model

The main function of a financial institution is to act as an intermediary between savers, by taking deposits, and investors, by granting loans.

In more common language, it can be said that a financial institution is engaged in buying and selling money, for which it pays and charges interest. In addition, it provides services to its customers for which it charges a series of fees.

Under this more common approach, there are different types of financial institutions (without attempting to be exhaustive and simply for the purposes of explanation):

1. Commercial banks: Their activity is focused on buying and selling money for households, businesses and corporations. Their results depend, to a large extent, on the evolution of the interest margin (NII hereinafter), with all that this implies, as they are highly exposed to the volatility of interest rate curves. This does not mean that commissions for the services they offer their clients are not important in their business, but they have less specific weight in their income statement with respect to total average assets.
2. Investment banks: These institutions generate most of their income from fees arising from advisory services, IPOs, debt issues on capital markets, M&A, etc., which are not subject to the volatility of interest rate curves but to financial markets' developments. They also buy and sell money on their balance sheets, but to a lesser extent.

There is a category of banks, which we can call universal banks, that are hybrids and are currently diversifying their activities and balancing their business between what would be traditional commercial banking and investment banking.

 | https://doi.org/10.1515/9783111328386-001

This handbook will focus on analysing the activities of all those financial institutions whose activities are centred on commercial banking.

1.1.1 Balance sheet and income statement

How are the operations of a financial institution reflected in their financial statements?

On the liability side (Figure 1.1), the balance sheet reflects the purchase of money from financial institutions. These financial resources may be raised through customer deposits, which can come from the retail sector – including households – or from wholesale counterparties, such as institutional investors like banks and insurance companies. Although to a lesser extent since the great financial crisis, financial institutions also obtain deposits through other financial institutions in the interbank market. Capital markets are widely used by banks to finance their growth through various instruments such as senior debt, senior non-preferred debt, covered bonds, etc. Finally, the equity, which includes issued capital, retained earnings and the net profit, as well as various items that reflect the changes in the fair value of financial instruments. Also, there are hybrid instruments (e.g., additional Tier 1 instruments) that share characteristics of both equity and debt, and depending on their specific features, they can be classified as equity. These instruments contain contractual clauses that trigger their conversion into equity when certain conditions are met.

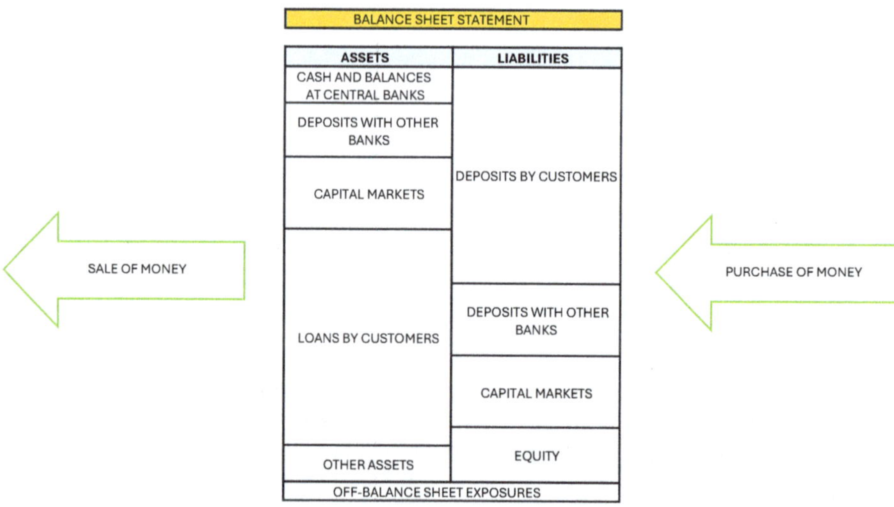

Figure 1.1: Balance Sheet Statement.
Source: Own elaboration.

On the asset side, the process of selling money, or in other words, investments, is reflected. In a commercial bank, loans to customers are the main item in which these institutions invest the resources obtained from customers, which may be classified depending on the type of borrower (households, corporates, institutions, etc.), the type of product (mortgage loans for home purchases, consumer loans, credit cards, commercial discounts, etc.) and the type of collateral securing the exposure (residential real estate, commercial real estate, securities, etc.). In addition, the surplus of deposits that is not invested in loans is placed in the interbank market via loans to other financial institutions (although currently with very low activity), in the capital markets through different instruments such as fixed income bonds or equity instruments, depending on their internal policies for liquidity management. Finally, institutions also keep a reasonable percentage of their reserves deposited with their central banks as a mechanism for maintaining a percentage of liquidity for their payments and also as an instrument for maintaining their central bank minimum reserves requirements, a monetary policy instrument for controlling liquidity in the banking system.

It is through this process of buying and selling money that the transformation of terms carried out by these types of entities takes place. Generally, commercial banks are financing in the short term, or at least in shorter terms, than those they use to invest that money. A positive interest rate slope, which is the most common form, indicates a certain economic growth and expected inflation, so long-term rates, which are those that must be used to set long-term operations, are often higher than short-term rates, which are used to reference short-term operations (or long-term operations when they are variable-rate) with which banks usually finance themselves, thereby obtaining a margin. The process by which commercial banks borrow funds on a short-term basis and lend them out over longer maturities, thereby earning a return or margin from the difference in interest rates, is known as 'maturity transformation'. There is also anti-transformation, which is when the interest rate curve is inverted, which is rather unusual, indicating that long-term rates are lower than short-term rates, where an entity has to adapt its business model in order to generate value.

A financial institution's profitability outlook is reflected in its profit and loss statement (Figure 1.2). Firstly, there is "net interest income", often described as the 'lungs' of a bank, representing the core strength of a commercial bank in carrying out its primary activity: the borrowing and lending of money. It consists of the "interest income" obtained from the investments it has made, such as loans granted, investments in bonds, mortgages, credit lines, etc. These investments may have been granted at a fixed or variable rate and, therefore, this item is sensitive to interest rate volatility. Similarly, there is "interest expense", which are the costs incurred by the banks to fund their activities, such as interest paid on deposits, wholesale debt or funds obtained from central banks or other institutions. Financing can be arranged at either a fixed or variable rate, with the latter typically referenced to a market benchmark such as the Euribor. It is important to note that, while customer deposits are the pri-

PROFIT AND LOSS STATEMENT
Interest Income
Interest Expense
Net Interest Income
Dividends
Commissions and fee income
Trading revenues
Net gains on financial asset/liability at fair value through profit or loss
Net gains (losses) on financial assets available for sale
Net Income (loss) from equity method investments
Other income (loss)
Total Operating Income
Compensation and benefits
General and adminsitrative expenses
Pre Provision Profit
Provisions for credit losses
Impairment of intangible assets
Profit before tax
Income tax expense
Profit after tax

Figure 1.2: Profit and Loss Statement.
Source: Own elaboration.

mary source of financing for commercial banks and are initially fixed-rate when made, they have a balance sheet renewal cycle of roughly six months to one year. As a result, they can be considered quasi-variable, since their interest rates are effectively reset with each renewal cycle.

The next item is total operating income, which is calculated by adding to net interest income the dividends from the bank's investments in shares, fees and commissions from various banking services (such as account maintenance, transfers, card issuance, and securities custody), and income from financial intermediation, including portfolio management advice and insurance activities. Trading revenues, derived from the active management of trading books, are also included, although they remain a residual source of income for a commercial bank.

'Pre-provision profit' is obtained after deducting from total operating income the expenses from employee compensation and benefits and the general expenses incurred in the course of business, such as rent, electricity, non-capitalisable technology expenses, etc. By analysing these expenses relative to the "pre-provision profit", institutions can assess the efficiency of their banking operations.

The assessment of provisions for credit losses—reflecting the materialisation of credit risk—leads to the calculation of "profit before tax". Deducting the applicable taxes from this amount produces "profit after tax".

1.1.1.1 Criteria for accounting for balance sheet items

In Europe, the majority of banks apply the International Financial Reporting Standards (hereinafter referred to as IFRS standards). In general, companies (including banks) whose debt or equity securities trade in a public market in a EU jurisdiction are required to use IFRS standards as adopted by the EU in their consolidated financial statements. For individual financial statements, banks apply the national accounting standards set out in each country's regulations. The most relevant accounting standard applied by banks applying IFRS standards is IFRS 9, which set out rules determining how financial instruments are valued and presented in financial statements, including the recognition of impairments. Despite the differences between IFRS and national accounting standards, the classification of financial instruments and the related impairment rules are often very similar.

The financial assets are classified according to the following categories:

1. Amortised Cost.
   In this classification, the assets are held to obtain their contractual cash flows. These cash flows stem solely from payments of principal and interest (also known as SPPI criterion – "Solely Payments of Principal and Interest"). Accounting of profits is carried out using the effective interest rate method and changes in the fair value of instruments do not affect results, except when the bank recognises a loss allowance for expected credit losses. These allowances reduce the accounting value of the instrument. The majority of loans in banks' balance sheets are classified in this category, but also bonds held to maturity. The 'amortised cost' is usually referred to as the banking book.
2. Fair Value Through Other Comprehensive Income (FVOCI).
   This category includes financial assets held with the aim to both collect and sell their contractual cash flows. Any changes in the fair value of these instruments are recognised in other comprehensive income (OCI). Accrued interest and impairments are recognised in profit or loss. On derecognition, except for equity investment under FVOCI option, fair value gains and losses recognised in profit and loss.
3. Fair Value Through Profit or Loss (FVTPL).
   It is a residual category to be applied when the criteria for amortised cost or FVOCI are not met. Products that fall under this classification criterion may include derivatives, trading book instruments or assets not meeting SPPI criteria. All gains and losses are recognised in profit and loss. The FVTPL category is usually referred to as the trading book.

2 Financial risk and capital

2.1 Financial risks as the banks' production factors

As noted above, a commercial bank's main activity is the purchase and sale of money. In the process of buying and selling money, financial institutions set interest rates on these operations. Price setting—whether fixed or variable, for different terms, and with varying rates across customers—depends, among other factors, on a range of financial risks that arise when origination decisions are made. These risks may be viewed as the production factors on which the banking business pivots. To achieve an appropriate margin, these production factors must also form part of the basis for pricing.

Pricing occurs at the moment an operation is originated; however, financial risks evolve over time and must be actively managed. This is why understanding these risks is essential for developing a comprehensive framework to identify, measure, monitor, control, and supervise each type of risk.

In the risk-identification process, when a bank evaluates which of its risk exposures may have the greatest impact, the answer is straightforward: it is the one that has not been correctly identified. If a risk goes unnoticed, it cannot be measured, monitored or controlled. Consequently, maintaining a rigorous and recurring process for accurately identifying risks is fundamental to the effective management of a commercial bank.

Risk assessment provides banks with a quantitative basis for how much risk they are taking on and provides the basis for correct pricing in the money buying and selling process. Assessment is key not only at the time of business origination, but it is also considered vitally important to reassess it periodically and whether risks are correctly remunerated.

The main financial risks[1] a commercial bank faces would be as follows:

- Credit risk, with concentration risk being a sub-type of credit risk
- Interest Rate Risk Banking Book
- Liquidity risk
- Currency risk

1 The manual focuses on the main risks incurred in the banking business of transforming maturities. Obviously, there are many other risks associated with other activities of financial institutions, such as market risk for trading activities, counterparty risk for all financial derivatives activities, etc.

 | https://doi.org/10.1515/9783111328386-002

2.1.1 Credit risk

Credit risk is one of the fundamental financial risks faced by banks and financial institutions in their operations, notably commercial banks. Historically, poor credit risk management has been a central factor in banking and financial crises, from classic bank failures to systemic ones as when the 2008 financial crisis caused by the collapse of the subprime mortgage market. In essence, credit risk refers to the possibility of losses arising from borrowers or counterparties of the institution being unable or unwilling to meet their payment obligations as agreed (Choudhry, 2023). In other words, it is the risk of default by a debtor, which would result in losses for the creditor in the form of non-payment of expected principal and interest. Given the nature of the banking business – based on credit intermediation and the assumption of credit exposures – rigorous management of this risk is crucial to the stability of banks and the financial system as a whole (Bessis, 2015). In other words, credit risk reflects the uncertainty surrounding the full and timely repayment of loans, investments or any type of credit exposure held by a financial institution (Saunders & Cornett, 2018).

In many instances, credit risk emerges as a consequence of weak governance standards. Poor governance manifests itself through lax lending standards, inadequate portfolio monitoring, or a lack of attention to economic developments that impair debtors' ability to pay. More importantly, deficiencies in governance are often reflected in the mispricing of credit risk.

Regulators and supervisors have significantly strengthened credit risk practices and requirements. European bodies such as the European Banking Authority (EBA) and the European Central Bank (ECB) have published detailed guidelines to promote prudent and consistent credit risk management. These regulatory initiatives are based on lessons learned from past crises. For all these reasons, international supervisory bodies emphasise that banks must adequately identify, measure, manage and control credit risk, as well as maintain sufficient capital to cover it and ensure that the return obtained[2] compensates for the risks assumed.

It should be noted that, although the general principles of credit risk management are applicable to any credit institution, their specific implementation varies according to the nature, size and complexity of each institution's operations. Even so, they all share the objective of maintaining the quality of their assets and avoiding losses that compromise their solvency.

2 The return obtained and within the scope of pricing always refers to pricing at the time of granting, an issue that will be addressed with a broader approach.

Identification of credit risk

Identifying credit risk is the first fundamental step in managing it, as it involves proactively recognising all exposures and factors that could lead to losses.

Credit risk covers a wide range of exposures in banking. It mainly includes traditional loans (retail loans, mortgages, corporate loans), but also off-balance sheet exposures (undrawn credit lines, guarantees, letters of credit) and credit exposures in either the banking or trading book (corporate bonds, counterparty positions in derivatives, etc.) (Casu, Girardone & Molyneux, 2015). Within this framework, a distinction is usually made between:

- Direct credit risk: associated with the possibility of a borrower defaulting on their obligations in active credit transactions (loans, credit accounts, etc.).
- Counterparty risk: a type of credit risk that arises in transactions involving derivative financial instruments or securities financing, where the counterparty may default on its obligations (e.g., in a derivative contract not cleared through a central clearing house) (Hull, 2015).
- Country or sovereign risk: related to exposures to governments or entities in certain countries whose credit risk is influenced by political or economic factors specific to the jurisdiction (Saunders & Cornett, 2018).
- Concentration risk: not a separate type of risk, but a characteristic of credit risk that arises when the credit portfolio is not sufficiently diversified and there are high exposures to a single debtor, economic sector or geographical region. High concentrations can magnify losses if correlated defaults occur in those exposures (Bessis, 2015).

Focusing on a financial institution's loan portfolio (i.e., the banking book), in banking practice, the identification of credit risk begins when a transaction is originated and continues throughout the life of the exposure. Institutions must have an appropriate risk environment and a sound and robust transaction approval process in place, as recommended by the Basel and EBA principles.[3] This involves having transparent policies for assessing applicants' creditworthiness, prudent approval criteria and a defined risk appetite, all of which are set out in their internal credit risk policy manuals.

Before approving a loan, the bank conducts a thorough analysis of the customers: it examines their financial information, credit history, available collateral, economic sector outlook, among other factors. The result of this analysis is reflected in an internal risk rating assigned to the debtor or the transaction. Risk ratings additionally incorporate a component of expert judgement, reflecting the opinion of an analyst or the risk committee. Having a robust internal rating system is vital for identifying the level of risk of each exposure and the portfolio as a whole. In fact, a good rating system allows for the uniform evaluation of all transactions and the detection of those with a higher probability of default, as opposed to a rating based primarily on expert judgement.

3 EBA/GL/2020/06, EBA/GL/2017/06 and Basel Committee on Banking Supervision (2025).

Risk identification should be a continuous process throughout the entire life of the loan. Banks should constantly monitor the credit quality of their debtors and identify early signs of deterioration. The risk monitoring function plays an important role in taking these early measures based on the information available. There are three different approaches to risk monitoring (see Figure 2.1):

1. Systematic monitoring: Defined as the periodic monitoring of risk carried out on individual borrowers or economic groups, based on an analysis of the aggregate position of borrowers using traditional risk reports.
2. Symptomatic monitoring. This monitoring consists of exploiting a series of early warnings that attempt to characterise the current and future payment behaviour of borrowers. These alerts include indicators related to payment behaviour from centralised records, central risk classifications from central bank risk information, changes in the average turnover periods of commercial paper discounted by companies, etc.
3. Management monitoring. This is monitoring in which dashboards are used to obtain a top-down view of the portfolio. It provides an overview of the borrowers positioning in terms of geography, sector, concentration of amounts, aggregate maps of early warnings from symptomatic monitoring, etc.

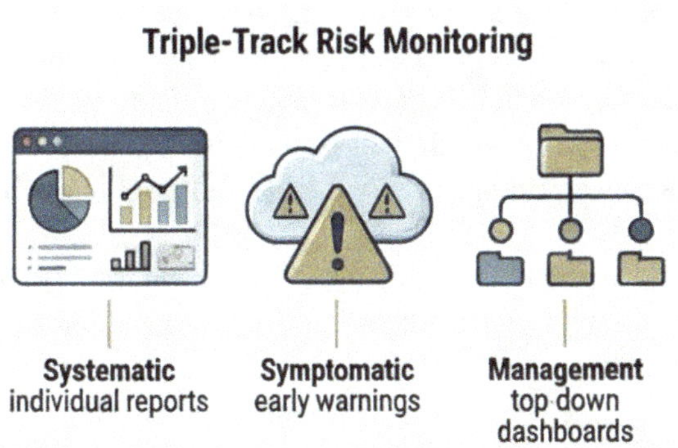

Figure 2.1: Monitoring Credit Risk.
Source: Own elaboration through NotebookLM.

Another critical aspect of risk identification is to clearly define when a loan is considered non-performing or in default. Once a customer defaults, specific management and provisioning measures are activated. It is therefore vital to establish uniform criteria. In the EU, the EBA[4] harmonised the definition of default through guidelines that ensure consistent application across all banks. These guidelines provide clarification

4 EBA/GL/2016/07

on elements such as the arrears threshold (typically, more than 90 days past due constitutes default), indicators of unlikeliness to pay (qualitative factors suggesting that the debtor is unlikely to meet its obligations even without formal arrears, e.g., recurrent negative EBITDA, borrowers operating in sectors facing difficulties, etc.), the criteria for reverting to non-default status, and the application of the definition within banking groups and for retail versus corporate portfolios. Thanks to this harmonisation, all European banks identify defaults using common criteria, improving the comparability of their risk metrics. Another key element of risk identification is the timely detection of default events according to regulatory standards. In some instances, the default event is easy to identify. For example, a loan that is more than 90 days past due or shows clear signs of inability to pay must be immediately recognised as non-performing in internal systems. However, in certain instances, the determination of default includes a substantial component of subjectivity or expert judgment (for example, unlikely-to-pay indicators), which may postpone its recognition.

Credit risk identification also operates at an aggregate level. Banks assess the composition of their portfolios to identify risk concentrations. For example, a high proportion of loans within the same sector or region creates vulnerability to a specific shock (e.g., a crisis in the local real estate sector) that could simultaneously affect many exposures. Similarly, concentration can also arise through significant exposures to individual borrowers or groups of borrowers with strong interrelationships. To address this, prudential regulation sets strict limits on large exposures. For example, in the EU, an institution cannot expose more than 25% of its capital to a single customer or economic group, precisely to prevent a single default from causing catastrophic losses. Early detection of excessive concentrations allows the bank to take action before such a risk materialises.

Banks also analyse the macroeconomic environment to identify emerging risks that could affect the loan portfolios. Factors such as recessions, rising unemployment, interest rate hikes or falling asset prices can foreshadow an increase in defaults. These analyses, which generally originate within the management monitoring function, enable banks to better understand the risk profile of the loan portfolio and thus take proactive measures to mitigate potential losses.

In summary, rigorous and early identification allows for the proper management of the subsequent stages of risk management. In line with the supervisory expectations and standards, proper risk identification ensures that management fully understands the risk profile of the portfolio and can take proactive measures to mitigate potential losses.

Credit risk measurement and quantification

Once the risk has been correctly identified, the measurement and quantification process must be carried out as objectively as possible.

Measurement assesses the magnitude of the risk (e.g., the probability of a customer defaulting and the potential loss given that default), while quantification expresses that risk in numerical values (e.g., expected loss expressed in euros). Accurate measurement and quantification of credit risk are essential for managing the portfolio in an informed manner, establishing sufficient provisions, allocating capital appropriately and ultimately setting prices consistent with risk.

Credit risk can be represented by a loss distribution, which is typically right-skewed (positively asymmetric). The information conveyed by this distribution is commonly summarised using two metrics: expected credit loss and the unexpected credit loss. The expected credit loss, corresponding to the mean of the loss distribution is used to determine the amount of credit-risk allowances a bank must allocate to cover expected losses. In contract, the unexpected loss, which corresponds to a high percentile of the statistical distribution at a specified confidence level, is used to calculate the amount of capital required to protect the bank against unexpected losses. In other words, the risk associated with expected losses is covered through accounting provisions, while the risk of unexpected losses is covered with capital.

The expected loss is determined by three fundamental parameters:

- Probability of default (PD): this is the estimated probability that a debtor will default within a specific time horizon, generally one year. Banks assign a PD to each debtor or instruments based on its risk. For example, a customer with a high internal rating will have a low PD (perhaps 0.5% per annum), while one with a speculative risk profile will have a much higher PD (e.g., 10% per annum). PDs can be derived from internal models based on historical default data or supported by external agency ratings. Banks estimate PDs both to calculate accounting allowances and to determine capital requirements for credit risk. For banks using advanced model approaches under Basel standards, rigorous PD estimation is essential and subject to detailed supervisory guidance.
- Loss Given Default (LGD): this is the percentage of the exposure that would be lost if a default occurred, i.e., 1 minus the expected recovery rate. It depends on factors such as the associated guarantees (type, value and liquidity of the collateral) and the bank's legal position, among others. For example, in a first-lien mortgage loan backed by strong collateral, the expected LGD may be low (e.g., 20% if 80% of the balance is expected to be recovered through collateral enforcement); in contrast, for an unsecured loan, the LGD could be high (e.g. >50%). Banks estimate LGD based on their historical recovery data.
- Exposure at Default (EAD): this is the amount exposed at the time of default. For disbursed loans, it is the outstanding balance; for unused credit lines or contingent products, EAD includes the portion that would likely be used by the customer before defaulting (estimated using conversion factors). EAD determines the basis on which the loss is calculated.

Using these parameters, the expected loss (EL) of an exposure is calculated as the product of the above parameters:

$$EL = PD \times LGD \times EAD$$

This product represents the average expected loss over a given time horizon. This expected loss is typically covered by provisions, as shown in Figure 2.2 (IFRS 9 will be discussed briefly later) and by the financial income from the loan (interest charged). For example, if a loan of €100 has an annual PD of 2% and an LGD of 50%, the expected annual loss is €1 (1% of the balance).

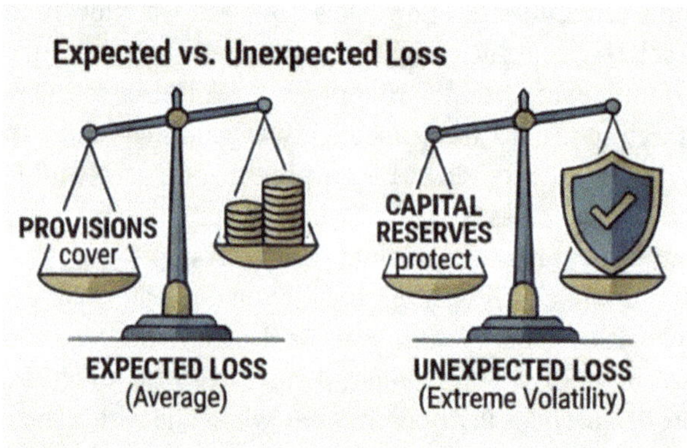

Figure 2.2: Expected vs. Unexpected Loss.
Source: Own elaboration through NotebookLM.

However, as noted above, it is also crucial to estimate the unexpected loss (UL), i.e., losses above expectations that could occur under extreme circumstances. The unexpected loss is associated with the *volatility* of losses (the dispersion around the mean value) and these are covered by capital.

$$UL = \sigma\,(EL)$$

Under the Basel framework, banks are required to hold capital to support unexpected credit losses with a 99.9% confidence level over one year (also known as Credit VaR). This means that capital must cover an extreme loss scenario that would only occur approximately once every 1,000 years. In practice, the difference between the 99.9% Credit VaR and the expected loss defines the unexpected loss that must be covered by capital to ensure solvency even in tail events.

In addition to these calculations, banks use portfolio models to estimate the total loss distribution of their portfolio, considering the possible correlation between defaults. For example, methodologies such as CreditRisk+ or single-factor models such as Vasicek or CreditMetrics allow the aggregate loss distribution function to be projected and loss percentiles to be derived. These models require extensive data and incorporate assumptions about default correlations, but they enable a more comprehensive quantification of overall portfolio risk and help highlight the benefits of diversification or, conversely, the impact of risk concentrations.

Finally, having a complementary measurement tool in stress situations is of high added value for assessing credit portfolios. Banks regularly perform stress tests to estimate how their credit losses would behave under adverse macroeconomic scenarios (e.g., severe recessions, falling real estate markets, sharp increases in interest rates, etc.). These tests provide a forward-looking and 'conditional' view: they allow for the assessment of potential losses in extreme scenarios that, while unlikely, are plausible. Supervisors also conduct periodic stress tests at the systemic level. Stress tests, therefore, serve to verify whether current capital and allowances would be sufficient in highly unfavourable environments, and to encourage preventive adjustments if they were not.

Chapter 8 will take a closer look at the stress tests carried out by the EBA and how they can be integrated into pricing policies.

In summary, credit risk measurement and quantification combine statistical parameters (PD, LGD, EAD) with portfolio models and scenario analysis, as well as accounting considerations (IFRS 9 expected losses). The objective is to obtain as complete a picture as possible of the magnitude of the risk: from average expected losses to unexpected losses in extreme events. Sound quantification lays the foundation for effective risk management, as detailed below.

Credit risk management

Credit risk management comprises the strategies and actions implemented by the institution to mitigate or limit exposure to risk, once it has been identified, measured and quantified. Managing risk does not mean eliminating it (the banking business consists precisely of taking on credit risk in a profitable manner) but rather keeping it within tolerable levels consistent with the bank's financial capacity. To this end, various mitigation techniques and active portfolio management are employed.

A basic principle is diversification: the bank seeks to lend to a wide variety of customers, sectors and geographies to dilute risk. Avoiding excessive concentrations ensures that the problems of a few debtors do not significantly compromise the entire portfolio. As mentioned, identifying concentrations is key; management consists of imposing appropriate limits. Internally, banks set exposure limits per individual customer, economic group, sector, country, product type, etc., in accordance with their risk appetite. These limits act as preventive barriers. Monitoring the use of limits and strict compliance with them is a fundamental part of management.

Another essential mitigation technique is obtaining guarantees that protect the bank in the event of default. Real or collateral guarantees (mortgages on real estate, pledges of securities, etc.) reduce the severity (LGD in other words) of the expected loss by providing alternative recovery assets. Personal guarantees (sureties, bonds) transfer part of the risk to third-party guarantors with better creditworthiness. Taken together, these credit risk mitigation techniques reduce the net risk of a transaction and are recognised by regulation for the purpose of reducing capital requirements, provided they meet certain quality criteria. In practice, the bank must ensure that the guarantees accepted are sufficiently liquid and stable in value and keep their valuation up to date. For example, if real estate is taken as collateral, a conservative haircut is usually applied to its value and it is revalued periodically; if the value falls, measures must be taken to replenish these guarantees.

Other mitigation techniques include netting exposures (offsetting credit and debit balances with the same counterparty, reducing effective exposure) and using credit derivatives to transfer risk. For example, banks can securitise or sell loan portfolios (e.g., NPL packages) to remove credit risk from their balance sheets, although these transactions involve costs and strategic considerations.

In addition to mitigating risk of individual loans, management focuses on actively managing the portfolio to improve its risk profile. This includes diligently managing defaulted assets. When certain loans become delinquent, the bank must act to maximise recovery and minimise the final loss. Some actions are internal: strengthening collection efforts, contacting the customer to renegotiate terms (e.g., granting additional time or grace periods) in order to restore their ability to pay, or formally restructuring the debt (postponing payments, granting partial write-offs, etc.) if this improves the likelihood of recovery. Other actions are external, for example, selling the non-performing portfolio to third parties (specialised investment funds) at a discount, or enforcing guarantees and taking legal action to collect. The choice between one strategy or another depends on the debtor's situation, the bank's position (e.g., whether it needs immediate liquidity) and the expectation of recovery.

In recent years, supervisors have insisted that banks proactively address their non-performing loans (NPLs). The EBA, for example, issued guidelines in 2018 for the management of non-performing and restructured exposures,[5] which require institutions with high levels of NPLs to establish medium-term NPL reduction strategies and strengthen their operational and governance capabilities to execute them. This involves setting quantitative targets for reducing delinquency, creating specialised recovery units, and adopting prudent provisioning and write-off policies.

The keys to good credit risk management include implementing tactical and strategic actions to keep risk within acceptable levels: diversifying the portfolio, establishing prudential limits, using collateral, hedging and other mitigations, actively managing impaired loans (collections, restructurings, loan sales) and adapting strategies to changes in the environment. All of this is supported by solid organisational structures (risk committees, recovery units) and timely information from the measurement and quantification stages. The entity's ability to effectively manage its credit risk and keep

5 EBA/GL/2018/06

it aligned with its risk appetite and loss absorption capacity is fundamental to its solvency and sustained success.

Credit risk control and supervision

Credit risk control refers to the set of mechanisms and governance structures that ensure that risk remains within established limits and that senior management has accurate information to take timely action (Choudhry, 2023).

Strong credit risk governance begins with the management team and Board of Directors: they define risk appetite, approve policies and procedures, and must ensure that there is an independent risk function with authority. Internal controls must be implemented, such as credit risk committees that approve the most relevant transactions involving risk, organisational separation between those who originate loans and those who analyse them, and the principle of dual approval for important decisions.

Similarly, continuous monitoring of the loan and credit portfolio and a transparent flow of information are essential. The management team should receive regular reports with key portfolio indicators (rating distribution, concentrations, delinquency levels, etc.) and any deviations from policies (e.g., limit overruns, approved exceptions), so that no problems go unnoticed.

In addition, banks establish independent review mechanisms. For example, it is good practice to have a credit audit or portfolio review department that regularly assesses the quality of the credit process. This unit reviews samples of loans to verify their correct classification, adherence to internal policies and the adequacy of collateral valuations, reporting its findings to the management team and the Board of Directors. Such independent reviews allow weaknesses in credit management to be detected and corrected as soon as possible. Similarly, internal and external audits periodically assess credit risk, providing recommendations for improving controls.

Another pillar of control is ensuring that the bank maintains sufficient provisions and capital in relation to its credit risk profile. Banks periodically assess, through internal exercises (e.g. ICAAP) and under supervision (SREP), whether their capital and reserves are adequate to cover unexpected credit losses in adverse scenarios. If deficiencies are found, the authorities may require additional prudential measures: for example, increasing regulatory capital (Pillar 2 requirements), limiting dividend distributions or implementing NPL reduction plans. In effect, external supervisors act as the last line of control: they review the entity's credit risk management and internal controls and, if necessary, impose adjustments to strengthen its resilience.

Finally, risk culture is a cross-cutting control factor. If the organisation, from senior management to business staff, shares values of prudence and responsibility in risk-taking, formal controls will work much better. In a strong culture, the spirit of policies is respected, employees are encouraged to report concerns in a timely manner, and excessive risk-taking is not rewarded, even if it generates short-term profits. Conversely, in a culture that prioritises growth at any cost, controls tend to be considerably laxer. Therefore, the management team and Board of Directors must promote an appropriate tone, integrating risk metrics (portfolio quality, compliance with limits, audit results) into performance evaluations and strategic decisions.

2.1.2 Interest rate risk banking book

Structural balance sheet interest rate risk (IRRBB) is an intrinsic aspect of the traditional banking model, stemming from the term and maturity transformation embedded in banking operations. Institutions take short-term deposits and grant longer-term loans, exposing themselves to interest rate fluctuations due to the mismatch between interest rates and maturities. When interest rates fluctuate, they can affect both the economic value of the institution's assets and liabilities and its future financial income, potentially jeopardising the bank's profitability and solvency (Saunders & Cornett, 2018; Lubinska, 2022).

For example, a bank that finances long-term fixed-rate loans with short-term variable-rate deposits faces the risk of rising rates: its deposit costs would increase rapidly while interest income from loans remains fixed, compressing its interest margin and reducing the net value of its assets relative to its liabilities (Bessis, 2015; Lubinska, 2022). Conversely, a liability-sensitive bank with more liabilities repricing ahead of its assets will suffer if interest rates fall, as the return on its assets will fall while its costs are already fixed at a higher level, also causing a decline in the margin. Moreover, many banking products contain explicit or implicit options (e.g., the possibility of early repayment of a loan or early withdrawal of deposits) that introduce uncertainty as to the actual maturity of the cash flows.

Consequently, all banks, regardless of their size, must carefully assess their exposure to IRRBB and explicitly incorporate it into their risk management and internal capital assessment processes (ICAAP), as emphasised in the most recent regulatory guidelines (EBA, 2022).

IRRBB is not just an abstract regulatory concept, but a risk factor that, if managed improperly, can lead to significant losses, capital erosion and financial stability problems for banks. A recent example of its importance was the sharp rise in interest rates that began in 2022 after a decade of ultra-low rates, which tested the measurement and hedging tools of many institutions designed during the period of 'low rates for a long time' (European Central Bank, 2022). Some banks even experienced substantial unrealised losses on their fair value portfolios, contributing to crises of confidence – as illustrated by the collapse of Silicon Valley Bank in 2023, precipitated by large losses from interest rate rises that had not been properly hedged (FDIC, 2024; Metrick, 2023).

In parallel with interest rate risk, banks also face what is known as credit spread risk in the banking book (CSRBB). This risk refers to potential economic losses caused by changes in the credit spreads (due to changes in the credit or liquidity risk premium) of instruments in the banking book, regardless of changes in pure interest rates and excluding the credit risk of specific defaults by individual issuers (EBA, 2022). In simple terms, CSRBB captures the sensitivity of the value of bonds and other fixed-income assets in the banking book to changes in market credit spreads. For example, a general increase in the risk premium demanded by investors on corporate or sovereign bonds will cause their price to fall, generating losses in such securities. This risk has become more relevant in recent years due to the huge volume of bonds that European banks held on their balance sheets as liquidity reserves (often classified in the banking book). In fact, more than 90% of CSRBB exposure in European banks comes from their liquid asset portfolios, such as sovereign debt and bank bonds, according to EBA impact studies. This prompted regulators to require explicit management of this risk alongside IRRBB (EBA, 2022).

Two main components of CSRBB are usually distinguished (EBA, 2022):

a) Changes in the market credit spread which reflect adjustments in the risk premium associated with the overall credit quality of an issuer or market segment. An example would be a broad-based widening of spreads on BBB corporate bonds in response to rising macroeconomic risk. Changes in the market credit spread, reflecting changes in the risk premium required for the overall credit quality of an issuer or segment, e.g., an increase in spreads on all BBB corporate bonds in response to a perception of higher macroeconomic risk.
b) Changes in the market liquidity spread, which reflect adjustments in the premium associated with the liquidity or illiquidity of specific instruments. For instance, during periods of market stress, investors typically require higher compensation to hold fewer liquid bonds, causing spreads to widen.

The correct identification, measurement and management of both IRRBB and CSRBB are essential for the financial stability of banking institutions. Proper management of these risks protects banks' net interest margin and equity value against adverse movements in yield curves or credit spreads, thereby contributing to long-term resilience. Conversely, poor management can lead to margin compression, volatility in results and erosion of the institution's capital.

Banking regulators and supervisors, aware of these dangers, have in recent years reinforced their expectations and requirements for institutions in this area. Bodies such as the EBA and the ECB have issued guidelines and carried out specific assessments on IRRBB/CSRBB, seeking to harmonise management practices and ensure that banks have sufficient capital and controls in place to cover these risks (EBA, 2022; ECB, 2022). In October 2022, the EBA published new final guidelines on IRRBB and CSRBB, replacing those of 2018, incorporating lessons from a prolonged low-interest rate environment and explicitly including credit *spread* risk within the scope of supervision (EBA, 2022). These guidelines, which came into force in 2023, emphasise that IRRBB is a material risk that must be managed in a 'comprehensive, explicit and exclusive' manner within banks' internal risk and capital management processes. The guidelines also require banks for the first time to rigorously assess and monitor CSRBB, although without prescribing methodologies as detailed as those for IRRBB.

Identification of IRRBB and CSRBB

The first step in managing structural interest rate risk is to comprehensively identify all on-balance sheet (and off-balance sheet) positions that are sensitive to interest rate changes. According to the EBA guidelines, the scope of IRRBB covers all banking book instruments that exhibit sensitivity to changes in interest rate, either because the instruments reach their maturity date or because their interest rates adjust periodically (also known as repricing), including assets, liabilities, off-balance sheet items (e.g., credit commitments) and even interest rate derivatives that are not included in the trading book. This identification must also consider non-performing exposures (doubtful assets), net of provisions, to the extent that they generate expected cash flows sensitive to interest rates, even if their recovery is uncertain. In summary, the bank must draw up a complete inventory of interest rate-sensitive items, covering a full range of instruments from fixed and variable rate loans, demand and term deposits, bonds in the banking book, to hedging derivatives (swaps, options) and any other instrument whose value or flow depends on the yield curve.

Within this risk identification process (Figure 2.3), it is crucial to review the different sources or subtypes of IRRBB to which the balance sheet is exposed:

- Gap risk. This is the most basic risk, arising from the mismatch between the interest rate fixation periods of assets and liabilities. If an institution has more assets than liabilities repricing in a certain time period (positive gap), it will be asset-sensitive and typically benefit from rate rises (because its assets reprice earlier at higher rates) and suffer from rate falls; conversely, a negative gap, in which repricing liabilities exceed repricing assets, renders the position rate-sensitive on the liability side. This exposes the bank to rising interest rates, as it is required to pay higher costs on liabilities prior to any repricing of assets. Gap analysis enables the quantification of positive and negative gaps by categorising all interest rate-sensitive instruments into time bands according to their next repricing. This approach allows the assessment of the effects of interest rate changes in each product segment on the bank's net interest margin. Repricing risk is usually measured both in terms of its impact on short-term net interest income (NII) and on long-term economic value.
- Yield curve risk. This corresponds to the risk of non-parallel shifts in the term structure of interest rates, which affect different segments of the curve unevenly. Even if a balance sheet were balanced for a parallel rise or fall in the curve, it could incur losses in the event of distortions in the slope or curvature of the yield curve (e.g., an unexpected flattening or steepening). This risk manifests in the economic value of the bank, defined as the net present value of its assets less liabilities, and is regarded as a component of medium- to long-term structural risk.

Curve simulation methodologies and sensitivity analysis to specific shocks (e.g., steepening or flattening scenarios) allow this component to be assessed. Regulatory standards such as the ones issued by Basel or the EBA propose six standard shock scenarios (parallel up/down, flattening, steepening, etc.) to capture curve shifts and estimate the impact on the economic value (ΔEVE) and net interest income (ΔNII).

- Basis risk. This is the risk that the various reference rates affecting a bank's assets and liabilities may not move in perfect synchronisation. Many banks finance assets referenced to a certain rate (e.g., loans linked to Euribor) with liabilities referenced to another (e.g., deposits whose rate is adjusted at the bank's discretion or debt linked to a different reference rate). If the correlations between these interest rates break down or adjustments occur with a lag, the bank is exposed to basis risk. A typical case is the divergence between market rates (e.g., Euribor, swap curve) and the administered rates that the bank itself sets on savings or loan products. Although the bank can change the remuneration of variable deposits or loans, in practice there is usually a lag in reflecting market movements. Basis risk materialises in losses if, for example, the Euribor falls, but the bank cannot reduce the rate it pays on customer deposits by the same amount.
- Optionality risk. This derives from the presence of explicit or implicit options in banking book products. Explicit options include, for example, early repayment clauses for loans (prepayment option) or early withdrawal clauses for term deposits, as well as bonds with early redemption clauses, etc. Implicit or behavioural options arise from customer behaviour in response to interest rate changes: for example, demand deposits and savings accounts without a defined maturity (non-maturity deposits) behave as options for customers (who can withdraw funds whenever they wish) and for the bank (which can vary the remuneration at any time), or mortgage loans when low interest rates encourage refinancing. These options mean that effective interest rate exposures may change non-linearly with interest rate movements. For example, in the event of a sharp fall in interest rates, many customers may exercise the option to prepay their fixed-rate mortgages in order to refinance at a lower interest rate, leaving the bank with long-term funds reinvested at lower rates (reinvestment risk). Conversely, when rates rise, depositors may move their balances to higher-yielding products or withdraw cash, which may create a risk of deposit run-off if withdrawals become significant. Optionality risk is particularly complex to model and requires behavioural assumptions (customer decisions) and statistical methods – for example, prepayment models based on interest rate spreads, or segmentation of non-maturing deposits into stable "core" and more volatile components (Bessis, 2015; Choudhry, 2023). It is crucial to emphasise that the correct modelling of these embedded options is vital, as incorrect modelling can lead the bank to make flawed balance sheet hedging decisions for IRRBB management, exposing it to losses if

behavioural assumptions are not met. For this reason, regulatory frameworks require rigorous documentation and validation of the behavioural assumptions used for these products (e.g., average life assigned to demand deposits, expected prepayment rates, etc.) and subject them to sensitivity analysis (EBA, 2022).

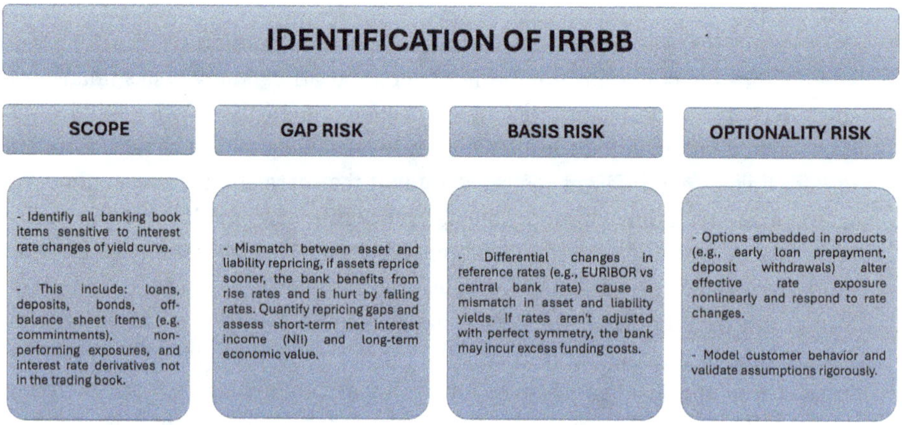

Figure 2.3: Identification of IRRBB.
Source: Own elaboration.

With regard to CSRBB, identification focuses on all balance sheet instruments (non-trading) whose value depends on market credit spreads. According to the EBA guidelines (2022), "no instrument in the banking book should be excluded from the CSRBB scope ex ante, regardless of its accounting treatment, unless it can be demonstrated that it is not sensitive to spreads". This means that even assets accounted for at amortised cost must be considered in the CSRBB assessment if their market value could be affected. Therefore, CSRBB identification should cover all banking book assets that are sensitive to changes in credit spreads. In practice, this will mainly be the treasury/ALM bond portfolio included as HQLA in the LCR, retained securitisations, and certain credit exposures traded in secondary markets. Banks must identify their exposures by rating, sector, and maturity, as spread movements are often linked to these factors. In addition, part of the identification process involves understanding how liquid assets are: the liquidity spread is part of the CSRBB, so highly illiquid assets may experience significant valuation fluctuations in times of liquidity stress.

IRRBB and CSRBB measurement

Risk measurement involves applying quantitative metrics and models to estimate how the bank's economic value and financial income will respond to hypothetical (or historical) movements in risk factors – whether these are variations in the interest rate curve for IRRBB, variations in credit spreads for CSRBB, or combinations of both.

The risk measured is then compared with the established appetite and limits, and management decisions are taken if needed, including hedging, balance sheet adjustments, economic capital allocation, etc.

There are two approaches to measuring IRRBB:

- Economic Value of Equity (EVE) perspective: This consists of calculating the net present value of all future cash flows from the banking book (assets minus liabilities, adjusted for derivatives) and estimating how that net value changes in response to interest rate shifts. It is essentially a long-term sensitivity measure that reflects the impact of interest rate shifts on the bank's equity. The typical metric is ΔEVE, which is measured under interest rate shock scenarios. This perspective is associated with the bank's solvency, as large declines in economic value due to interest rate movements could eventually translate into capital issues (even if they do not immediately show up in the accounts). Regulatory standards issued by Basel and the EBA have paid considerable attention on ΔEVE, establishing a standard to identify banks as "outliers" if the estimated loss exceeds a certain percentage of capital equivalent to 15% of Tier 1 (under different scenarios of shocks). To calculate EVE, it is necessary to have: the expected inflows and outflows for each instrument (considering assumptions about prepayments, deposit behaviour, etc.), an appropriate discount curve, and apply the rate shock to the yield curve to recalculate the values of the different instruments.
- Net Interest Income (NII) perspective: Evaluates the effect of rate changes on the bank's net interest margin (interest income minus interest expense) over a short-term horizon, typically 1 year. This metric reflects the impact on the income statement (profitability flow) rather than on equity value. For example, the NII for the next 12 months is projected under a base scenario (assuming constant rates or using forward rates to roll-out the cash flows of the instruments) and compared with the NII projected under a scenario of rates shift (e.g., +100 bp in the first period and the rest constant). The outcome of this exercise is the sensitivity of the NII. This measure captures the risk of refinancing and repricing in the short term. Many banks calculate ΔNII for time horizons of 1 year and 2 years for various shocks (e.g., parallel shifts and curve movements). It is sometimes expressed as a percentage of base NII or capital. The EBA defines the IRRBB "large decline in NII" threshold (Supervisory Outlier Test) as a 12-month NII reduction. Under the prescribed supervisory interest-rate shocks that exceeds 5% of Tier 1 capital, measured as ΔNII_{12m}/Tier 1.

To quantify sensitivities, regulators have defined a series of standardised shock scenarios that banks must apply when measuring their IRRBB. According to EBA guidelines (aligned with the Basel standard), six interest rate shock scenarios should be considered when calculating the EVE:

1. Parallel upward shock: Sudden increase in all tenors of the yield curve (e.g., +200 bp across the curve, although the exact magnitude may be adjusted by currency, according to Basel standards).
2. Parallel downward shock: Decline in all rates by a certain margin (e.g., –200 bp), except when clauses or instruments with floors are triggered. These floors mitigate the risk of negative rates.
3. Steepening: Non-parallel movement in which the curve's slope becomes positive, i.e. short-term rates fall and long-term rates rise.
4. Flattening: The opposite, where short-term rates rise while long-term rates fall, thus flattening/inverting the curve.
5. Short-term rise scenario: A sharp increase in short-term rates (perhaps reflecting abrupt monetary policy action) while long-term rates rise only slightly.
6. Short-term decline scenario: A sharp decline in short-term rates (e.g., official rate cuts) compared with little change in long-term rates.

Each of these shocks is applied to the entire term structure of rates (in all relevant currencies) and the bank recalculates its economic balance sheet under the new term structure, thus obtaining ΔEVE for each scenario. In addition, for the income metric (NII), at least two main scenarios are usually considered: a parallel upward shock and a downward shock, and the impact on the projected 1-year margin under each scenario is then assessed. Some regulators also require an analysis of a scenario of gradual rate increases and decreases throughout the year. The typical horizon for NII is 12 months, assuming a static balance sheet (no growth) or a dynamic one with certain assumptions.

On the other hand, behavioural models in IRRBB are of vital importance. The most important ones are the behavioural models applied to non-maturity deposits and loan prepayments, as they are essential tools for understanding the real sensitivity of a bank's balance sheet. Their purpose is to estimate how customer decisions in response to interest rate changes affect future cash flows and, consequently, EVE and NII metrics.

Non-maturing deposits are liabilities that are contractually payable on demand, but in practice they tend to be highly stable for two main reasons. First, they are protected by deposit guarantee schemes, so in periods of financial instability customers – primarily households – know they will be repaid by the scheme. Second, these customers exhibit slower withdrawal behaviour than institutional counterparties, who typically reallocate their positions more rapidly due to the absence of deposit-guarantee protection on their balances. Part of households' balances, known as core deposits, behave predictably even in stressful market conditions. To estimate their effective duration, institutions use econometric models or replicating portfolios that transform these non-maturing deposits into theoretical combinations of term instruments. This allows IRRBB measurement teams to assign them an interest rate sensitivity consistently with the rest of the balance sheet. However, these models rely on assumptions about average life, rate elasticity and customer base stability which, if overly optimistic, can lead to an underestimation of risk. The ECB and EBA guidelines therefore recommend limiting the duration of non-maturing deposits, applying conservative horizons and ensuring that results are subject to robust validation.

Prepayment models, meanwhile, seek to quantify the optionality implicit in fixed-rate assets, mainly mortgages and retail loans. Early prepayment affects expected cash flows, reducing the effective duration of the instrument and modifying its sensitivity to interest rates. The simplest approaches use constant prepayment rates, while conditional prepayment rate and multifactorial models incorporate variables such as the interest rate spread, the loan's maturity vintage, seasonality and the borrower's demographic characteristics. The most advanced models integrate macroeconomic and behavioural factors, offering a more realistic view of customer decisions.

Together, non-maturing deposits and prepayment models are essential components of the IRRBB framework, as they allow for a more accurate estimation of structural exposure to interest rate risk. Their effectiveness does not depend solely on statistical sophistication, but also on data quality, methodological consistency and continuous validation. Ultimately, these models must serve a prudential purpose: to provide a reasonably stable and conservative representation of customer behaviour that supports ALCO decision-making and underpins the long-term sustainability of the bank's balance sheet.

In addition to these two macro views, there is a more granular set of tools and metrics that complement IRRBB measurement (EBA, 2015; Lubinska, 2022):

- PV01/DV01 (dollar value of 1 basis point): Indicates the change in the EVE of an instrument (usually in monetary units) in response to a small change of 1 bp in interest rates. It is essentially the first derivative of value with respect to rates (i.e., a measure of linear sensitivity). It is sometimes calculated in aggregate (for the entire balance sheet) or by segments of the curve, providing a quick measure of the exposure to IRRBB.
- Duration and duration gap: Modified duration is another measure of EVE sensitivity that can be applied to net worth (difference between average duration of assets and liabilities, adjusted for size). The duration gap is defined as the difference between the weighted-average modified durations of a bank's assets and liabilities. A duration gap other than zero indicates a mismatch in the balance sheet. If the effective duration of assets is greater than that of liabilities, the entity tends to lose value when interest rates rise, as its long-term assets are more sensitive to interest rate shifts than liabilities.
- Bucket sensitivities: Breaking down EVE sensitivity by maturity bands (e.g., 0–1 year, 1–3 years, 3–5 years, etc.) is useful for identifying the segments of the yield curve where the bank is most exposed. This approach builds on traditional gap analysis but expresses the results in present value terms.
- IRRBB "earnings at risk": Similar to VaR but applied to interest margins. Some institutions employ stochastic interest rate simulations to estimate the statistical distri-

bution of potential NII over a one-year horizon, deriving metrics such as the 95th percentile worst-case outcome, which is equivalent to NII-at-Risk. This incorporates volatility and market correlations. EVaR (Economic Value at Risk) would apply a similar concept to economic value, measuring the loss of value with a given confidence level. It is not an explicit regulatory requirement, but some advanced institutions use it to capture a broader spectrum of scenarios than the six standards.
- Idiosyncratic or historical scenarios: In addition to regulatory shocks, banks frequently assess bespoke stress scenarios, such as replicating the impact of the 2008 financial crisis on the yield curve or a scenario of abrupt rate increases similar to those observed in 2022–2023. This helps to understand impacts in more realistic extreme conditions or scenarios tailored to the bank's risk profile.

The quantification of spread risk in the banking book (CSRBB) remains less mature; however, certain practices are being consolidated following the 2022 EBA guidelines. These guidelines deliberately allowed for flexibility, requiring measurement and control of CSRBB without prescribing a specific methodology:
- CS01/CS02 sensitivity: CS01 measures the change in the economic value of the bank's equity given a one basis point (1 bp) change in credit spreads, showing linear sensitivity to spread risk. CS02, on the other hand, assesses the impact of a two-basis point (2 bp) movement and incorporates non-linear effects (e.g., convexity effects) of a bank's equity value into changes in the credit spreads. Together, these metrics enable the estimation of the impact of credit spread movements on the bank's equity, accounting for both linear and non-linear effects. They are used to identify risk concentrations and calibrate hedging strategies within the ALM framework.
- Deterministic spread scenarios: For example, a parallel upward shock of 50 basis points can be applied across all credit spreads. Alternatively, historical events—such as the 2008 financial crisis, the 2011–2012 sovereign debt crisis, or the COVID-19 shock in 2020—can be analysed to quantify the widening of spreads, which are then applied as adverse scenario shocks. This approach provides a CSRBB stress test. This gives a CSRBB stress test with estimated loss.
- NII or capital horizon: Changes in credit spreads do not necessarily affect contractual interest flows immediately, except in the case of instruments with variable coupons linked to spreads, which are uncommon in typical portfolios. Nevertheless, income may be impacted if the bank chooses to sell assets and realise gains or losses, or if certain instruments—particularly those classified as FVTPL—affect the P&L. To address this, the EBA guidelines recommend that institutions assess CSRBB using the "net interest income plus market value" metric, which captures both dimensions—reflecting impacts on either NII or the capital position (bank's equity).

Although IRRBB and CSRBB are measured separately, it should be noted that, in a real stress scenario, interest rate and credit spread shocks can occur simultaneously. For instance, during a financial crisis there may be a "flight to quality" effect: base rates decline due to central bank cuts, while credit spreads widen. This produces opposing effects—IRRBB may generate gains from falling rates, whereas CSRBB may generate losses from widening spreads. Conversely, an economic expansion could lead to rising rates and spread compression.

In integrated risk management, banks sometimes analyse such combined scenarios. However, for analytical clarity, IRRBB is typically assessed assuming constant credit spreads, and CSRBB is evaluated assuming a constant base curve. Constructing a fully coherent global scenario would require modelling interest rate–spread correlations, which may vary by economic regime. For the time being, regulatory frameworks treat each risk separately to ensure that neither is overlooked.

IRRBB and CSRBB management and control

Effective management of balance sheet interest rate risk requires a comprehensive framework of governance, policies, limits, monitoring and internal controls to ensure that risk remains within the institution's appetite and financial capacity.

In terms of governance and risk appetite, the Board of Directors is ultimately responsible for overseeing the IRRBB management framework and approving the corresponding risk appetite. According to EBA guidelines, senior management should treat IRRBB as a significant risk, explicitly assessing it in its risk management and ICAAP processes. In practice, the Board of Directors approves a specific risk appetite statement for IRRBB, which sets out how much interest rate risk the bank is willing to take on the basis of its capital and business model. These appetite metrics must be aligned with the institution's strategic objectives and business plan.

For day-to-day management, responsibilities are normally assigned at executive level through the Asset and Liability Committee (ALCO) or similar body, which includes senior management members (finance, treasury, risk) and meets regularly, although the ideal approach is to establish an asset and liability management area as the first line of defence within a finance department, where the entire cross-cutting vision of a financial institution's ALM activities is carried out, together with business, funding, treasury and capital planning teams. The ALCO is primarily responsible for making strategic decisions regarding the balance sheet structure to manage IRRBB: for example, deciding on hedging certain exposures, changing the funding structure or adjusting the duration of the banking portfolio. The EBA expects there to be a clear organisational structure, differentiating between first, second and third lines of defence.

The bank must have a written IRRBB management policy, reviewed at least annually, detailing: the objectives of managing this risk, the metrics used, the frequency of measurement, the limits set, the actions to be taken in the event of limit overruns, the modelling assumptions (and procedures for their validation) and the internal reporting mechanisms. This policy should also cover how new products or activities are incorporated.

Subsequently, and based on its risk appetite, the institution must establish a system of internal limits for IRRBB. These limits are usually calibrated using the quantitative metrics mentioned above. Limits must be calibrated in accordance with the bank's risk appetite, which should be more conservative than regulatory thresholds to allow for operational flexibility. They are typically accompanied by lower early-warning triggers to facilitate timely preventive actions (e.g., hedging with derivatives, changes in commercial policies, and financial strategies). When an internal limit is exceeded or is close to being exceeded, the framework should provide for management actions and appropriate escalation. Any breach of the bank's limits should be reported to senior management and the Board, along with a remediation plan. This disciplined framework of limits and corrective actions is essential to ensuring that risk remains under ongoing control.

Among the mitigation strategies for actively managing IRRBB risk, the following classification of strategies can be identified (see Table 2.1):

Table 2.1: IRRBB Strategies.

IRRBB STRATEGIES		
FINANCIAL STRATEGIES	**COMMERCIAL STRATEGIES**	**DERIVATIVES STRATEGIES**
The objective is to match the durations of assets and liabilities through debt issuance or purchased of fixed-income securities	Risk is managed through the use of various loan-based instruments	Derivatives are used to adjust the interest rate sensitivity of assets and liabilities. These instruments are generally employed to hedge structural positions and are typically managed within the interest rate risk book by the entity's treasury, separate from the trading portfolio

– Active ALCO portfolio management
– Extension or shortening of interbank lines
– Asset securitisation
– Issuance of certificates, promissory notes, senior bonds, subordinated debt, etc.
	– Customer deposits:
	  – Structured
	  – Fixed/variable rate
	– Reference-linked demand accounts
	– Mortgage loans
	  – Mixed rate
	  – Fixed rate
	  – Featuring explicitly defined contractual floors, caps, or collars
	– Transaction pricing, including spreads, reference indices, repricing frequencies, early cancellation fees
		– FRAs
		– Interest rate futures
		– Plain vanilla IRS, Amortising Swaps
		– Call Money Swaps
		– Cap/Floor/Collar
		– Swaptions

Source: Own elaboration.

IRRBB and CSRBB monitoring and control

IRRBB must be monitored frequently, with key metrics such as (ΔEVE, ΔNII) calculated monthly and reported on a weekly basis if balance sheet positions change rapidly or economic conditions change. Standard reporting typically includes, among other items:

- Current risk situation relative to limits, including the evolution of ΔEVE, ΔNII.
- Breakdown by factors, showing the contribution of each currency, tranche, and product type to total risk.
- Monitoring of model assumptions, including comparisons between observed prepayment or deposit outflow behaviour against modelled projections.

All this information should be presented to the ALCO and senior risk management. According to the EBA, monitoring systems and standards should include procedures for updating shocks, parameters and scenarios as conditions change (e.g., incorporating a reverse rate stress scenario if the curve inverts).

A crucial control element is independent validation and auditing. IRRBB metrics rely heavily on models (e.g., valuation models, deposit/customer behaviour models). Therefore, there must be periodic independent validation of these models: reviewing methodologies, testing sensitivity to assumptions, backtesting (comparing predictions vs. realities). The IRRBB framework should also be subject to periodic review by internal audit: checking policy compliance, the integrity of the data used in measurements, the effectiveness of daily controls, etc. Supervisors require that validation tests are documented and that any deficiencies detected in models or processes are promptly remedied.

Finally, as part of the ICAAP (Internal Capital Adequacy Assessment Process), banks must assess the amount of own funds allocated to IRRBB. This assessment involves considering extreme scenarios beyond regulatory standards and integrating IRRBB into the bank's overall stress testing framework. If IRRBB indicates the potential for significant losses, the bank may allocate additional economic capital as a buffer. Supervisors, via SREP, review this allocation and may impose additional Pillar 2 capital requirements if the bank's IRRBB risk is deemed high.

In terms of governance, CSRBB should be integrated into the same framework as IRRBB. The bank's risk strategy should explicitly include appetite for CSRBB, possibly with dedicated limits. Operationally, the management of CSRBB risk within the banking book is carried out strategically by the ALCO and tactically by the asset and liability management unit.

CSRBB mitigation tools include:

- Portfolio diversification: mitigate excessive concentrations in exposures that may be subject to correlated spread widening.
- Spread hedging: although more complex and costly, instruments such as credit default swaps (CDS) or CDS indices can be used to partially hedge spread risk, while introducing counterparty and cost risks.

- Active management: in contrast to IRRBB, where the repricing structure cannot easily be changed without significantly affecting the core business, in CSRBB the bank has the flexibility to sell or refrain from purchasing certain bonds. In other words, the bank can manage the portfolio similarly to an investment manager: reducing positions in assets with high spread risk if a widening is anticipated and rotating into safer or shorter-maturity assets. Naturally, such decisions depend on the function of the assets (e.g. liquidity, collateral, etc.). Nonetheless, in principle, the bank could decide to reduce CSRBB risk by voluntarily selling certain positions, assuming the associated losses or costs, if it considers this preferable to incurring larger potential losses.

For CSRBB, as with IRRBB, internal limits should be established. These may include limits on sensitivity measured by CS01, loss limits under stressed credit spread scenarios, and restrictions on bond holdings by credit rating. Active management of these limits should be carried out through ALCO to trigger actions as defined in the governance framework.

In terms of monitoring and incorporating CSRBB into the ICAAP, this should be performed in parallel and in a manner consistent with IRRBB, with stress scenarios designed in an integrated way for both IRRBB and CSRBB being particularly important.

2.1.3 Liquidity risk

Liquidity risk is one of the most critical financial risks that banks and other financial institutions face. In essence, commercial banks transform short-term deposits into long-term loans, thereby assuming the risk of being unable to obtain sufficient liquidity—or only at an unfavourable cost—when demanded by depositors or creditors.

Recent history has demonstrated that inadequate liquidity management can rapidly precipitate severe banking crises. During the 2007–2008 financial crisis, a regulatory "liquidity gap" was exposed. Furthermore, prior to the crisis, existing rules and guidelines on liquidity risk were not sufficiently stringent, which allowed what began as a relatively contained issue to escalate into a widespread banking crisis. It was after this crisis that regulators and supervisors significantly increased their focus on this risk, introducing specific quantitative standards and management guidelines. Both the EBA and the ECB have issued regulations and guidelines to ensure that banks maintain adequate liquidity buffers and sound control practices.

However, recent events, including the collapses of Silicon Valley Bank and Credit Suisse, have highlighted that existing standards remain incomplete, as liquidity risk is inherently complex and closely interconnected with other risks, such as IRRBB, which will be discussed later.

Recent events, including the collapses of Silicon Valley Bank and Credit Suisse, have highlighted that liquidity risk is inherently complex to manage. Similar to capital standards, current liquidity regulations aim to improve the management of these risks; however, they cannot fully prevent a liquidity crisis. Moreover, liquidity risk is often closely interconnected with other risks, such as IRRBB, capital adequacy, and the business model risk, which will be discussed later. In the Silicon Valley Bank and Credit Suisse cases, banks failed due to a liquidity event. However, the underlying causes were typically weaknesses in governance, which led banks to assume risks that crystallised as hidden losses or to maintain unsustainable business models that persisted until investor confidence eroded.

As such, liquidity risk is a fundamental concern for institutional survival, with Choudhry (2023) describing effective liquidity management as "a matter of life and death for the bank".

Now, turning to the definition of liquidity risk, it could be defined, in general terms, as the probability that a financial institution will be unable to meet its payment obligations at the appropriate time and without incurring unacceptably high losses. This risk can be divided into two types:

- Funding liquidity risk: This is the possibility of not obtaining sufficient funds at a reasonable cost when they are needed, leading to the extreme case of being unable to refinance at all. In other words, it is the risk that the bank will be unable to meet cash outflows (e.g., deposit withdrawals, debt maturities) either by obtaining new debt or by selling assets without incurring significant losses. A typical example is a bank run, where a sudden increase in deposit withdrawals forces the hasty sale of assets at fire-sale prices.
- Market liquidity risk: This refers to the difficulty of quickly selling assets or securities on the secondary market at prices close to their fair value. It arises when certain assets are illiquid—such as complex loans or bonds—and the bank incurs significant price discounts when attempting to convert them into cash. Although this risk is typically idiosyncratic or specific to individual banks, during periods of stress it can become systemic, as the realisable value of assets across multiple banks may decline simultaneously
- Contingent liquidity risk: the risk that unexpected cash outflows arise from contingent or off-balance-sheet exposures (draws on committed credit lines, margin/collateral calls on derivatives, guarantees/LCs, or early-redemption options) which typically spike under stress, forcing the bank to secure funding on adverse terms.

Conceptually, it is useful to distinguish between market illiquidity and institutional illiquidity. Adam (2007) refers to market illiquidity risk as the inability to sell an asset quickly without loss of value, and institutional liquidity risk as the inability of a firm to obtain the funds necessary for its operations. In practice, the two aspects are interrelated: in a stressed situation, a bank facing deposit outflows (a funding problem) may be compelled to sell assets at a discount (a market liquidity problem) to raise cash. Conversely, illiquid market conditions further exacerbate the difficulties in converting assets into available cash.

In short, liquidity risk refers both to a lack of liquidity (not having enough money or borrowing capacity when needed) and to a lack of market liquidity (not being able to convert assets into cash without loss). It is a highly non-linear risk: it generally remains latent in normal times, but can materialise suddenly and self-perpetuate under stress, due to panic or loss of confidence leading to massive withdrawals and fire sales of assets. Rigorous management of this risk is therefore essential for the financial stability of institutions and the system as a whole.

As noted above, liquidity risk is not a risk that can be analysed in isolation and is closely related to other risks such as IRRBB. It is recognised that effective analysis and management of this risk require banks to adopt a three-tier activation mechanism based on the evolution of liquidity risk (see Figure 2.4):

1. ASSET PROFITABILITY MODEL: Banks must ensure that the assets on their balance sheets generate returns consistent with the prevailing interest rates indicated by market curves (e.g., the Euro-swap curve in Europe). Why is this necessary? To maintain the financial capacity -specifically sufficient income-, to respond to customer demands for deposit returns. Silicon Valley Bank exemplified this risk: its balance sheet consisted of high-quality, long-term fixed-rate assets funded by substantial deposits from non-household customers, which are typically less stable than household deposits. When the FED abruptly changed monetary policy, money markets offered more attractive interest rates with relatively low risk. Confronted with customer demand for higher returns, the bank was unable to respond, contributing to deposit outflows. This case illustrates the strong correlation between liquidity risk and IRRBB.
   In conclusion, a good asset profitability model is the best natural hedge against funding liquidity risk and will always act as the first line of defence.
2. HIGH-QUALITY LIQUID ASSETS (HQLA): The interest rates offered on customer deposits are typically set above prevailing market rates as customers demand liquidity premiums above the market curve. When the return on assets is not sufficient to remunerate customers, banks must have a buffer of HQLA to address potential accelerated deposit outflows that excess expected progressive outflows. Basically, Essentially, these HQLA are built through prudent management of liquidity buffers, which, when converted to cash, can accommodate accelerated deposit outflows.
3. CONTINGENCY PLANS. If the level of HQLA is not sufficient to address deposit outflows, banks must have a contingency plan in place to convert all the most illiquid assets on the balance sheet, such as customer mortgages, loans to companies, etc., into cash within a very short period of time. This can be achieved, for example, through retained issuances of covered bonds or by mobilizing such col-

lateral via monetary policy facilities, thereby maximising the liquidity of the financial instruments held as assets. The contingency plan, along with its periodic reassessment, serves as a third line of defence, enabling banks to respond effectively to extreme liquidity events.

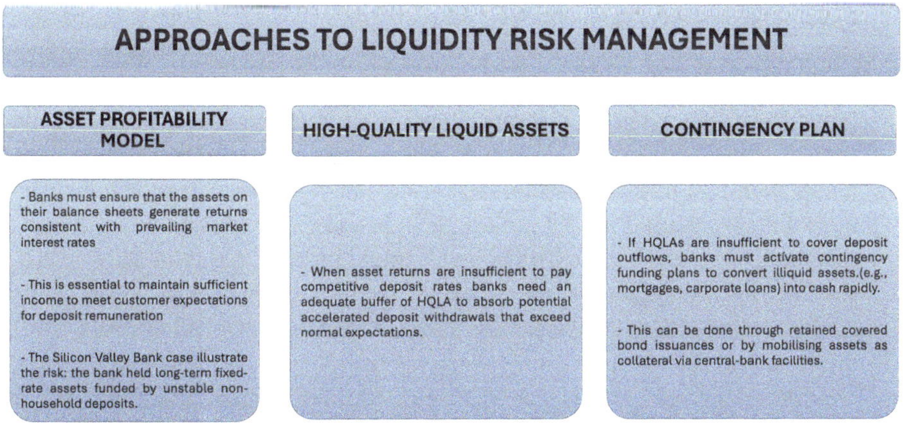

Figure 2.4: Approach to Liquidity Risk Management.
Source: Own elaboration through Copilot.

Identification of liquidity risk

Early identification of liquidity risk exposures is the first step in managing them. It involves recognising where an institution may face a shortage of funds. Some of the key practices and approaches for identifying liquidity risk are:

– Liquidity gap analysis: Banks prepare maturity ladders and projected cash flows for their assets and liabilities over different time horizons (e.g., one day, one week, one month, three months, etc.). This tool shows the time lags between expected cash inflows and outflows. An excess of outflows over inflows in a given interval indicates a liquidity gap that must be covered with liquidity reserves, new sources of funding or, ultimately, by assuming the stability of non-maturity deposits by customers. In banks relying on a retail funding structure, non-maturity deposits are generally allocated to the shorter-term maturity buckets.

  Gap analysis allows for the identification of maturity concentrations (e.g., many bank bonds maturing on the same day) and scenarios in which the bank would depend on external refinancing. Standards (EBA) often require standardised reporting (e.g., maturity ladders) to monitor banks' liquidity positions.

– Review of funding sources and concentration: Identifying liquidity risk involves mapping who the banks' fund providers are (depositor base, wholesale debt investors, counterparty banks, central banks) and assessing how stable those sources are. A bank that is heavily dependent on very short-term wholesale funding, or on a few large depositors, is more exposed to a sudden withdrawal than one with a broad base of stable retail deposits. In its supervisory exercises and guidelines, the EBA emphasises the importance of analysing liability concentration and excessive dependence from a few counterparties: for example, measuring the percentage of funds that come from the 10 largest depositors or the repo market, etc., to detect excessive dependence. Developing deposit matrices based on balance ranges on the one hand and interest rates on the other provides relevant information about the risk of deposit runs. Factors such as the proportion of insured deposits (covered by deposit insurance) versus uninsured deposits are also examined, as the latter are more likely to be redeemed at any sign of trouble.

- Identification of off-balance sheet risks and contingent liabilities: Many obligations with a potential impact on liquidity are not fully reflected in the balance sheet until they materialise. For example, unused credit lines granted to customers (contingent liabilities) could be called upon in a stress scenario, forcing the bank to finance these customers. Similarly, guarantees or letters of credit issued may result in cash outflows under certain conditions. Identifying liquidity risks requires taking stock of these off-balance sheet commitments and estimating how much additional liquidity might be required under different scenarios (e.g., how many credit lines might be drawn if the economy deteriorates).
- Early warning indicators: Banks develop a set of qualitative and quantitative indicators that signal potential liquidity stresses. Some typical examples include:
  - Unusual rates of deposit withdrawals in a day or week compared to historical averages.
  - Significant increases in the cost of short-term funding (e.g., widening of the spread on wholesale deposits or bank notes in the market).
  - Sharp falls in the prices of the bank's bonds or rises in its credit default swaps (CDS) spreads. These indicators reflect the market's perception of higher credit risk and, therefore, its effect on liquidity conditions.

  These warning signs allow emerging problems to be identified before they become critical. For example, if a bank observes net deposit outflows well above normal for several days, this could indicate a loss of customer confidence and require preventive action, which is usually, first and foremost, higher remuneration of customer deposits. Internal risk management usually sets thresholds for these indicators, which, when exceeded, trigger crisis committees or contingency protocols.

- Qualitative assessments and internal processes: Identification is also supported by periodic qualitative reviews. Asset and liability committees (ALCO) assess overall exposure to liquidity risk by considering macroeconomic factors, market perceptions and hypothetical scenarios. In addition, banks document their liquidity processes in an Internal Liquidity Adequacy Assessment Process (ILAAP) report, as required by European standards (ECB/EBA). In the ILAAP, the institution identifies and describes all relevant sources of liquidity risk, its risk appetite in this area, the measurement methodologies used and contingency plans. Supervisors expect banks to consistently integrate the identification of liquidity risks with that of other risks (capital, credit, etc.), reflecting interdependencies, and to update this identification at least annually or more frequently if conditions change.

Liquidity risk measurement

Once the identification process has been completed, it is necessary to rigorously measure and quantify the exposure to liquidity risk. This involves using quantitative metrics and tools to estimate how much liquidity the bank needs under normal and stress scenarios and to assess whether its reserves are sufficient. Among the main measures and quantification approaches are different metrics (LCR and NSFR) that emerged as an evolution of prudential regulation in response to the great financial crisis of 2008/2009 and to address shortcomings in liquidity risk management by banks:

- Liquidity Covered Ratio (LCR): Introduced by the Basel Committee and implemented in the EU since 2015, with phased implementation, the LCR is now the standard metric for quantifying short-term liquidity resilience, under certain assumptions. It is defined as the ratio between the stock of High Quality Liquid Assets (HQLA) and expected net cash outflows over 30 days under a severe stress scenario. Liquid assets are classified into categories according to their liquidity and are computed into the numerator of the LCR after applying haircuts, e.g., Level 1 assets such as sovereign bonds have no discount, Levels 2A and 2B have discounts and volatility limits. A minimum LCR value of 100% means that the bank has sufficient liquid assets convertible into cash (government bonds, central bank reserves, etc.) or cash on hand to withstand 30 days of intensive withdrawals without the need for additional funding. In calculating the LCR, cash inflows and outflows are standardised by applying stress factors defined by regulators. Regulatory standards establish haircuts on HQLA based on the quality and liquidity of the assets, while run-off rates are applied to different balance sheet liabilities according to their stability. For example, it is typically assumed that retail deposits have lower run-off rates compared with wholesale deposits, that a significant percentage of uninsured wholesale deposits will be withdrawn, that certain credit lines will be partially utilised, etc. Banks report their LCR regularly and must disclose it publicly.
- Net Stable Funding Ratio (NSFR): Complementing the LCR, the NSFR is a structural indicator with a longer horizon (one year). It came into force in the EU in 2021. The NSFR relates the amount of available stable funding to the required stable funding that the bank has for its assets and off-balance sheet exposures over one year. In simplified terms, it requires that assets and positions with greater illiquidity or longer maturities (e.g., long-term loans, less liquid investments) be financed largely with stable liabilities (capital, long-term debt, stable retail depos-

its, etc.), avoiding excessive reliance on very short-term funding. An NSFR ≥100% indicates that the institution has sufficient funding considered "stable" for at least one year to support its assets and activities. Measuring the NSFR involves assigning factors to each component of the balance sheet: liabilities are weighted according to their expected stability (e.g., capital and liabilities ≥1 year count as 100%, stable retail deposits ~95%, wholesale deposits <6 months ~50% or 0% depending on category, etc.), and assets according to their need for stable funding (short-term liquid assets require little or no stable funding, long-term illiquid loans require 100% stable funding, etc.). High NSFR levels indicate a balanced funding structure, while low NSFR levels indicate excessive reliance on volatile funding for long-maturity assets.

The LCR and NSFR ratios have contributed to more robust liquidity management practices; however, they are not without limitations, as they rely on assumptions that may not capture all possible stress scenarios, some examples of this may be the concentration of both deposits and clients and illiquid investments.

- Internal liquidity indicators and ratios: Beyond the LCR and NSFR, banks use various internal ratios to assess liquidity over multiple horizons. A common indicator is the loan-to-deposit ratio, which indicates the extent to which the loan portfolio (illiquid in the first instance, as securitisation transactions can be carried out) is financed by deposits, which are traditionally more stable. A loan-to-deposit ratio well above 100% may indicate that the bank is relying heavily on additional wholesale funding to finance its loans, reflecting greater vulnerability. Other ratios include, for example, liquid assets/total assets or liquid assets/total deposits, giving an idea of immediate repayment capacity. Similarly, the liquidity gap analysis mentioned above translates into liquidity indicators by maturity: for example, the cumulative mismatch at 7, 30, and 90 days as a percentage of total assets or total funds, showing the relative magnitude of liquidity shortfalls in those windows. Another useful metric is the survival horizon, which estimates how many days the bank could survive solely on its net liquidity reserve under different scenarios of outflows (expressed in days of survival without new funding).
- Stress models and scenario simulations: The quantification of liquidity risk is particularly dependent on the analysis of adverse scenarios, as it usually manifests itself under stress. Banks perform liquidity stress tests, simulating extreme but plausible conditions to assess the impact of these scenarios on their liquidity position. These scenarios may include, for example:
  - Idiosyncratic shock: A negative event specific to the bank (rumours of insolvency, massive loss of reputation) that causes a massive outflow of depositors and the closure of funding markets for that institution.

  - Systemic market shock: General freeze of wholesale markets, falls in liquid asset prices (due to increased risk aversion), moderate outflows of deposits from many banks at the same time.
  - Combination of both. In each scenario, conservative assumptions are applied (e.g., run rate on different deposits, ability to sell liquid assets at a discount, use of contingent lines, additional collateral requirements, etc.) to calculate the cumulative funding gap over the duration of the stress in different periods.

  This exercise quantifies how much liquidity the bank would lack or have in excess in each case, serving to gauge the necessary buffers. European standards (ECB/EBA) require banks to perform these liquidity stress tests as part of the ILAAP and the supervisory review process (SREP), covering short- and medium-term horizons and considering systemic and idiosyncratic scenarios. A key result is the determination of the worst projected cash deficit, which ideally should be covered by available liquidity reserves; if not, the institution has a liquidity gap that needs to be remedied (either by accumulating more liquid assets or reducing outflows).

  In addition, stress tests are used to design contingency plans and are often reviewed by supervisors to assess the bank's robustness. It should be noted that supervisors also conduct liquidity stress tests at the sectoral or individual level, sometimes executed without the involvement of banks, to compare results and draw conclusions about the robustness of the system and the interconnections within it.

- Additional regulatory liquidity monitoring tools: Basel III and EU standards have also introduced complementary monitoring metrics that banks must report to provide a more granular view of their liquidity risk. These include, for example:
  - Distribution of contractual maturities of cash flows or maturity ladder detailing inflows and outflows on a weekly basis.
  - Concentration of funding by significant counterparty, identifying dependence on a few large funding providers.
  - Concentration by type/instrument. For example, percentage of short-term wholesale funding.
  - Measurement of unencumbered available assets that could be used as collateral.
  - Intraday liquidity metrics. Monitoring of peaks in intraday payment needs. For example, the Basel standards require banks to monitor their intraday liquidity positions on a daily basis (maximum debit peaks, available intraday collateral, etc.), recognising that even banks with sufficient liquidity on a daily basis could fail to make critical payments within the same day. These additional metrics do not currently carry standardised minimum limits such as LCR/NSFR, but they provide crucial information for supervisors and for internal management.

- Measuring market liquidity: Institutions also quantify the market liquidity risk of their positions. For example:
  - Assigning "liquidity levels" to each asset:
    - Level 1: immediately tradable without material loss
    - Level 2: saleable at some discount
    - Level 3: illiquid or sellable only at a large discount or over a long period of time

    This can be based on bid-ask spreads, daily trading volumes, number of market participants, etc. One indicator used is the price spread. Assets with very wide spreads or that spike under stress are more illiquid.
  - Settlement time: how long it would take the entity to liquidate a position given its size without moving the price by more than X%. For example, a bank might estimate that to sell its corporate bond portfolio (worth, say, €100 million) in 5 days, it would have to accept a discount of Y%. These estimates can be incorporated into stress tests (applying stronger haircuts to less liquid assets).

Liquidity risk management and control

Liquidity risk management consists of a set of policies, procedures and actions that institutions implement to maintain their liquidity profile within acceptable levels, all within their risk appetite or tolerance, thereby ensuring their ability to meet their obligations even in adverse scenarios. The fundamental components of liquidity management are discussed below:

- Corporate governance and organisational framework: Effective management begins with strong involvement of the governing bodies in liquidity and liquidity risk management. The Board of Directors and senior management must define a clear appetite for liquidity risk, i.e., how much liquidity stress they are willing to tolerate. This appetite is translated into specific limits and targets (e.g., minimum internal LCR level above the regulatory 100%, target size of the liquidity buffer, limits on negative liquidity gaps, etc.). The asset and liability committee (ALCO) or, failing that, the asset and liability management unit as the first line of defence, is usually responsible for day-to-day monitoring of the liquidity position, reviewing periodic reports on metrics and raising alerts when limits are approached. Likewise, the second line of defence, the risk function, must have an independent role in measuring and reporting liquidity risk, validating liquidity models and monitoring policy compliance. The EBA and the ECB emphasise that institutions must include liquidity risk in their comprehensive risk frameworks and in their recovery plans (in case emergency measures need to be activated). In addition, there should be a Contingency Funding Plan (CFP) approved at the highest level, detailing the actions to be taken in response to different levels of severity of idiosyncratic or systemic liquidity crises (e.g., sale of specific assets, use of credit lines, activation of central bank financing, communication to the market, etc.)

and those responsible for executing them. This plan should be tested periodically to ensure its effectiveness.

- Incorporation of liquidity costs into financial management: Good liquidity risk management is not limited to the treasury department. When banks grant long-term fixed-rate loans, where liabilities have a considerably shorter duration, future problems may arise in scenarios of rising interest rates. When depositors demand higher returns, and loans have not been properly hedged against interest rate risk, financial institutions may fail to generate enough income to meet these demands. As a result, even under moderately challenging conditions, they might have to sell or discount deposits at central banks, and in more severe scenarios, activate contingency plans. For all the above reasons, banks must have adequate incentives in place for the correct setting of interest rates, at least at the time of origination of the transaction. This is typically achieved through a Funds Transfer Pricing (FTP) mechanism that assigns a cost to liquidity for transactions and products according to their liquidity cost, which is based on the assessment of structural risks including structural interest rate risks on the balance sheet, liquidity risk and currency risk. In this way, business units incorporate the correct pricing of liquidity risks into their decisions, aligning their incentives with the bank's overall liquidity strategy.
- Liquidity buffer and liquid asset management: Banks should maintain a sufficient buffer of high-quality liquid assets (HQLA) that can be quickly converted into cash. This issue is regulated by the aforementioned LCR. However, institutions must make their own estimates based on their experience. Therefore, financial institutions must work along the following lines. Assets typically include central bank reserves, sovereign bonds and other eligible securities that can be sold or repoed with minimal loss of value even under stress. The composition and size of this liquidity buffer are calibrated based on the results of the measurements and stress tests described above. The quality of the buffer is crucial: treasury managers must ensure diversification in this portfolio of liquid assets (avoiding concentration in a single issuer or asset type) and monitor associated risks such as market or interest rate risks of these assets (although they are high quality, their value may fluctuate). A related concept is counterbalancing capacity, which encompasses not only HQLA but also the ability other reliable sources (e.g., committed credit lines with other institutions or the central bank's discount facility). Part of day-to-day management involves monitoring the intraday and short-term liquidity position, optimising the use of a temporary surplus of cash and investing it without compromising its availability in the short-term.
- Diversification of funding sources: A basic rule for mitigating liquidity risk is to seek a diversified funding base in several areas: by type of investor (retail vs. institutional), by instrument (deposits, bonds, commercial paper, interbank loans, etc.), by term (combining short, medium and long maturities, avoiding excessive reliance on a single date), and by markets/geographies. Diversification reduces

dependence on any single source which, if it were to suddenly dry up, would put a bank in difficulty. The EBA[6] has published specific guidelines on the preparation of medium-term funding plans, urging banks to project their expected funding needs and sources and to proactively manage risks such as large refinancing needs or high dependence on funding that is susceptible to withdrawal (e.g., large uninsured wholesale deposits, which in LCR carry high withdrawal coefficients). In practice, banks often set internal limits on the maximum proportion of funds that can come from a single source or counterparty. Another dimension is currency diversification, i.e. ensuring that sufficient liquidity is available in each relevant currency (or access to currency swaps) to cover needs in that currency, thus minimising conversion risks in times of market stress.

- Continuous monitoring and internal controls: Effective control requires close and frequent monitoring of the liquidity position. Banks maintain daily liquidity dashboards reporting cash balances, liquid asset positions, daily LCR (even if regulatory requirements are monthly), daily and weekly liquidity gaps, etc. The risk function independently verifies the integrity of these metrics and ensures that established limits are met. If any metric approaches a risk threshold (e.g., LCR falls to a certain internal level), an early warning should be triggered. In addition, internal controls include periodic audits of liquidity management processes to ensure that approved policies (e.g., limits, liquid buffer composition, quarterly stress tests, contingency plan updates) are being executed correctly and that the information reported to senior management is reliable.
- Intraday liquidity management: An often underestimated but increasingly important element is the management of intraday liquidity risk. This is the risk of not being able to meet payments on time throughout the day (e.g., payments in real-time settlement systems, margin calls from clearing houses, etc.). Traditionally, it was assumed that if the net position was solvent at the end of the day, intraday liquidity was not a problem, but it can precipitate a crisis of confidence. European supervisors[7] conducted a thematic review of intraday liquidity practices in 2023-2024, identifying good practices such as: real-time monitoring of intraday flows and collateral positions, setting intraday limits, explicitly incorporating intraday risk into risk appetite and contingency plans, and ensuring that banks have sufficient pre-positioned collateral at central banks or payment systems to meet peaks in intraday liquidity demand. Incorporating intraday management means that treasury closely coordinates payment outflows to minimise gaps during the day and maintains intraday credit lines with counterparties or the central bank to cover hour-to-hour imbalances.

6 EBA/GL/2019/05

7 European Central Bank (ECB). (2024). Sound practices for intraday liquidity risk management. Supervision Newsletter, 13 November 2024.

- Preparation for using last-resort liquidity support: As part of their management, institutions also consider extreme scenarios where they exhaust their private sources of liquidity and must resort to the lender of last resort (central banks). Banks therefore pre-qualify eligible assets as collateral for emergency credit from the central bank (e.g., in Europe, the ECB has lists of eligible assets that banks can deliver in exchange for liquidity). Having a reserve of discountable assets (e.g., securitised loan portfolios or illiquid but eligible bonds) ready and uncommitted is a prudent strategy.

Finally, effective control is also achieved through independent oversight: internal and external auditors periodically assess whether the institution complies with liquidity policies and whether the assumptions used (e.g., in stress tests) remain valid. All of this is also under the control of supervisors, who, through the Supervisory Review and Evaluation Process (SREP), examine each bank's liquidity management and can demand improvements or even impose restrictions if they find material deficiencies.

2.1.4 Currency risk

Currency risk arises from the exposure of balance sheet items to movements in exchange rates. In the financial literature, Choudhry (2023) distinguishes between two main categories of currency risk.

- Transaction risk: This is the most immediate and "contractable" risk. It arises when there is a contractual cash flow in foreign currency. The risk is that, between the date the transaction is fixed and the settlement date (payments or collections), the exchange rate may change unfavourably, affecting the final amount in the domestic currency. Transaction risk, also called contractual risk, covers accounts payable and receivable, loans receivable or payable in foreign currency, dividends to be repatriated, etc. Its management is usually a priority, as it directly affects cash flows. The key feature of this risk is that it is associated with items already contracted (committed exposure) with future maturity in foreign currency.
- Translation risk: This affects multinational financial institutions or those with assets and liabilities denominated in currencies other than the currency in which their financial statements are presented. It occurs when converting the accounts of subsidiaries or items in foreign currency into the parent company's currency in order to prepare consolidated financial statements. This risk, also known as accounting risk, does not involve immediate cash inflows or outflows (it does not affect daily cash flow), but it can influence shareholders' decisions (for example, when evaluating the value of foreign investments) or have a direct impact on the capital position of a group.

Identification of currency risk

Identifying currency risk in a financial institution involves recognising all sources and magnitudes of exposure that the entity has to movements in exchange rates. Given that virtually all areas of a bank's business can generate some form of currency exposure, the task of identification requires a comprehensive approach, covering the balance sheet, off-balance sheet operations and projections of future cash flows in foreign currency. A basic principle is that the bank must know its net open position in each relevant currency, understood as the (algebraic) difference between all assets denominated in that currency and all liabilities denominated in that same currency. In addition, off-balance sheet positions involving foreign exchange risk (e.g., notional amounts of exchange rate derivatives, currency positions for contingent transactions, etc.) must be incorporated. The net open position per currency shows whether the bank is "long" in a currency (i.e., it has more assets than liabilities in that currency, making a gain if the foreign currency appreciates, or a loss if it depreciates) or "short" in it (more liabilities than assets, a situation in which an appreciation of the foreign currency results in losses for the bank because it increases the cost of its net liabilities). These positions by currency constitute the base exposure that the bank faces to movements in each exchange rate and quantifying them is the first step in measuring the exchange rate risk.

It is important to note that currency risk is considered a structural risk, as it can arise from the entire balance sheet, affecting both assets and liabilities in the banking and trading books.

Effective identification is usually organised by differentiating the sources of currency risk that exist in the bank's operations. In general terms, the currency risk can be originated in three main areas (in line with the two conceptual categories discussed above):

- Exposures from commercial transactions and operations: These arise from day-to-day banking activities involving foreign currencies. Examples include loans granted to customers in foreign currency, deposits taken in foreign currency, international trade financing, international payments and transfers, etc. A commercial bank may have a portfolio of loans in dollars or Swiss francs granted to local residents; at the same time, it could take deposits in those or other currencies, or issue dollar-denominated bonds on the international market. Each of these transactions generates a future inflow or outflow of foreign currency and therefore an exposure to currency risk. These exposures are typically identified in the relevant business unit (corporate banking, treasury, foreign trade, etc.) and their management is centralised in the bank's asset and liability management (ALM) area.[8]

8 For reasons of focus, the concepts of indirect exposure are not introduced, where a customer is financed in one currency, but their operating income is in another, generating a potential credit risk in the event of volatility scenarios that are not managed correctly.

- Structural exposures from investments in foreign entities: These are linked to the aforementioned conversion or translation risk. If a bank has subsidiaries or branches in other countries with different currencies, the bank's equity interest in those entities, as well as the portion of profits reinvested there, constitute a long-term exposure to currency risks. When preparing consolidated financial statements, these foreign investments must be converted to the parent bank's functional currency at the closing exchange rate, generating potential accumulated exchange differences in equity (other comprehensive income). These structural exposures are identified by quantifying, for each currency, the value of investments in foreign subsidiaries (generally equivalent to the net equity in local currency of each subsidiary). This figure indicates how much of the bank's capital is exposed to fluctuations in that currency. Due to their long-term nature, many banks choose not to fully hedge these exposures, or do so only partially, as hedging would involve costs and eliminate the geographical diversification of foreign investment. Therefore, in terms of identification, the bank must maintain an up-to-date inventory of its structural foreign currency positions (capital invested in subsidiaries, undistributed earnings abroad, etc.) and quantify the sensitivity of its capital ratio to different exchange rate scenarios. The internal capital adequacy assessment reports (ICAAP) required by the supervisors typically include this analysis, in which the bank demonstrates how its CET1 ratio varies in response to exchange rate shocks, identifying the most influential currencies.

Currency risk measurement

Once foreign currency exposures have been identified, the bank must quantitatively measure currency risk to understand the magnitude of potential losses under different market conditions. Currency risk is measured using various metrics and approaches, ranging from simple calculations based on nominal positions to complex statistical models that estimate distributions of losses and gains, analogous to those employed in quantifying market risk. Below is a very brief overview of some of the quantification techniques used in currency risk management:

- Net open position by currency and aggregate exposure: The starting point for measurement is the net open position in each currency, defined as value of assets and net of liabilities (including derivatives) in that currency. This net position, typically expressed in the original foreign currency and sometimes also converted to the bank's functional currency at the current exchange rate, indicates the amount of the bank's exposure to changes in that exchange rate. In the standard Basel methodology, it is the basis for calculating capital requirements for currency risk. This approach has limitations: it does not consider diversification across currencies. Even so, the calculation of net open position remains a key metric reported in financial and regulatory reports; many banks set internal limits on this metric.

- Sensitivities and simple scenario analysis: Another way to quantify currency risk is to calculate the sensitivity of the value of the bank's position to hypothetical changes in exchange rates (also called delta). This is sometimes expressed as "how much money would the bank lose or gain if each currency depreciated by X % against our base currency?" For example, the ECB sometimes includes adverse currency shocks in its stress tests and observes the projected decline in banks' capital under those scenarios.[9] The results of such scenarios provide a measure of "unexpected" or tail risk, complementing the view of milder scenarios.
- Value at Risk (VaR) and statistical models: For more sophisticated quantification, especially of the market risk associated with foreign currency trading operations, large banks generally use the VaR approach. VaR estimates the maximum probable loss over a given time horizon, with a specified confidence level, under normal market conditions. To calculate exchange rate VaR, the bank uses historical volatility data for each currency and correlations between currencies. Typical methods are historical simulation, variance-covariance methodology, or Monte Carlo simulations. VaR has the advantage of providing a single aggregate measure of risk that incorporates diversification.

Currency risk management and control

Currency risk management comprises the set of policies, procedures, and actions that a bank implements to mitigate and control potential losses arising from exchange rate fluctuations, keeping such losses within acceptable levels in line with its risk appetite.

Financial institutions must promote a strong risk culture, ensuring that traders, managers and executives understand the risks associated with foreign currency transactions and act prudently. Implementing a control environment involves establishing robust mechanisms and proactive strategies. Below are some of the best practices for managing and controlling currency risk in financial institutions:

- Hedging policies: One of the most direct responses to currency risk is to use derivative or cash financial instruments to hedge identified exposures to currency risks. This means taking positions that offset potential losses in the event of adverse exchange rate movements.

  Banks must monitor the effectiveness of hedges in mitigating price risk, while also considering liquidity issues in contract settlement and counterparty risk associated with derivatives. To manage this, banks handle collateral with counterparties through CSA (Credit Support Annex) agreements.

9 In the 2025 stress test, the adverse scenario assumed a significant appreciation of the euro against certain currencies, which for some European banks with high exposures in those currencies meant notable reductions in their projected operating margin and income.

- Foreign exchange risk limits and alerts: A central element of control is the establishment of quantitative limits on exposures and losses related to currency risk. These limits are approved by the risk committee or senior management and reflect the bank's risk tolerance. Generally, several types of complementary limits are implemented:
  - Net position limits by currency
  - Aggregate net position limits
  - Loss or stop-loss limits
  - Valuation limits per currency
  - Intraday limits

All these limits function as early warning signals. The risk management function track exposures in real time and sends alerts if any position approaches or exceeds the calibrated limits set according to the risk level. This enables traders to take corrective action or request approval for exceptions. A sound risk requires strict adherence to these limits, with any deviations escalated to higher management and properly justified. Finally, auditors and supervisors periodically review compliance with limits, as sustained breaches may indicate weaknesses in internal controls.

A sound control and risk management environment in currency risk management requires clear segregation of duties and organisational oversight, ensuring a separation between those who take positions and those who supervise them. At the front line are the currency desks, where traders handle both customer transactions and proprietary balance sheet management activities. The second line is the market risk area, which operates independently from the business and monitors risk. Additionally, structural and balance sheet exposures are typically overseen by the Asset and Liability Committee (ALCO), which aligns these exposures with the overall financial strategy.

Monitoring and reporting tools are important in ensuring that currency risk management is on the radar of both internal management and supervisors and facilitates internal and supervisory decision-making. Key elements include market risk reports that include positions on a set of risk metrics for each currency. At the supervisory level, the annual ICAAP must include an analysis of currency risk under adverse scenarios.

In terms of corrective actions, if risk thresholds are breached due to a sudden increase in the exposure to currency risk or unusual losses, the bank should have predefined procedures in place, including risk mitigating measures such as immediate additional hedging, exposure reduction, or in extreme cases, temporary suspension of speculative trading in that currency. Contingency plans are also key to managing currency risk actively. These plans define the course of actions if an extremely rare but possible event occurs (e.g., collapse of an emerging currency, etc.). Such plans may involve activating crisis committees and communicating with central banks to secure access to liquidity in foreign currency if necessary.

2.2 Bank capital

Bank capital represents the equity owned by shareholders, see Figure 2.5. It is composed of the share capital, premiums, various types of reserves and the net profit of the current financial year. It contrasts with the funds obtained from depositors or other creditors, which are classified as liabilities. Unlike deposits or loans, capital is ultra-subordinated, meaning that in the event of insolvency it is repaid last. As such, it functions as a safety net against unforeseen losses and constitutes the last line of defence against bank failures.

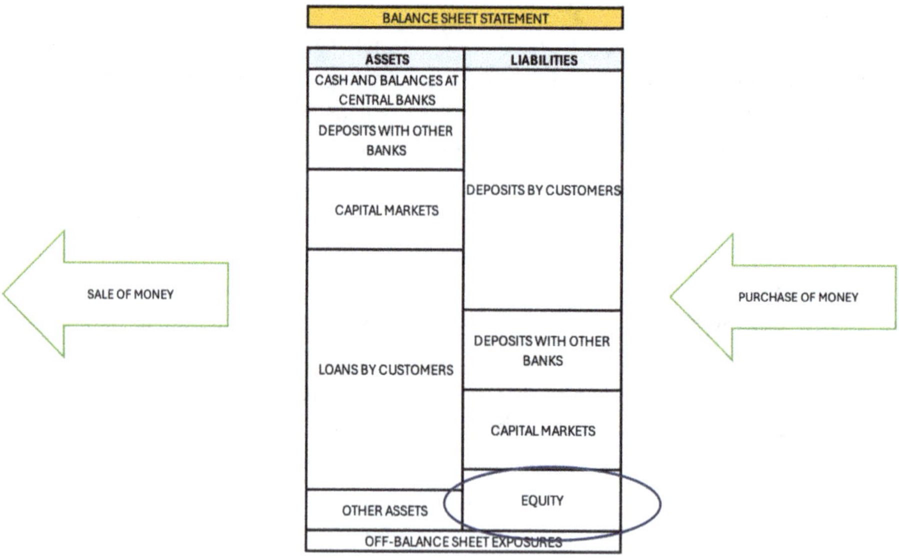

Figure 2.5: Bank Capital.
Source: Own elaboration.

The importance of bank capital is justified for several reasons:
1. Protection of depositors and creditors: in the event of losses, these are charged against capital (i.e., absorbed by shareholders) before compromising depositors' funds. Losses may stem from credit risk or the materialisation of other risks inherent in a financial institution's business model.
2. Preservation of confidence and financial stability. Well-capitalised banks inspire greater confidence and are better able to continue operating under adverse conditions without requiring external assistance.
3. Mitigation of systemic risk: risk by reducing the likelihood of chain bank failures. High capital levels reduce the probability of contagious bank failures. Regulators explicitly aim to avoid situations in which banks must be rescued with public funds; sufficient capital buffers diminish the likelihood of such bailouts.

4. Counteracting moral hazard from deposit insurance: Deposit insurance—present in most jurisdictions—guarantees depositors' funds up to a certain limit, which may weaken market discipline because insured depositors do not punish risk-taking behaviours. Capital requirements offset this moral hazard by ensuring that bank owners bear sufficient risk, thereby encouraging prudent management and limiting excessive risk-taking driven by expectations of public support.

Basel committee and its evolution

International capital standards are developed by the Basel Committee on Banking Supervision (BCBS), a forum created by the central banks of major economies. This committee was established in 1974 in response to high-profile bank failures in Germany and the US, with the aim of improving the quality of banking supervision worldwide. Although the BCBS does not possess supranational authority – its agreements do not have direct legal force – its members agree on principles and standards, which are subsequently implemented by national authorities through their own laws or regulations. Initially, the BCBS aimed to strengthen global financial stability by harmonising supervisory practices and closing regulatory gaps between countries. Over time, its focus shifted toward ensuring the capital adequacy of international banks and the banking system in general.

Before Basel I, each country applied its own solvency standards. The financial globalisation of the 1970s and 1980s highlighted the need for a common approach, prompting the BCBS to develop a unified international capital adequacy framework.

Basel I

The Basel I Accord, announced in 1988, was the first global standard for bank capital. Its objective was to ensure that international banks maintained a uniform minimum level of capital relative to their credit risk.

As it core, Basel I introduced the notion of "risk-weighted assets" (RWA) and set a minimum capital requirement equal to 8% of RWA. In practice, each bank was required to maintain capital – divided into two categories, Tier 1 and Tier 2 – equivalent to 8% of its RWAs. RWAs were calculated by classifying the bank's assets into five standard risk categories, with weightings of 0%, 10%, 20%, 50% and 100%, depending on the type of counterparty or exposure.

Basel I also defined the composition of regulatory capital into two tiers. Tier 1, or core capital, included the most robust capital components – ordinary shares and retained earnings – representing high-quality items from a loss-absorbing capacity perspective. Tier 2, or supplementary capital, allowed for lower-quality instruments, subject to certain limits (e.g., Tier 2 could not exceed Tier 1). The sum of Tier 1 and Tier 2 constituted the total regulatory capital to meet the required 8%. This distinction reflected the concern that elements of "capital" lacked the same loss-absorbing capacity as core capital so their proportion was restricted.

Basel I was widely adopted internationally beyond the original G-10. By the early 1990s, over 100 countries had incorporated similar minimum capital standards into their banking regulations. In the European Union, for example, Basel I was implemented through the 1989 Capital Adequacy Directive,[10] applicable to banks and investment firms, establishing the 8% requirement on risk-weighted assets. This convergence successfully strengthened the solvency of global banks and levelled the competitive playing field, preventing banks in countries with looser regulations from gaining an unfair advantage. Studies show that, throughout the 1990s, major international banks strengthened their capital ratios to meet at least the 8% requirement.

However, Based I had limitations. One criticism was its excessive simplification of risk: the standard weightings were too broad (for example, treating all private companies equally at 100%, without differentiating creditworthiness). Nor did it explicitly consider risks other than credit risk, such as market risk (fluctuations in interest rates, currencies, etc., in the trading portfolio) or operational risk (losses from internal failures or fraud). Furthermore, advances in risk management during the 1990s rendered Basel I's approach increasingly inadequate. By the late 1990s, it became clear that Basel I was not well suited to the sophisticated risk measurement practices that many banks adopted or to the growing complexity of financial activities.

Recognising these shortcomings, the BCBS began developing a more complex and risk-sensitive framework, leading to the development of a new capital agreement, Basel II.

Basel II (2004): A comprehensive approach and risk sensitivity

In June 2004, the central bank governors and heads of supervision of the BCBS countries approved the New Capital Accord, known as Basel II. This accord replaced the 1988 accord, with implementation planned for the end of 2006 in many jurisdictions.

This new agreement introduced a broader and more dynamic framework for capital adequacy, structured around three mutually reinforcing pillars:

- **Pillar 1**: Minimum capital requirements – Maintains a quantitative capital requirement similar to that of Basel I, 8% on RWAs, but with an expanded definition of risks and more sophisticated methods for calculating RWAs. Basel II not only covered credit risk, but also market risk – revising the treatment introduced in the 1990s – and, for the first time, operational risk (losses due to errors, systems, internal crimes, disasters, etc.). For each type of risk, it offered several calculation methods of increasing complexity:

10 Directive 89/647/CEE

- For credit risk: from a standard method (a refined version of Basel I, with more nuanced risk weights based on each exposer's external credit rating) Basel accord evolved to introduce methods based on banks' internal ratings (IRB), where banks, with the approval of the supervisor, were allowed to use their own internal models to estimate risk parameters (probability of default, loss given default, etc.). A basic IRB approach and an advanced IRB[11] approach were introduced, allowing sophisticated banks to align capital requirements with their internal risk measurements. The goal was for regulatory requirements to better reflect the actual risk of each portfolio.
- For operational risk, three alternatives were introduced: the Basic Indicator Approach, which required capital equal to a fixed percentage of the bank's gross income; the Standardised Approach, which subdivided income by business lines with different percentages; and the Advanced Measurement Approaches (AMA), which allowed banks to use internal models to estimate the operational loss distribution and calculate its associated capital requirement. This was a revolutionary step, formally integrating operational risk management into the capital framework.
- For market risk: Basel II incorporated the improvements already introduced in 1996 (which allowed banks to use VaR models for their trading portfolios, subject to validation) and adjusted some details. In 2006, the Committee would combine Basel II with the Market Risk Amendment to form a single consolidated framework.

Overall, Basel II retained the minimum total ratio of 8% capital to RWAs, but with RWAs calculated in a way that more accurately reflected each bank's actual risk profile.

Regarding the numerator of the solvency ratio, it should be noted that Basel II also formally added a Tier 3 capital (tertiary capital) to specifically cover market and commodity risk in the trading portfolio. Tier 3 consisted of subordinated short-term debt and other lower-quality instruments and was subject to strict limits (it could only be used after Tier 1 and Tier 2 had been exhausted for market risk). However, Basel III subsequently eliminated Tier 3, considering it to have low loss-absorbing capacity.

- **Pillar 2 – Supervisory Review** – Recognising that a standard requirement cannot cover all individual situations, Basel II established a process whereby supervisors assess the capital adequacy of each bank based on its overall risk profile and may require additional capital beyond the minimum (this is known as Pillar 2 requirement). It also encourages banks to develop internal processes called ICAAP (Inter-

11 The basic IRB allows institutions to estimate PD internally. LGD and EAD are provided by the regulator. In the advanced IRB, PD, LGD and EAD are all estimated internally by financial institutions.

nal Capital Adequacy Assessment Process) to assess how well or poorly they cover their risks and plan their capital prospectively. In short, Pillar 2 seeks to make supervision and capital requirements more tailored to the specific risk profile of each bank. This strengthens prudential discipline, ensuring that well-managed banks are not penalised for the risks of others, while allowing supervisors to act promptly and impose additional buffers on a case-by-case basis. In Europe, the Single Supervision Mechanism (SSM) conducts annual assessments (SREP) for each significant bank, in which it can impose additional Pillar 2 capital requirements if it considers that a bank's risks justify it. Supervisors also set capital expectations (Pillar 2 Guidance) and verify that banks comply not only with the Pillar 1 and Pillar 2 minimums, but also with macroprudential buffers – explained in a subsequent section – at all times.

- **Pillar 3 – Market Discipline** – The third pillar of Basel II established requirements for the public disclosure of banks' financial and risk information, with the idea that investors, analysts and the market in general can assess the soundness of each institution and thus exert pressure for prudent management. Transparency regarding capital structure, risks assumed, exposure by asset type, etc., allows the market itself to reward or penalise banks (e.g., through the price of their bonds or shares) according to their level of risk. This "market discipline" complements official supervision. Basel II detailed a comprehensive set of data that banks must disclose periodically, seeking to improve the comparability and trustworthiness of institutions.

Overall, Basel II aspired to be much more than a simple numerical capital requirement; its fundamental objective was to stimulate improvements in the comprehensive risk management of institutions as a means of ensuring financial stability. By better aligning requirements with actual risks and incorporating active supervision and market discipline, banks were expected to strengthen their internal capital control and planning practices. In fact, it was conceived as an evolutionary framework, designed to adapt as new methods and best practices emerged, gradually integrating them.

Basel II was implemented between 2007 and 2009 in many jurisdictions, although not without difficulties. The EU, for example, adopted Basel II through Directives 2006/48/EC and 2006/49/EC (Capital Requirements Directives) which came into force at the end of 2007. By the end of 2008, most large European banks were calculating their ratios using the advanced approaches of Basel II. In the US, however, Basel II implementation was delayed: it was applied mandatorily to the largest banks only and was still in the early stages of implementation in 2008.

The great financial crisis revealed the shortcomings of Basel II: it permitted extremely high leverage ratios in absolute terms – banks could hold assets 30 or 40 times their capital on an unweighted basis, provided they meet the 8% APR – and it did not account for liquidity risk. Consequently, the international community (G-20, BCBS) embarked on an even more far-reaching reform: Basel III.

Basel III (2010–2017): Strengthening the framework after the global financial crisis

Basel III[12] is the set of reforms agreed at international level in direct response to the global financial crisis of 2007-2009. The G-20 leaders tasked the Basel Committee with reviewing and strengthening prudential regulation to address the shortcomings revealed by the crisis. In November 2010, an agreement was reached on the overall design of Basel III, with further details finalised in subsequent years (up to 2017). The central objectives of Basel III were to increase both the quantity and quality of bank capital, limit excessive leverage, incorporate capital buffers to absorb macroeconomic shocks, and address other risks not previously covered, notably liquidity risk. The main elements are summarised below:

- Higher capital quality: Basel III increased the importance of Tier 1 capital, and especially Common Equity Tier 1 (CET1) capital. CET1 (highest quality common capital: ordinary shares and tangible reserves) became the main focus. It was established that banks must maintain a minimum of 4.5% CET1 on their risk-weighted assets (RWA), compared to the explicit 2% required under Basel II. In addition, total Tier 1 (which includes some additional high-quality hybrid instruments) rose to a minimum of 6%. The total capital requirement (Tier 1 + Tier 2) remained at 8% of RWA as in Basel I/II, but with the condition that a much larger proportion now had to be in the form of fully loss-absorbing capital (CET1). It is also important to note that Basel III introduces an extensive set of capital deductions – to address double counting of capital and to adopt a more conservative valuation approach for assets with higher valuation uncertainty – which further strengthens the definition of high-quality capital.

  Tier 3 (capital for market risk) was eliminated and the conditions for hybrid or preferred debt to count as Tier 1 were tightened (requiring that it be convertible into shares or absorb losses upon reaching the point of non-viability, i.e., incorporating loss absorption clauses). Thus, regulatory capital became closer to tangible book capital, reducing the gap between regulatory requirements and the true capacity to absorb losses.
- Capital buffers: A key innovation was the introduction of the capital conservation and countercyclical buffers. Specifically, Basel III added:
  - A Capital Conservation Buffer (CCB), mandatory at 2.5% of RWA, composed entirely of CET1 capital. This buffer is added to the 8% minimum, effectively

12 In Europe, it has been partially implemented through Regulation 575/2013, which supplements Directive 2013/36

bringing the total requirement to 10.5% (of which at least 7% must be CET1: 4.5% minimum + 2.5% buffer). The purpose of the CCB is to ensure that banks accumulate extra capital in normal times. In time of stress, if a bank incurs losses and its capital ratio falls within the buffer range (below 10.5% but above the 8% minimum), automatic restrictions on profit distribution are triggered. These restrictions limit or prohibit dividends to shareholders, share buybacks and bonuses to senior management. As the capital ratio approaches the regulatory minimum, these restrictions intensify, forcing banks to recapitalise by retaining profits until the full buffer is restored. The mechanism is designed to "conserve capital" during times of stress: instead of distributing profits, banks strengthen their equity. This mechanism disciplines banks to avoid depleting the buffer; if they draw on it to absorb losses during crisis times, they must replenish it before resuming normal distributions. Importantly, operating within the conservation buffer does not prevent the bank from continuing to operate – it is not a regulatory breach per se as long as the 8% minimum is maintained.

- A Countercyclical Buffer (CCyB) of up to another 2.5% on RWA (also to be met with CET1). Unlike the CCB (which is the same for all banks globally), the CCyB is set by each national designated authority in accordance with the financial cycle of its economy. The idea is that in times of excessive credit growth – when latent systemic risks accumulate – authorities can activate an additional buffer, compelling banks to accumulate more capital. This helps moderate credit expansion and prepares banks to absorb potential losses when the euphoria reverses. Then, in a recessionary or crisis phase, this countercyclical requirement can be reduced to 0%, freeing up capital for banks to use to absorb losses and continue lending – thus avoiding a credit crunch. The CCyB is a macroprudential tool that allows supervisors to "adjust the volume" of capital according to conditions of the economy in order to build reserves in good times and release them in bad times. Basel III provides that the CCyB decided by a country also applies to foreign banks for their exposures in that country (principle of international reciprocity, up to 2.5%). Similarly, falling below the CCyB requirement entails the same restrictions on dividend distribution as the capital conservation buffer.
- In addition, Basel III established buffers for systemically important banks, or Global Systemically Important Banks (G-SIBs). Each year the FSB publishes a list of G-SIBs, which must maintain an additional CET1 buffer above the above, ranging from 1% to 3.5% of APR depending on the entity's level of global systemic importance. Likewise, many jurisdictions implemented buffers for Domestic Systemically Important Banks (D-SIBs), typically up to an additional 2%. These buffers seek to ensure that institutions whose failure would have major consequences have "extra" capital to internalise that po-

tential cost. As with other buffers, falling below the requirement entails dividend restrictions.

- Finally, some jurisdictions have adopted additional buffers such as the Systemic Risk Buffer (SRB) for structural risks not covered by the above (e.g., country-specific vulnerabilities).

With all these buffers, the effective capital required of a large bank in normal times increases substantially under Basel III. Including minimums requirements and buffers, a typical bank must maintain at least 10.5% total capital (8% minimum plus 2.5% conservation buffer), of which 7% must be CET1. For a systemic bank, total capital requirements may reach 12-13%, with CET1 around 9-10%, not including any CCyB that may be activated. This represents a significant increase from Basel II, where total capital requirements were 8%, with 4% as Tier 1 capital.

- Leverage ratio: One lesson from the financial crisis was that some banks had extreme leverage ratios (very high assets compared to their capital) despite complying with RWA-based regulatory ratios. Those RWAs underestimated certain risks. To add a complementary unweighted measure, Basel III introduced the Leverage Ratio, which requires Tier 1 capital to represent at least 3% of total exposures[13] (unweighted assets plus certain off-balance sheet items). This metric acts as a safety net to complement risk models that determine RWA), preventing banks from becoming overly indebted even when holding assets deemed "safe".
- Liquidity coverage and stable funding: Although this falls outside the strict concept of "capital", Basel III included prudential liquidity metrics to ensure that banks can withstand short- and medium-term liquidity stresses. It introduced the Liquidity Covered Ratio (LCR), which requires banks to hold sufficient high-quality liquid assets to cover 30-day net cash outflows, and the Net Stable Funding Ratio (NSFR), which ensures that assets with a maturity of more than one year are financed with stable sources (capital or stable liabilities) in a minimum proportion.
- Other technical improvements: Basel III also refined risk calculation methods (e.g., increasing requirements for complex trading book exposures, re-securitisations, etc., and imposed capital requirements for credit valuation adjustment (CVA) risk in derivatives, among others. In addition, it promoted the use of periodic stress tests to assess whether banks had sufficient capital under severe adverse scenarios.

Implementation of Basel III

Given the magnitude of the changes, Basel III was implemented gradually. The new capital minimums and buffers were introduced between 2013 and 2023, giving banks

13 The United States and Switzerland, for example, set different levels.

time to raise capital in an orderly manner. By 2019, most of the requirements (CET1 4.5%, Tier 1 6%, CCB 2.5%, LCR, etc.) were already in force in the major economies. The final risk requirements – often referred to as "Basel 3.5" or even "Basel 4"– were agreed in 2017. They include revisions to both standardised and internal credit risk methods, such as limits on excessive reductions in APR by internal models (the so-called 72.5% output floor), as well as a new market risk approach (FRTB), with a target implementation period of 2023-2028.

However, implementation has been delayed somewhat: in the EU, for example, full implementation will be in 2025-2028, and in the US, proposals were submitted in 2023 to align with these final rules from 2025 onwards.

MREL and TLAC: loss instruments in resolution

Following the financial crisis, the concept of bank resolution was introduced as an alternative to bankruptcies supported by public bailouts. In this context, two complementary requirements were defined to ensure sufficient resources for recapitalisation purposes: MREL (in Europe) and TLAC (for global G-SIB banks).

- MREL (Minimum Requirement for own funds and Eligible Liabilities): this is the minimum threshold of capital and eligible debt that each bank must maintain in order to support an orderly resolution. As indicated by the Bank of Spain,[14] this requirement "ensures that institutions have sufficient own funds and debt instruments to absorb losses and, if necessary, recapitalise the institution in the event of resolution, ensuring that shareholders and creditors bear the losses first". The Single Resolution Board defines it by stating that MREL seeks to ensure that the institution has sufficient eligible instruments at all times to implement its preferred resolution strategy, thereby improving its resolvability. In practice, MREL is usually expressed as a percentage of RWA and exposure (TREA or LRE) and consists of a loss absorption amount (essentially equivalent to regulatory capital plus other amounts) and a recapitalisation amount intended to rebuild own funds post-crisis. The SRB adjusts the MREL according to factors such as subordination (degree of subordination required), the legal geography of the debt and the principle that no creditor should suffer greater losses in a resolution process than they would have suffered if the institution had been wound up through ordinary insolvency proceedings. If a bank fails to meet its MREL, the resolution authority may impose restrictions (e.g., limiting dividends) to prevent transfers to shareholders or preferred creditors.
- TLAC (Total Loss-Absorbing Capacity): this is a global standard of the Financial Stability Board (FSB, 2015) aimed at global systemically important banks (G-SIBs).

14 https://www.bde.es/wbe/es/areas-actuacion/resolucion/mrel-y-tlac/

It requires G-SIBs to maintain a level of capital and liabilities with high loss-absorbing capacity sufficient to support their resolution. Its objective is that, in a resolution scenario, shareholders and creditors of subordinated debt and non-preferred senior debt cover the losses, avoiding bailouts with public funds. The original TLAC standard set specific levels (Term Sheet): for example, 16% of RWA plus 6% of initial exposure in 2019, reaching 18% and 6.75% in 2022. In the EU, TLAC was incorporated via Regulation (EU) 2019/876 (CRR2) and applies to G-SIB banks in the Banking Union. The key differences between MREL and TLAC, according to the Bank of Spain, are: TLAC only applies to G-SIBs (fewer entities) and is set in advance (18% RWA + 6.75% LRE); in addition, TLAC requires liabilities to be contractually or structurally subordinated. Therefore, in the EU, a G-SIB must simultaneously comply with the national MREL set by the resolution authority and the global TLAC required by its home country.

In both cases, the existence of sufficient eligible instruments (equity, subordinated debt, non-preferred senior debt, etc.) is essential. These instruments must meet eligibility criteria (minimum maturity, subordination and contractual bail-in clauses). The EBA supervises and periodically updates the universe of eligible liabilities.

Finally, MREL and TLAC support a hypothetical implementation of the resolution strategy. They allow an intervened bank to absorb losses and rebuild capital without relying on public support, ensuring the continuity of its critical functions, in line with the principle of avoiding the use of public funds in bank failures.

2.2.1 Capital-focused regulation

A review of the events that led to the great financial crisis of 2008 (a crisis driven by a phenomenon known as the credit boom) has led most of the literature to various conclusions,[15] which are summarised below:

1. Failures in risk management:
   a. Underestimation of credit risk: Institutions granted loans to subprime customers, trusting that underlying properties would suffice to cover the risk.
   b. Poorly calibrated internal models: PDs and LGDs were based on data from boom periods, without considering adverse scenarios.
   c. Excessive reliance on external ratings: Banks and investors relied blindly on rating agencies, without conducting their own due diligence.
   d. Lack of a comprehensive view of risk: Risk, finance and business areas operated in silos. Structural balance sheet risks (IRRBB, liquidity) were not viewed in a holistic manner.

15 The failures in the origination of complex and opaque financial products are not detailed, as this is not the subject of this manual.

2. Poor liquidity management
   a. Short-term financing for long-term assets: Mortgages and structured loans were financed with very short-term interbank market instruments.
   b. False sense of liquidity: It was assumed that wholesale markets would always be liquid. When these markets froze, institutions lost their source of funding.
   c. Lack of structural buffers (LCR, NSFR): There were no mandatory regulatory metrics for stable liquidity, which led to immediate tensions when confidence was lost.
3. Inadequate governance and corporate culture
   a. Lack of control by the Board and ALCO: ALM was treated as a technical, not a strategic, function. Balance sheet committees had no real authority.
   b. Short-term profit culture: Decisions were geared towards quarterly profit growth, not balance sheet sustainability.
   c. Poor internal transparency: Off-balance sheet risks were not fully known to management or supervisors.
4. Insufficient supervision and regulation
   a. Procyclical accounting standards: Under IAS 39, only *incurred* losses were recognised, not *expected losses* (which delayed provisioning).
   b. Low-quality capital: Hybrid instruments were accepted as Tier 1 capital but did not effectively absorb losses.
   c. Lack of international coordination: Prudential frameworks were inconsistent across countries and there were no macroprudential standards.

The regulatory response has been through the implementation of Basel III. The introduction of the new liquidity standards, through the LCR and NSFR metrics in addition to the ILAAP exercises, is considered positive because it has compelled the industry to operate with greater prudence in terms of liquidity. However, these metrics will need to evolve in the future, as there is room for improvement given the experiences with the recent bankruptcies of Silicon Valley Bank and Credit Suisse.

For failures in risk management, regulators have responded by continually increasing capital requirements, guided by the seemingly obvious conclusion that financial institutions with more capital are better prepared for future crisis. This is unquestionably true, but it is worth asking whether this approach is fully justified.

Improvements have been required in the quality of instruments assimilable to capital (a positive development). However, a series of macroprudential capital buffers has also been introduced, whose calibration is not justified by a comprehensive analysis of the root causes of banking problems. Instead, these buffers were designed primarily as tools to limit the procyclicality of lending during period of turmoil, by allowing their release. Yet, as the experience of the COVID crisis showed, almost no banks made use of these buffers due to concerns about how doing so might expose them or negatively affect their share prices. In practice, credit expansion during the pandemic was sustained mainly through state guarantee schemes that enabled companies to obtain bank loans.

MREL/TLAC requirements have been created, to build layers of loss-absorbing instruments similar to capital, with the aim to avoid reliance on public resources.

In addition to the above, the regulation modulates the risk weights (RW) of assets according to the economic revitalisation interests of certain segments/sectors. The results of IRB credit risk models implementing an output floor are not entirely credible. In short, the capital framework needs an in-depth review, where the principle of parsimony should prevail, accompanied by a comprehensive analysis of the origins of banking crises. It is time to stop, reflect and simplify, always with a view to improving the professionalisation of banking management.

For the analysis of banking crises, there is a need—beyond the academic sphere—for a more intensive debate within the industry and among supervisors and regulators. The origins of crises rooted in credit-boom-driven risk accumulation can often be better understood from a practical, experience-based perspective. It should also be remembered that the function of capital, by definition, is to absorb unexpected losses incurred by banks; it should not be used as a substitute for improvements in management or as an instrument for purposes that can be addressed through better governance and oversight.[16]

For all these reasons, regulation/supervision should devote much greater attention to promoting best management practices within financial institutions. One issue that has not been sufficiently highlighted is that risks are inherent and must be continuously assessed. In the banking business, the prices that reflect these risks are set at the time of origination, and they cannot be adjusted thereafter except through balance sheet management exercises using interest rate derivatives. Through these instruments, institutions modify the profile of certain balance sheet items to manage their sensitivity to, or benefit from, movements in interest rates. Yet these adjustments are typically carried out from an aggregate perspective, which can lead to a loss of microeconomic focus on where risks are actually accumulating within banks' balance sheets.

However, adjusting the balance sheet's sensitivity to interest rate risk through derivative instruments—an essential activity within ALM management—does not, in itself, ensure the sustainability of the underlying business model. Sustainability exists only when the assets and liabilities on the balance sheet, with their current and measurable financial risks, are priced appropriately for those risks, allowing the institution to operate soundly over time. Maintaining this perspective is fundamental to effective management: when risks exceed the thresholds for which positions were

---

16 European Central Bank. (2023). Assessment of the European Central Bank's Supervisory Review and Evaluation Process: Report by the Expert Group to the Chair of the Supervisory Board of the ECB (Annex). https://www.bankingsupervision.europa.eu/ecb/pub/pdf/annex/ssm.pr230417_annex.en.pdf

originally priced, and even when stress tests confirm potential vulnerabilities, institutions must adopt a proactive strategy. This may involve modifying their business model or securing alternative sources of funding in order to withstand the consequences of emerging problems. Ultimately, the core issue is the imbalance between risk and price, and it is from this starting point that corrective action must be taken.

This handbook will develop the definition and cross-cutting integration—at both the macro and micro levels—of two metrics for the management of financial institutions: PRICING GAP annual and PRICING GAP total. These metrics aim to support a more comprehensive approach to bank management and will assist both supervisors/regulators and bank managers in designing sustainable and viable banking business models over time.

3 Distorting aspects of the banking business

As far as concerns the pricing gap, the banking business is subject to distorting phenomena that affect how the business of buying and selling money is originated, how credit risk impairment is recognised within the accounting sphere, which amplifies aspects of competition, as well as the idiosyncrasies of bank pricing.

3.1 Banking competition

Competition in the banking sector is one of the most decisive factors in the functioning of modern economies. Its influence on the profitability, stability and risk behaviour of financial institutions has been the subject of intense academic debate. The work of Xavier Vives (2016) represents one of the most comprehensive contributions to this discussion, integrating economic theory on competition with prudential regulation and financial stability. In his analysis, Vives demonstrates that the relationship between competition and banking risk is not linear, but rather articulated through a complex balance between efficiency, incentives and systemic fragility.

In classical literature, the link between competition and banking risk has been explained by the so-called "charter value effect". According to Keeley (1990), institutions with greater market power and monopoly rents have more incentives to maintain prudent behaviour, as they seek to protect their franchise value. Conversely, financial liberalisation and the reduction of barriers to entry erode these rents and encourage the pursuit of profitability through excessive risk-taking. However, Boyd and De Nicoló (2005) quantify this relationship, showing that greater competition can reduce aggregate risk if lower interest rates on loans decrease the probability of borrower default.

These authors, however, overlook practical evidence that lower rates, although easing the financial burden, simultaneously reduce banks' ability to absorb the financial risks they face, which must be duly reflected in pricing. Despite this, empirical evidence tends to confirm that in highly competitive environments, banks tend to relax credit standards in order to preserve market share (Jiménez & Saurina, 2006). This phenomenon translates into credit expansion, a decrease in collateral and a progressive deterioration in asset quality, increasing the probability of financial crises. If this rivalry exposed by Jiménez and Saurina leads to lower lending standards and is not accompanied by pricing that appropriately reflects these risks, it may create conditions conducive to future financial crises.

On the other hand, Vives (2016) points out that competition, although disciplinary, can induce short-term behaviour. Commercial pressure intensifies the search for volume at the expense of risk-adjusted profitability, a phenomenon that is particularly visible in the expansionary phases of the economic cycle. This situation creates per-

 | https://doi.org/10.1515/9783111328386-003

verse incentives within institutions, as executive compensation is often linked to business growth and not necessarily to margin sustainability or credit quality.

Another way of analysing competition between financial institutions is the effect of deposit insurance in financial systems and moral hazard problems. According to Matutes and Vives (2000), when insurance premiums are uniform, depositors no longer distinguish between safe and risky banks, reducing market discipline. As a result, weaker institutions tend to compete aggressively for deposits, raising interest rates to attract liquidity, thereby driving up financing costs, reducing margins, and increasing systemic risk. This phenomenon was experienced intensely during the aftermath of the Spanish banking crisis of 2008-2012.

Regarding the effect of competition on pricing, Vives (2016) argues that competitive pressure acts as a disciplinary mechanism but can also lead to price cannibalisation: banks reduce their margins to levels that do not cover the costs of risk or capital. This erosion of the financial margin compromises structural profitability and can lead to internal imbalances in the balance sheet. Along the same lines, Repullo and Suárez (2013) show that when banks set prices below their risk-adjusted cost of capital, they distort the allocation of resources and reduce the aggregate resilience of the banking system. This could signal the onset of a banking crisis, as insufficient profitability may limit the ability to absorb future losses.

The link between competition and banking crises has been addressed by other authors too. Beck, Demirgüç-Kunt and Levine (2006) document that more competitive systems are more likely to experience crises in the absence of effective regulation. In Europe, Egan, Hortaçsu and Matvos (2017) show that competition for deposits increased the fragility of banks during the financial crisis, in line with the findings of Vives (2016). In the case of Spain, Jiménez, Ongena, Peydró and Saurina (2014) observed that, in expansionary phases, competition reduces credit standards and increases banks' exposure to risk.

In response to this evidence, regulators have implemented macroprudential measures, including the countercyclical capital buffer, to dampen the impact of credit booms; however, the underlying causes of these issues have received little attention. Rather than relying solely on additional capital—which may not address all of a bank's deficiencies, such as weaknesses in governance or business models, and does not always have a clear link to the identified risks—supervisors should more proactively enforce corrective measures (other than capital) when pricing does not adequately reflect the financial risks being assumed.

3.2 IFRS 9 in the treatment of provisions

Financial institutions currently apply IFRS 9, or a national equivalent under national GAAP standards, to estimate provisions for credit risk. Unlike the previous IAS 39 standard, which was based on the incurred loss model, IFRS 9 uses a forward-looking expected credit loss (ECL) approach. This model applies to financial assets at amortised cost and at fair value through other comprehensive income (FVOCI), as well as to loan commitments and financial guarantees not measured at fair value through profit or loss. The model is defined as follows:

$$ECL = PD * LGD * EAD$$

Where:

PD = Probability of default.
LGD = Loss given default.
EAD = Exposure at default.

For the purposes of this handbook, it is important to note that according to IFRS 9 standards instruments subject to impairment are classified into three stages (see Figure 3.1):

- Stage 1: These are instruments that do not present a significant increase in risk since origination. Their expected loss should be recognised over the next 12 months.
- Stage 2: These are instrument that present a significant increase in risk since origination. Their expected loss is calculated using the lifetime ECL.
- Stage 3: These are instruments that meet the entity's definition of default. Their expected loss is also estimated using the lifetime ECL.

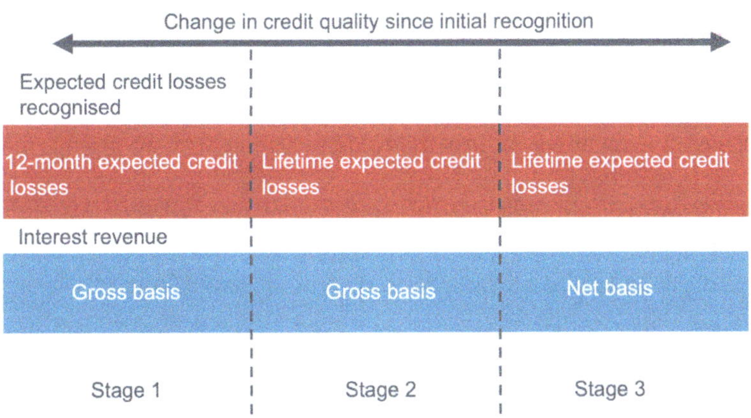

Figure 3.1: IFRS 9 – Stages.
Source: https://www.ifrs.org/content/dam/ifrs/project/fi-impairment/exposure-draft-2013/webcast/expected-credit-losses-slides.pdf?utm_source=chatgpt.com.

The issue with IFRS 9 arises from its interplay with the competitive pricing scheme. As mentioned in the previous section, Vives (2016) argued that banks cannibalise prices to such an extent that they do not cover the costs of risk. When considering that provisions in Stage 1 are based on 12-month expected credit losses (ECLs)—which are significantly lower than lifetime ECLs—financial institutions face little accounting pressure to recognize provisions over the life of the exposure. As a result, they may not accumulate a sufficient volume of provisions to cover expected losses arising beyond the initial 12 months, i.e., over the full economic cycle.

When a negative cycle emerges, as during the COVID-19 crisis, supervisors typically issue recommendations to restrict dividend distributions and to release macroprudential buffers to absorb losses so that credit can continue to flow to the economy.[17] In the past these recommendations were received with discontent by institutions, as their implementation could affect stock market price. Additionally, the use of macroprudential capital buffers may single out certain institutions and adversely affect market perception, which may be remediated by placing greater emphasis on IFRS9 provisions. However, the application of IFRS 9 required further evolution. The industry knows how to calculate lifetime PDs, so an evolution of the approach for Stage 1 transactions towards a lifetime ECL approach would ensure that the possible losses arising at any point in the economic cycle are adequately provisioned. Such an approach would also enhance pricing discipline and contribute to greater financial stability.

3.3 Distortions of the accounting view in the analysis of financial institutions

One of the main difficulties in decision-making in a financial institution is at the moment of origination, when taking funding and especially when financing its customers.

In loan financing, banks set the prices of transactions at the time of origination. For performing such lending banks incur in financial risks for which banks should be properly remunerated. In other words, banks should be remunerated, via pricing, for the risks taken.

In a long-term mortgage, how will it be financed in the coming years? What difficulties might a lender face in the future when renewing it? If a bank takes out a fixed-rate loan, will rates evolve as predicted by the markets at the time of origination? All these issues are not reflected nor factored into the accounting information, which may be inconclusive when analysing financial institutions in times of volatility and even without it, greatly limiting its use for drawing conclusions about the performance and the long-term sustainability of banks. This makes it necessary to use other analytical resources.

Example:

Let us assume a newly created financial institution that has a set of very recently granted mortgages on its balance sheet and the "snapshot" it shows on 30 December 2019 is as follows: €1 billion at a fixed rate, financed with 1-year customer deposits at 0.10% for €200 million and the rest in customer non-maturing

17 ECB/2020/62

deposits for €800 million. The bank has a balance sheet structure as shown in Figure 3.3, constructed under a yield curve such as that shown in Figure 3.2.

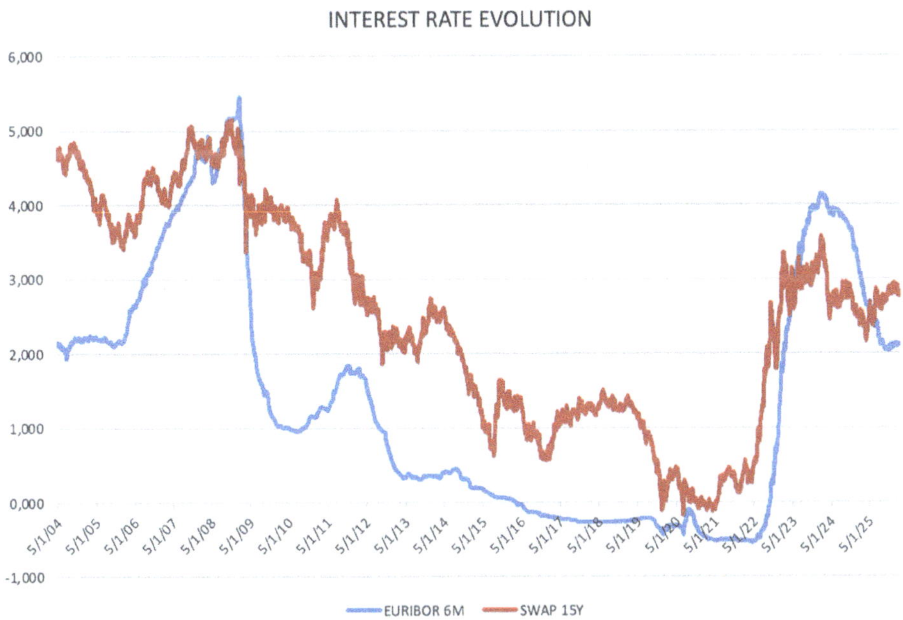

Figure 3.2: Interest Rate Evolution.
Source: Own elaboration based on data from Bloomberg.

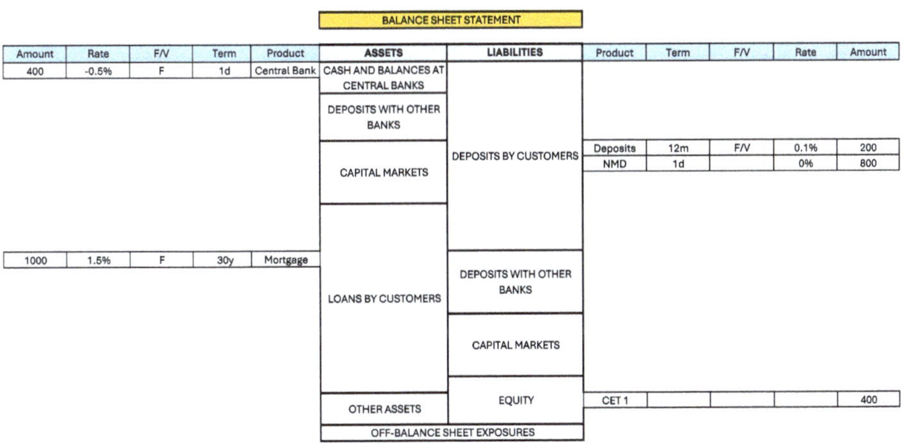

Figure 3.3: Balance Sheet Example.
Source: Own elaboration.

The interest rates' path on 30 December 2019 are shown in Figure 3.4

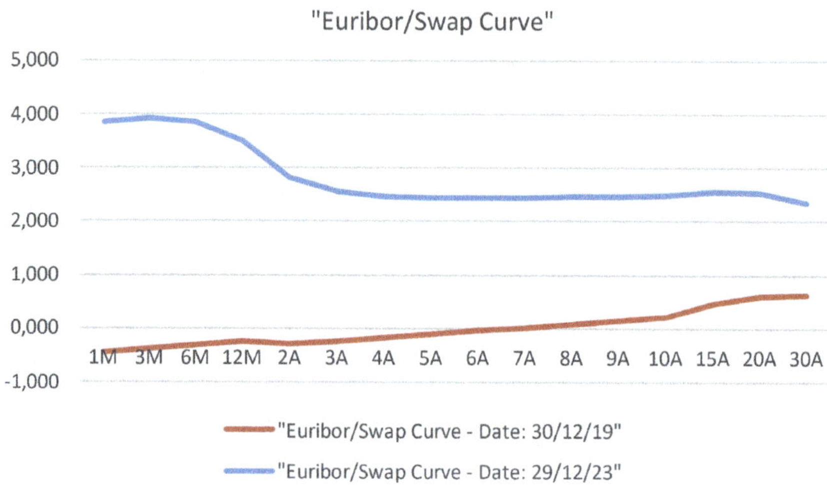

Figure 3.4: Yield Curve.
Source: Own elaboration based on data from Bloomberg.

This bank reports a net interest income (NII) of 12.8 million (see Table 3.1). It grants fixed-rate loans at 1.5%, compared with the 15-year swap rate at 0.468%,[18] which appears reasonable, since, although we will see this in more detail later, this transaction would be equivalent to the 6-month Euribor plus a spread of 1.032%. Its funding structure, with a strong reliance on non-maturing deposits, may provide some protection against interest-rate hikes. If the 6M Euribor spot rate is -0.388% and the 10-year swap is 0.212%, the market-implied 6M Euribor in 10 years' time would be approximately 0.75%.[19] This forward rate should serve as the benchmark against which customer deposits would normally be remunerated under standard market conditions.

Assuming a constant balance sheet and allowing time to pass until the end of 2023, different scenarios interest-rate curve scenarios may materialise by that date, as shown in Table 3.2.

Case A reflects a situation in which the institution has focused on extracting value from its deposit customers by keeping remuneration low, as it did in 2019, while repricing its treasury position (i.e., deposits placed with the central bank). Fixed-rate loans at 1.50% now contrast with a 14-year swap rate at approximately 2.50%, revealing hidden valuation losses. Such lending is offset by a short-term financing structure that is vulnerable to future instability. In this scenario, NII increases from 12.8 to 30.8. Accounting therefore shows a positive effect, while the internal dynamics of the balance sheet remain concealed: the vulnerabilities and actual risks embedded in this balance sheet structure are not fully perceived.

18 The 15-year swap can be taken as an instrument with similar sensitivity to the interest rate risk of a 30-year mortgage with a French-type amortisation payment system, since the modified duration of this type of loan is approximately its term divided by 2.

19 The implied rate has been calculated in a rough and simplistic manner as follows: (Swap 10Y *2 – E6). This would give us the implied 6M Euribor rate in 10 years' time in a very approximate manner, but it is sufficient for the illustrative purposes of the handbook.

Table 3.1: P&L – Date: 30 December 2019.

PROFIT AND LOSS STATEMENT	Product	Amount	F/V	Rate	Carry
Interest Income	Mortgage	1000	F	1.5%	15
	Central Bank	400	FMD	-0.5%	-2
Interest Expense	Deposits	200	F	0.1%	-0.2
	NMD	800		0	0
Net Interest Income					**12.8**

Source: Own elaboration.

Table 3.2: P&L – Date: 29 December 23 – Case A.

PROFIT AND LOSS STATEMENT	Product	Amount	F/V	Rate	Carry
Interest Income	Mortgage	1000	F	1.5%	15
	Central Bank	400	FMD	4%	16
Interest Expense	Deposits	200	F	0.1%	-0.2
	NMD	800		0	0
Net Interest Income					**30.8**

Source: Own elaboration.

Case B, see Table 3.3, reflects a situation in which the entity reprices its cash position, followed by a shift of non-maturing deposits into term deposits remunerated at the 6-month Euribor rate. Keeping the loan position constant, the main difference in results compared with case A becomes evident. In this case, unlike in case A, part of the liquidity risks embedded in the balance sheet have materialised through higher deposit remuneration consistently with the market yield curve.

Table 3.3: P&L – Date: 29 December 2023 – Case B.

PROFIT AND LOSS STATEMENT	Product	Amount	F/V	Rate	Carry
Interest Income	Mortgage	1000	F	1.5%	15
	Central Bank	400	FMD	4%	16
Interest Expense	Deposits	500	F	3.86%	-19.3
	NMD	500		0	0
Net Interest Income					**11.7**

Source: Own elaboration.

Finally, Case C, see Table 3.4, reflects a situation in which the market is actively competing for customer deposits, resulting in a larger shift of non-maturing deposits into terms deposits. As in case B, the materialisation of liquidity risks is driven by this transfer, but in this case the effect is more pronounced, reducing the entity's NII from 12.8 to 4 million.

Table 3.4: P&L – Date: 29 December 2023 – Case C.

PROFIT AND LOSS STATEMENT					
	Product	Amount	F/V	Rate	Carry
Interest Income	Mortgage	1000	F	1.5%	15
	Central Bank	400	FMD	4%	16
Interest Expense	Deposits	700	F	3.86%	-27
	NMD	300		0	0
Net Interest Income					**4**

Source: Own elaboration.

What conclusion can be drawn from these examples?

The analysis of Cases A, B, and C illustrates that conclusions drawn from a bank's accounting information must be treated with caution, especially in volatile market environments. In Case A, accounting shows strong NII growth despite hidden vulnerabilities in the balance sheet. In Cases B and C, the materialisation of liquidity risks through higher deposit remuneration reveals that apparent stability can quickly deteriorate. These scenarios highlight that accounting figures alone may give the illusion of solvency and financial stability, while the true risk-return profile of the balance sheet can be significantly challenged.

External financial analyses of banks tend to focus heavily on accounting information reported in quarterly results, relying on key metrics such as ROE, market capitalisation or comparison with the cost of capital. However, the usefulness of this accounting indicators is rather limited: they reflect current profitability relative to the spot yield curve but do not capture the underlying risks or the hidden value that may emerge during periods of market turbulence. Therefore, conclusions about a bank's valuation based solely on accounting information should be treated with caution.

4 Asset and liability management (ALM) in financial institutions

Asset and liability management is a fundamental function within modern financial institutions, basically comparable to the "nerve centre" of a bank. As noted above, a bank's activity can be defined as the buying and selling of money. In this process, the production factors or elements to be taken into account when setting prices – including the financial risks described above – are crucial, highlighting the vital importance of this function within financial institutions.

The ALM function is responsible for the strategic management of a bank's balance sheet (assets and liabilities) with the aim of managing key financial risks, ensuring liquidity and optimising profitability in a sustainable manner. Far from being a purely tactical or "back-office" activity, the ALM discipline has become a strategic pillar of financial planning and comprehensive risk management in today's banking sector. In fact, expert authors such as Moorad Choudhry describe ALM as a high-level discipline that encompasses the entire bank's organisation and whose scope transcends day-to-day treasury management, integrating itself into the formulation of the business strategy and the definition of the institution's risk appetite.

In recent years, various events and trends have underscored the critical importance of a robust ALM function. The 2008 financial crisis, prolonged periods of ultra-low interest rates followed by rapid increases, and recent cases of troubled banks (such as the collapse of Silicon Valley Bank in 2023) show that poor management of the asset-liability gap can expose banks to serious financial difficulties and, in extreme cases, compromise their viability. Conversely, proactive ALM management allows institutions to cover risks properly, maintain stability in their revenues and margins, and meet their obligations even under adverse scenarios.

What is the role of ALM? As it is not a standardised function within financial institutions, there is no standardised role definition and, depending on the risk culture of each financial institution, different definitions or approaches may be used. The preferred definition is that the ALM function should be a front-line, first-line-of-defence function. This process enables financial institutions to manage their balance sheet structure and mitigate risks arising from mismatches between assets and liabilities, while ensuring adequate levels of liquidity, profitability, provisions, and capital. In other words, the ALM function aims to balance items of balance sheet so that financial risks remain within the bank's defined risk appetite. The ALM function should also oversee the profitability model, reflected in the P&L statement, where the pricing of operations (e.g., interest rates on interest-bearing assets and liabilities) reflects the financial risks embedded in the balance sheet, enabling banks to maintain a sustainable business model over time. It also assesses whether the level of provisions and capital are sufficient to ensure a bank's viability in all scenarios, including adverse scenarios. The ALM function should also oversee and anticipate how assets and liabil-

 | https://doi.org/10.1515/9783111328386-004

ities will react to changes in the financial environment (e.g., interest rates, market conditions, depositor behaviour, etc.) and make decisions to align the bank's financial structure with its business strategy and risk-taking capacity.

From an operational point of view, ALM combines different dimensions, with long-term financial planning and the strategic dimension of management at its core. Key dimensions include profitability risk (from both capital and accounting perspectives) and liquidity, among others.

Traditionally, different risks – such as interest rate, liquidity and credit risk – were managed separately in silos; however, the ALM approach integrates these elements into a holistic view of the balance sheet, monitoring all of the entity's structural risks in a coordinated manner. The ALM approach operates at the macro level of the organisation, integrating these elements to provide a holistic view of the balance sheet, monitoring all of the institution's structural risks in a coordinated manner.

The ALM function is applicable across different types of banks, including commercial banks, investment banks, credit unions, insurance companies, and even pension funds or any financial institution where there are temporal or structural gaps between collections and payments. In the case of banking, Moorad Choudhry points out that, although the basic principles of ALM seem to be more oriented towards traditional commercial banking, it is actually essential to apply them in all areas, including investment banking and trading treasuries, since ultimately, they all operate with assets and liabilities. A well-integrated ALM function typically covers both retail banking (banking book) and market or treasury activities (trading book), so that the entire organisation is aligned in terms of balance sheet and risk management.

Risks managed by the ALM function

Among its various responsibilities, a key function of ALM is risk management. Predominantly, the literature and practice agree that the main risks covered by the ALM function are:

- Structural interest rate risk (IRRBB and CSRBB): ALM must measure and limit the sensitivity of the balance sheet to rate movements using tools such as gap analysis, duration and convexity, income simulations under different scenarios, and stress testing. The objective is to ensure that a reasonable adverse movement in interest rates does not compromise either the solvency (economic value of equity) or the profitability of the bank.
- Liquidity risk. A crucial function of ALM is to ensure that there is a sufficient liquidity buffer (compliance with the LCR) and a balance between the maturities of assets and liabilities (compliance with the NSFR) that minimises the risk of running out of available funds. The ALM function devotes considerable attention to liquidity management, monitoring expected cash flows on a daily basis, identifying deposit concentrations, planning for adverse scenarios (mass withdrawals,

market closures, etc.) and establishing contingency financing plans to withstand stress situations.

- Currency risk. The ALM function manages currency risks by monitoring and coordinating the institution's foreign exchange exposures, ensuring that currency mismatches do not threaten capital, liquidity, or profitability, and that all positions remain within the bank's defined risk appetite.
- Credit Risk (in the ALM context). Credit risk is generally managed by specialised areas (e.g., credit risk department). While ALM does not directly manage individual credit risk (that is a separate function), it does consider credit risk at the aggregate level to the extent that it influences the balance sheet structure and investment policies. In fact, Moorad Choudhry points out that the ALM function should focus on strategic aspects such as establishing the credit risk policies, while the tactical management of credit risk (loan concession, scoring models, rating, IRB models, monitoring and workout strategies) should be delegated to other committees. From an ALM perspective, the main concern is how expected and unexpected credit losses may affect capital and liquidity under different scenarios and, ultimately, how these losses are reflected in banks' profitability and pricing models. Therefore, ALM should influence the composition of the asset portfolio (what proportion of the balance sheet is allocated to loans vs. liquid investments, diversification by sector, concentration limits) to ensure that overall credit risk remains within parameters consistent with the desired financial resilience.

The ALM function also plays a key role in capital management. Capital management within ALM involves planning future capital requirements based on asset growth, dividend policies, regulatory requirements and stress scenarios. Many banks integrate capital planning (including metrics such as leverage and regulatory capital ratios) into strategic ALM, as capital adequacy is the ultimate safeguard against losses arising from any of the above risks.

The philosophy of ALM is to balance risks and returns in a comprehensive manner, seeking appropriate trade-offs. A key point highlighted by Moorad Choudhry is that ALM is not just about mitigating risks, but about balancing them with margin objectives. The bank must take on a certain amount of risk to achieve profitability, but in a conscious and controlled manner. The true essence of good banking lies in deliberately achieving this risk-margin balance, which should be the cornerstone of every ALCO committee.

Mission and objectives of the ALM function

The main mission of the ALM function in a financial institution is to ensure the long-term sustainability of the institution, including optimising profitability through proactive management of structural balance sheet risks. This general statement can be broken down into several specific objectives:

- **Manage interest rate risk and liquidity risk within the defined appetite**. The ALM function establishes policies and quantitative limits in accordance with the risk appetite approved by the Board of Directors. The ALM function monitors these risks and takes action (hedging, changes in the term structure, etc.) to keep effective exposure under control. The aim is to ensure that neither market fluctuations nor liquidity stress scenarios jeopardise the viability of the institution.
- **Preserving financial margin and medium-term profitability**. Good ALM does not simply seek to minimise risk by eliminating all exposure, but rather to protect and stabilise the net interest margin (NIM) within acceptable levels. This involves, for example, mitigating excessive volatility in financial income caused by sudden changes in interest rates. ALM management seeks to ensure that the bank can maintain NIM in different scenarios, or at least that any reduction is gradual and manageable. This objective is aligned with maximising long-term shareholder value: if the financial margin is stable and sufficient, the bank will be solvent and profitable and may even distribute dividends to its shareholders.
- **Optimising the balance sheet structure and allocation of capital and provisions**. ALM plays a role in vital strategic balance sheet planning, as it decides to what extent asset growth will be financed with certain liabilities, what is the optimal mix between retail deposits versus wholesale debt, or between liquid investments versus long-term loans, etc., to achieve the best risk-return combination. It also helps determine the bank's capital and provision strategy. An explicit objective is to maximise the bank's economic value in the long term, which is achieved when the balance sheet is structured efficiently (taking advantage of profitability opportunities, but without taking on disproportionate risks). In a sense, ALM seeks to ensure that each part of the balance sheet yields an adequate return for the risks taken. Such balance between risk and revenues can be measures with risk-adjusted performance measurement such as ROAC, EVA, etc.
- **Ensuring regulatory compliance and a reputation for soundness**. Another fundamental mission of ALM is to keep the bank in compliance with regulatory requirements related to the balance sheet. This includes not only the aforementioned LCR, NSFR for liquidity and IRRBB (Interest Rate Risk in Banking Book) for interest rates, but also concentration limits, supervisory guidelines on ALM corporate governance, etc. A robust ALM will give confidence to supervisors and stakeholders in general. In contrast, the absence of adequate controls can lead to red flags from supervisors. Protecting the institution's reputation is part of ALM's mission, as a bank that manages its structural risks well is less prone to unpleasant surprises that erode public confidence. In an environment where information travels fast (social media, real-time news), any sign of liquidity problems or large unexpected losses can trigger a bank run. Therefore, by fulfilling its mission, ALM is also preserving confidence in the institution.

Implementation of strategic ALM in a financial institution[20]

Implementing the ALM function in a bank is not simply a matter of creating a department, but rather establishing a function along with processes, policies, tools and governance that enable the above objectives to be put into practice.

When it comes to implementing strategic ALM, i.e., an ALM approach that is closely linked to business planning and high-level decision-making, it is more than just an isolated technical exercise. The ALM function must necessarily be strongly embraced by senior management for proper implementation. Strategic ALM, as Choudhry (2018) explains, seeks to optimise three dimensions:

1. Regulatory compliance: capital, liquidity and leverage, and solvency according to Basel III.
2. Profitability: net interest margin (NIM) stability and risk-adjusted return maximisation.
3. Business sustainability: maintaining customer confidence and satisfaction (banking franchise).

The key components and steps for effective implementation of the ALM function are described below:

1. **Definition of the Governance Framework**: The first step is to define who will be responsible for the ALM function, with the CFO being the most suitable person for this role, and how it will be integrated into the corporate governance structure. Typically, entities create an Asset and Liability Committee (ALCO), which provides the governance architecture for ALM management, ensuring that there is a collegiate, high-level body with a strategic vision dedicated to "steering" the bank's balance sheet, although it should be emphasised that ultimate responsibility for financial risk must lie with the Board of Directors and operational management with the ALCO, acting as the central executive committee for the balance sheet. The members should be at the highest level within the organisation in terms of their responsibilities, and the committee is usually made up of senior management, C-suite executives, commercial banking managers, etc. The ALCO should ideally report directly to the Board of Directors or be a subcommittee of the latter, to ensure that the highest governing body is involved and has direct visibility of balance sheet risks and business model sustainability. Therefore, it is recommended that the ALCO have explicit delegated powers from the Board of Directors to manage the balance sheet with a long-term perspective, and that at least one member of the Board be present or informed in detail of the ALCO's

20 This point is taken from the author who coined this term, which has been key in the development of the ALM function in the banking industry. Choudhry, M. (2018). The Moorad Choudhry Anthology: Past, Present and Future Principles of Banking and Finance (Chapter 11: Strategic ALM). John Wiley & Sons.

decisions, with meaningful two-way communication. This elevation of ALCO's profile in the hierarchy seeks to recognise that ALM discipline is as critical as, for example, the internal audit function (which typically reports to the Board's Audit Committee). In short, governance must ensure that ALM has a "voice and vote" at the highest level and that strategic balance sheet management decisions are not lost in intermediate layers of management.

ALCO should promote a culture of debate between business lines, risks and finance. In addition, it should have a clear mandate, formalised in statutes or policies approved by the Board of Directors. This mandate includes its objectives, responsibilities and the frequency of its meetings and reporting. In accordance with best practices, ALCO members should receive, prior to each meeting, an information package covering various aspects such as financial planning (balance sheet and profitability), capital and provision planning, details of the Fund Transfer Pricing (FTP) model, etc. Specific policies under the remit of ALCO include the Liquidity Management Policy (and the Contingency Fund Plan), the Interest Rate Risk Management Policy (including the methodology for measuring income sensitivity and economic value), the FTP Policy, etc. The ALCO must review and approve these policies at least once a year, ensuring that they translate the Board of Directors' objectives and tolerances into clear operating standards.

2. **Development of the ALM Strategy and Risk Appetite**: In parallel with the formation of the governance structure, the institution must articulate its ALM strategy and define its structural risk appetite. The ALM strategy consists of establishing how the balance sheet will be managed to support the overall business strategy. For example, if the bank's strategy is to grow strongly in fixed-rate mortgage loans, the ALM strategy should consider how to finance this (perhaps by incentivising longer-term deposits or using swaps to convert fixed rates to variable rates). Part of this strategy is to explicitly formulate the ALM Risk Appetite, i.e., how much variable- or fixed-rate interest-bearing assets and liabilities, as well as liquidity risk, the bank is willing to take while ensuring its meets its profitability targets.

   The ALM strategy also includes principles on balance sheet composition (loan-to-deposit targets, mix of funding sources, mix of liquid assets, etc.). It also determines the overall stance on interest rate exposure (neutral, directional, but without speculation).

   At this strategic stage, the "rules of the game" for ALM are established, aligning it with the bank's overall vision. In other words, effective strategic ALM connects daily business decisions with the implications for balance sheet risk.

3. **Implementation of Tools, Systems and Risk Models**: With governance and strategy already defined, the next step is to equip the ALM function with the necessary analytical and technological tools. Comprehensive balance sheet management requires handling large volumes of data (all asset and liability positions, with their characteristics in terms of maturity, interest rate type, early repayment

options, etc.) and projecting complex scenarios. Many banks implement specialised ALM or Balance Sheet Management systems, which allow them to perform interest rate simulations, liquidity calculations under different assumptions, market value assessments of instruments, etc. It is important that the systems are capable of processing portfolios at a very granular level (ideally contract by contract), as excessive aggregation can obscure risks.

Among the methodological tools, Fund Transfer Pricing (FTP) stands out. As part of its implementation, the FTP scheme must be defined. FTP assigns an internal price to funds transferred between treasury (ALM centre) and business units or areas. For example, if the treasury receives deposits from retail depositors, it "pays" an internal rate to the retail business unit; if it grants funds for loans, it "charges" a rate to that unit. A good FTP reflects the marginal cost of liquidity and capital at each horizon, so that business areas can make the right decisions. For example, an area that originates a long-term fixed-rate loan understands that it must immobilise liquidity and assume interest-rate risk, accordingly, its profitability must be sufficient to cover the associated costs. A well-designed FTP helps to incorporate the cost of liquidity into the pricing of entity's lending.

The implementation of all these tools usually requires a competent ALM team with staff specialised in quantitative finance, market knowledge, and analytical skills to interpret the results. In large entities, there may be subdivisions (e.g., one team focused on IRRBB, another on liquidity, another on FTP and capital). In smaller banks, a compact planning/treasury/balance sheet risk team can take on multiple roles. In any case, training and culture are important: ALCO members and related areas must be trained to understand ALM concepts so that committee discussions are fruitful.

4. **Integration into Decision-Making and Daily Operations**: Once the ALM framework, governance, policies, and tools are in place, the crucial step is to effectively integrate the ALM function into the bank's daily operations and decisions, thus achieving truly strategic ALM. This means that before launching a new product or changing a major business or investment strategy, these decisions are discussed within the ALCO. Ideally, the head of ALM should be included in committee discussions on new product proposals, business planning, and other strategic topics.
5. **Monitoring, feedback and continuous improvement**: The work of ALCO should include periodic monitoring to verify whether the strategies are delivering the desired results or whether adjustments are required. The ALCO should receive periodic reporting to be able to give answers to questions such as: Are rate and liquidity sensitivity limits being met? What is the current position vs. appetite? What have the latest stress tests revealed? Has anything changed in the environment (new regulations, competition for deposits, etc.) that requires modifying the ALM strategy? A strategic ALM learns from these events and updates its assumptions and policies.

The most advanced banks, and not always the largest, see ALM not only as centre of risk control, but as a driver of strategic decision-making and performance optimisation. For example, a modern approach is to use ALM to transform risk management from a defensive task to a proactive growth strategy. This implies that ALCO discussions cover not only how to protect the bank against risks, but also how to optimise the balance sheet to create value – for example, by adjusting the mix of deposits and loans to enhance margins without exceeding limits, or by using hedges creatively to enable new products while keeping risks under control.

5 Pricing/funds transfer pricing (FTPs)

So far, the main activities of a commercial bank have been defined in previous chapters. Its primary mission is to buy and sell money, while also providing a range of services for which it charges fees or commissions. In the process of buying and selling money, prices are set for different transactions, which vary according to their characteristics such as transaction duration, whether the rate is fixed or variable, the currency involved, and the type of borrower. These characteristics give rise to a variety of risks, the identification of which has been highlighted in earlier chapters. Measuring and quantifying these risks is the foundation for setting transaction prices. Capital, as a buffer against unexpected losses, is another factor to bear in mind. Pricing in banking should therefore account not only for expected losses arising from identified risks, but also but also for potential unexpected losses, which must be absorbed by the bank's own funds.

The role of ALM within financial institutions is essential for the identification, measurement and management of financial risks. It is the function within a bank that provides a holistic, aggregated view of all financial risks, which form the basis for setting prices for the purchase and sale of money. Consequently, ALM becomes the nerve centre for decision-making, guiding both tactical and strategic decisions.

In this sense, Fund Transfer Pricing (FTPs) is a fundamental component of the ALM function, serving as the cornerstone for pricing within financial institutions. The construction methodology – covering both liabilities and assets, as well as balance sheet stock and new production – must be carefully supervised and agreed upon at the institutional level to ensure proper integration into the management of the different business units.

A review of the literature reveals that there is no single, structured or universally accepted definition of FTP. For example, without attempting to be exhaustive in citing all authors, the following contributions from notable authors illustrate the range of perspectives:

- Choudhry (2018) defines FTP as "*the internal rate at which the funding desk lends or borrows from business lines*".
- Schäfer et al. (2017) define FTP as "*a term used to describe the sum of policies and methodologies that a bank applies in its internal governance system to charge/credit for the use/obtaining of funding and liquidity*".
- Dermine (2009) does not provide a definitive definition and bases his arguments regarding its calculation by saying that "*FTP is used to evaluate the profitability of deposits and loans*".
- Bessis (2015) states that "*FTP serves to transfer funds from units with excess liquidity to units with liquidity needs through a pool of funds located in the Treasury*".

Note: Extracted from the author's doctoral thesis. https://repositorio.uam.es/handle/10486/686795

 | https://doi.org/10.1515/9783111328386-005

He also argues that "FTP is a system of income allocation, breaking down the overall profits from the financial institution's portfolio into profits allocated to each line of business".

- Wilson (2015) states that "*FTP is the target transfer price of financial risk from an individual product to the ALM portfolio. Each transfer price is associated with a financial representation or replica portfolio, i.e., a portfolio of cash and derivative instruments that replicates the financial risks of the underlying product. The replication portfolio is precisely what the ALM function sees*".

Given the objective of separating origination decisions for both investment and financing operations, Wilson (2015) suggests that an FTP system should adhere to the following principles:
1. FTP should be calculated using actual market prices.
2. FTP should reflect, as closely as possible, the specific characteristics of the product's financial cash flow.
3. FTP should capture the marginal cost of hedging financial risks for a financial institution with the highest rating in wholesale, liquid markets, and in the same currency as the underlying product.
4. FTP should, in principle, allow the institution to "purchase" the replication portfolio or hedge the cash flows that neutralise the financial risk of the product.
5. Since FTP is primarily used to calculate the contribution to margin in product origination and influences management decisions, it should be established in a clear and transparent manner.

Again, according to Wilson (2015), FTP is designed to ensure that the true costs and benefits of financial institutions' liquidity are allocated across all products, and it does not necessarily need to be equivalent to the institution's actual funding cost.

The ALM function, see Figure 5.1, typically managed through a central unit – often referred to as the ALM desk, Treasury or similar – generally acts as a clearing house for structural balance sheet risks, including interest rate, liquidity, and currency risks. The various business units lend and borrow funds, incorporating these structural risks into the balance sheet, which are then managed centrally. This central management isolates the business units – and their profitability measures – from market movements beyond their control. This centralisation of risk is implemented through FTPs. When calculating their contribution to the institution's margin, business units compare the origination price of a transaction with the corresponding FTPs. For asset transactions, the FTP reflects the price or valuation of the risks a similar transaction would carry, incorporating the same risks as the originated transaction. If the result is positive, the transaction adds value. For liability transactions, the price paid at the origination of the transaction is subtracted from the FTP (Wilson, 2015).

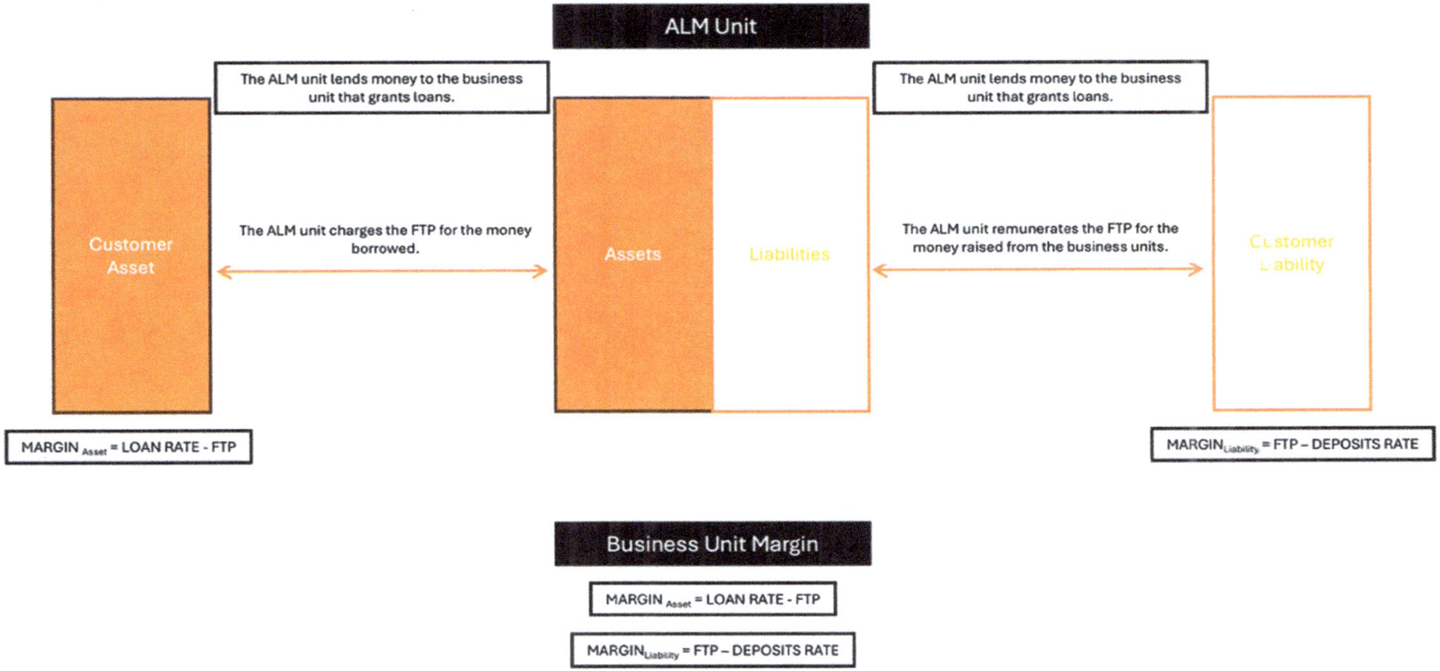

Figure 5.1: Diagram Showing How FTPs Work as a Mechanism for Obtaining Profitability From Business Units.
Source: Own elaboration.

With the correct application of the FTP methodology, financial institutions ensure that business units do not face perverse incentives that could lead to excessive risk-taking or a misallocation of resources, potentially jeopardising the sustainability of the business. FTPs also help ensure that business units act appropriately, avoiding the creation of internal imbalances, as business units are incentivised to contract only products that generate a positive margin for their unit.

Applying the rates resulting from the FTP calculation to customer rates allows for a commercial margin that remains stable over time, with performance unaffected by market fluctuations. This consistency in margin is a key feature of an FTP system. The ALM function, through the treasury, assumes financial risks and makes management decisions based on the internally approved risk-return profile, particularly in the context of dynamic risk management. However, in practice, institutions may not fully implement this segregation of information, nor manage dynamically the risks embedded in the balance sheet. The results of the treasury's decisions regarding the synthetic positions created through the FTP system are referred to as the treasury margin or ALM unit margin (Wilson, 2015).

5.1 FTP models

In the specialised literature, three main types of FTP models are identified: the single pool model, the multiple-pool model, and the matched-maturity model.

5.1.1 Single pool model

This establishes a single rate as FTPs for all assets and liabilities subject to the FTP system, without considering the explicit or implicit financial risk characteristics of the transactions.

The rate can be set internally or by taking a market rate.

Table 5.1 shows the advantages and disadvantages of this single pool model (Pushkina (2013)).

Given the complexity of today's environment and the importance of the subject in management decision-making, this method can be considered outdated and of limited practical use. Nevertheless, it represents a first step towards obtaining initial figures from an analytical perspective, provided that the conclusions drawn from the extracted information are interpreted with caution.

Table 5.1: Advantages and Disadvantages. Single Pool Model of FTPs.

Advantages	Disadvantages
It is the simplest method to implement in terms of cost	There is no separation of interest rate risk from credit risk
Does not require significant investment in data systems	There is a single transfer price, which minimises management incentives
Requires little IT knowledge compared to other FTP systems	There is no differentiation in the transfer of results in line with the temporary structure of the portfolio
Allows for the allocation of an average cost to transactions	Does not take historical interest rates into account.
It is suitable for small banks, especially those that operate with only one business unit	Behavioural measures are not valid as prices are not assigned to each transaction

Source: *Pushkina (2013)*

5.1.2 Multiple pool model

In this model, assets and liabilities are classified into different pools, with separation criteria that can include tenors, interest rate type (fixed or variable), credit quality, product type, etc. These characteristics determine the choice of transfer rate for each pool.

Consequently, each financial institution must establish a set of rates, which can be determined internally or obtained from market data. As Pushkina (2013) notes, a lack of objectivity in the deriving internal rates can lead to significant errors, so greater emphasis should be placed on market-based rates.

However, if market rates are used without adjusting for the age or maturity of transactions, business units may engage in arbitrage by exploiting interest rate fluctuations to improve the profitability of their units. Nonetheless, market rates can be appropriate for pricing new transaction inflows.

Table 5.2 shows the advantages and disadvantages of this model (Pushkina (2013)).

5.1.3 Matched-maturity model

The main feature of this model is that transfer rates are set on a transaction-by-transaction basis, allowing the characteristics of each contract's cash flow – including interest rate risk (including optionality), liquidity and credit – to be incorporated into the FTP. This ensures that the margin achieved on each transaction remains constant throughout its life. Market movements do not affect this margin, as the associated risks are managed centrally by the ALM function through the treasury.

Table 5.2: Advantages and Disadvantages. Multiple FTP Pool Model.

Advantages	Disadvantages
Does not require complex computer systems.	It is subject to changes in interest rates, as the profitability of the products depends on them.
Does not require detailed transaction information.	Does not take into account the effect of historical interest rates.
Can be implemented using internal software developments.	It is suitable for short-term fixed-rate transactions and long-term transactions.
It allows accurate profitability calculations for *pools* of variable-rate products.	There is no separation of interest rate risk from credit risk.
It incorporates the term structure of assets and liabilities while allowing for adjustments.	There is considerable variation in the accuracy of management results.
Valuable for commercial banks with many branches that use interbank transactions.	There is more disparity between management interest and accounting interest.
Facilitates objective performance evaluation and assists in management decision-making regarding product structure.	Requires more IT resources than the single *pool* model.

Source: Pushkina (2013)

Table 5.3 shows the main advantages and disadvantages of this model (Pushkina (2013)).

Table 5.3: Advantages and Disadvantages. Matched-Maturity Model of FTPs.

Advantages	Disadvantages
Separates credit risk and interest rate risk.	It is the most expensive method to implement.
All business transactions are based on a fixed interest margin.	Requires the acquisition of expensive IT tools.
Facilitates impartial commercial decisions by enabling accurate assessment and motivation.	It is not suitable for small banks that do not have the resources or knowledge to use it.
It allows for the centralisation of interest risk and its subsequent transfer to the responsible business unit.	

Source: Pushkina (2013)

One of the main issues with this model is the potential misuse of information from the analytical FTP in other internal analyses within financial institutions. For example, consider a customer who was granted a mortgage loan in 2021 at a fixed rate of 2% (Figure 5.2). Based on the FTP margin, without performing precise calculations and noting that the rate is well above the 15-year swap curve, which serves as a reference basis for calculating the cost of liquidity (excluding any premiums) this transaction would appear to contribute positively to the margin. However, the same customer in 2023, as shown in Figure 5.2, made a deposit at 3.5%, assuming the same amount as the outstanding loan balance. Given that this rate is below the 6-month Euribor, it could also be concluded (i.e., without making more precise calculations) that this transaction contributes positively to the margin of the business unit to which this customer belongs.

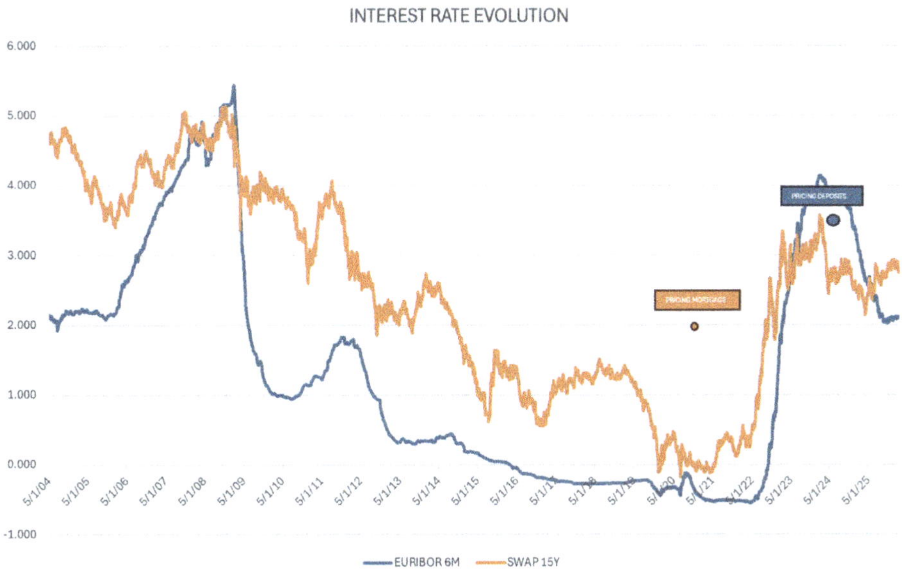

Figure 5.2: Example of Distortion in the Matched-Maturity Model.
Source: Own elaboration based on data from Bloomberg.

When analysing the customer from the perspective of value creation in a bank's commercial information systems, this customer would appear to generate positive margins under the FTP model, that is, from the ALM perspective, both for the mortgage loan and for the deposit. However, if the financial institution decides not to cover these positions and based on the actual rates, this customer is effectively engaging in a carry trade, holding a loan at 2% and a deposit at 3.5%. Whether the ALM function has hedged this position is a matter of balance sheet management and it makes sense that this client has a positive margin with the coverage of the positions. From a commercial point of view, this customer should be assessed without the margin models of FTP systems in order to correctly identify the value contribution and better orient commercial strategies at the customer level.

5.2 Purpose of using FTPs

Choudhry (2018) identifies three potential uses of FTPs: as a tool for product pricing, as a tool for profit management, and as a risk management tool.

5.2.1 FTP as a tool for product pricing

This approach involves establishing an internal barrier rate – minimum for loans and maximum for deposits – used as the reference for negotiating transactions with customers. Using FTP in this way for product pricing ensures that a customer transaction is only executed if it generates a positive commercial margin for the bank over the life of the transaction. The margin obtained at origination remains constant throughout the transaction's life and is not affected by the risk of mismatch, which is managed centrally by the ALM function within the treasury area (Choudhry, 2018).

In general terms, profitability thresholds are set by the various business units within a financial institution. However, the production factors associated with any asset or liability product are best understood by the ALM function. The ALM function should therefore be responsible for ensuring that profitability thresholds derived from the construction of FTPs are correctly established for pricing purposes (Choudhry, 2018).

5.2.2 FTP as a tool for profit management

When comparing the profitability of operations using an FTP curve – established as an internal system of profitability thresholds – financial institutions can break down profitability into three components (Choudhry, 2018):

a. Commercial margin on asset operations.
b. Commercial margin on liability operations.
c. Treasury margin due to maturity transformation.

Both commercial margins remain constant throughout the life of the transaction, even if the FTP curve changes – assuming a market-oriented FTP system where the treasury can operate freely in capital markets and the FTP curve reflects current market conditions. Any variations in the FTP curve are absorbed by the treasury, which is responsible for managing balance sheet mismatches of the financial institutions (Choudhry, 2018).

The treasury margin generated from the transformation of maturities is managed centrally. Specifically, it is the difference between the rate received from investment operations minus the rate paid for financing operations. Whether or not it is covered depends on the entity's risk appetite.

Under this market-oriented FTP scheme, management of assets and liabilities by each business unit is mutually exclusive in terms of price, volume, and maturities (Choudhry, 2018).

5.2.3 FTP as a risk management tool

Transfer prices are constructed under the principle of "matched maturity", whereby the rates embedded in a portfolio of instruments that would represent a micro-hedge of the mismatch (including interest rates and liquidity premium, depending on whether these are considered) are assigned as FTP rates for customer transactions. This applies to both asset and liability transactions. The decision to hedge, however, rests with the treasury department, which is not obliged to execute it. Treasury retains discretion to take positions on market movements that may benefit the entity (Choudhry, 2018).

This approach can be extended to more complex product features, such as prepayments on asset products (valued as an embedded options), credit accounts, non-maturing products, etc. (Choudhry, 2018).

Centralising all these risks in the treasury area facilitates the identification, measurement, monitoring and control of risks through the implementation of an FTP system.

From a risk management perspective, certain options are difficult to manage, either due to the absence of a liquid market in which they are quoted or the difficulty of calculating them internally within institutions. Including these characteristics in FTP calculations may not be practical if the treasury function lacks the mandate or the necessary resources to manage these risks effectively. In some cases, it may also be impractical to centralise these "more exotic" risks from the business units to the treasury due to the inherent difficulty of managing them (Choudhry, 2018).

5.3 Construction of FTPs as pricing in investment operations

As a reminder of earlier chapters, when analysing the financial intermediation model of banks, their activity can be summarised as follows: a financial institution borrows money and then lends it to its customers at longer maturities, thereby performing maturity transforming. This process exposes the institution to interest rate risk, which depends on the rate at which funds were borrowed and the rate at which they are lent, as well as liquidity risk arising from the need to roll over borrowings.

Additionally, a credit risk arises depending on the characteristics of the borrowers. This risk must be assessed and estimated and as noted in previous chapters, can be parametrised through the concept of ECL.

Own funds or capital must also be considered – not only as a regulatory requirement but for their fundamental economic function: to cover unexpected losses under worst-case scenarios. As such, capital represents a cost, since it belongs to shareholders and must therefore be remunerated.

Finally, carrying out banking activities involves a series of transformation costs, including administrative expenses such as staff costs, which must necessarily be reflected in the pricing of the operations offered to customers.

From the above, it follows that the costs to be considered in credit investment operations carried out in commercial banking, which should be reflected in FTP, are:
- Cost of funding.
- Operating costs.
- Credit risk or expected loss.
- Capital or unexpected loss.

As shown in Figure 5.3, these costs are reflected either in the P&L statement or in the balance sheet (via equity or regulatory capital) of the institution.

5.3.1 Cost of funding

Dermine (2009) highlights the difficulty of determining the cost of financing for a credit investment operation, due to the different sources of financing available to banks. To address this problem, the author draws on the theory developed by Monti (1971) and Klein (1972). As explained by Dermine (2009), the starting points is a bank's balance sheet as shown in Figure 5.4:

On the asset side, this bank holds central bank reserves "R", loans "L", and market-traded assets such as bonds and interbank loans "B". On the liability side, it has deposits "D" and capital "E". Reserves do not earn interest and are assumed to be a fixed proportion "r" of deposits. Bonds, Interbank "B" yield an interest rate "b". Bonds and interbank markets are perfectly elastic in a competitive market – in other words, the market is large and highly liquid, so individual transactions do not affect prices.

Loan demand "L" is a decreasing function of the loan interest rate "l", while deposits "D" are an increasing function of the deposit rate "d". It is assumed that all assets and liabilities have the same duration and that all parameters are known. The cost of capital in the model is given by the bond rate "b". It is assumed that there is no risk. The specification of the financial institution's balance sheet model is determined by the maximisation of its economic profit, represented as follows:

$$Max\,EP = (l * L + b * B - d * D) - b * E$$

Subject to the following balance sheet restriction:

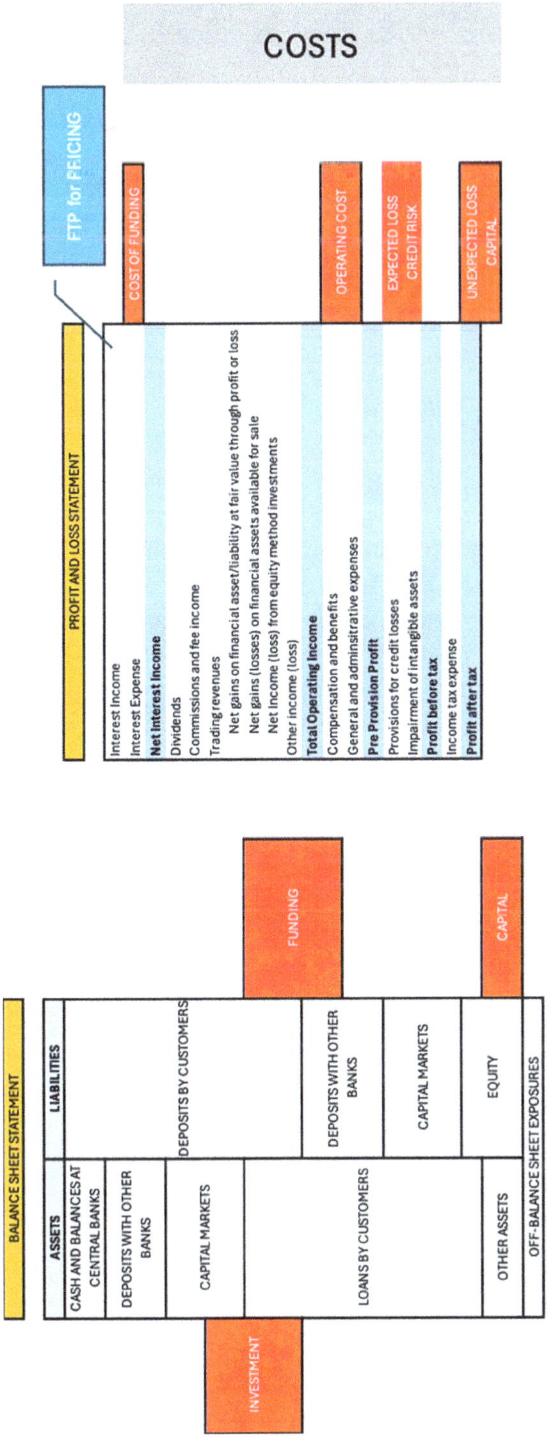

Figure 5.3: Balance Sheet and P&L Movements for FTP Construction as Price Setting.
Source: Own elaboration.

Assets	Liabilities
Reserves **R** Loans **L** Bonds, Interbank **B**	Deposits **D** Capital **E**

Figure 5.4: Financial Institution Balance Sheet. Separation Theorem in Banking (Monti, 1971 and Klein, 1972). Source: Dermine, J. (2009).

$$R + L + B = D + E$$

Substituting the balance sheet restriction into the objective function, the objective function can be rewritten as follows:

$$Max\,EP = [(l - b) * L] + \{(b * (1 - r) - d] * D\}$$

Dermine (2009) shows that economic profit can be decomposed into two components: (i) income from loans net of the opportunity cost of capital, and (ii) income from deposits that are invested in assets that yield "b". However, that yield cannot be applied to the entire deposit base because a fraction must be held as non-remunerated central banks reserves, net of the interest paid to depositors. This decomposition gives rise to the *separation theorem* in banking, which states that the pricing of loans and deposits is independent and is referenced to the market rate for bonds and interbank loans "b". Graphically, the separation theorem can be represented as in Figure 5.5:

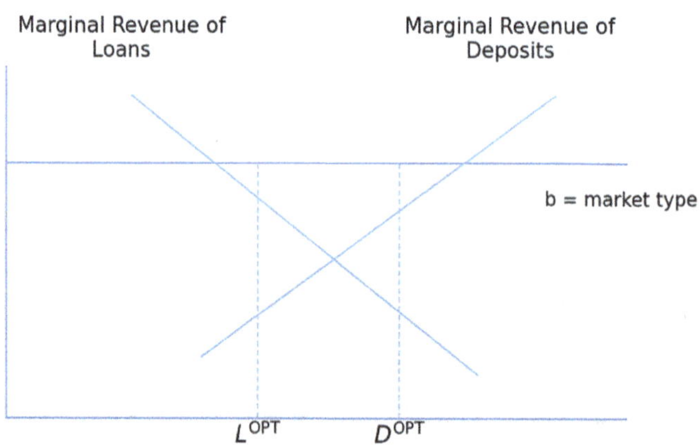

Figure 5.5: Separation Theorem (Monti, 1971 and Klein, 1972).
Source: *Dermine (2009).*

When a financial institution seeks to expand its loan portfolio, the marginal income generated from additional loans decreases. This is because the bank either lowers its lending rate to attract new borrowers or accepts borrowers with higher risk. Likewise, the marginal cost of increasing the deposit base increases, either because the bank needs to raise the interest rate to attract new depositors or expand its commercial network into new areas where it currently has no presence. These mechanisms illustrate how banking competition directly affects the pricing of both loans and deposits.

The graph shows that the optimal deposit volume, D^{OPT}, is reached when the marginal cost of new deposits equals the market rate "b". It would not be optimal for an institution to attract deposits above its optimal level, since the marginal cost of doing so would exceed the cost of obtaining funds directly the capital market at rate "b". Similarly, the optional volume of loans, L^{OPT}, is reached when the marginal income from new loans equals the marginal return on market investments at rate "b". The separation theorem therefore states that both loan and deposit pricing must be referenced to the market interest rate and that these decisions are independent of one another. The difference between the optimal levels of loans and deposits determine the institution's position in cash, bonds and interbank loans (Dermine, 2009).

An alternative and intuitive reasoning for using the interbank market rate as the fund transfer price, which Dermine (2009) emphasises himself, is the following: if a business unit succeeds in significantly increasing its deposit base, the resulting effect on the balance sheet will be an expansion of the institution's holdings of interbank loans or sovereign bonds. In this situation, transfer prices should indicate a signal about the optimal level of funding, based on the interest rates the unit pays for those deposits. Similarly, this reasoning can be applied to loans.

The Monti-Klein model provides a microeconomic foundation for the use of interbank market interest rates as reference rates for pricing. In the matched-maturity framework described above, the inherent maturity *mismatches* in banking imply that FTP, when set on a transaction-by-transaction basis, must accurately reflect the cash-flow profile of each contract and incorporate interest rate risk (including optionality), liquidity and credit risk. In this regard, it is primarily through the interbank markets, especially the money market and swap markets, that these characteristics can be most effectively captured. This is consistent with the model present earlier: using interbank market rates as transfer princes enables business units to be immunised from structural risks, allowing these risks to be managed centrally by the ALM function through the treasury.

However, in practice, distortions arise in the pricing of assets and liabilities. These do not invalidate Dermine's (2009) argument. Rather, due to actual market prices, combined with short-term ambitions based on expected cross-selling opportunities with customers, and assumptions of yield-compensation schemes between balance sheet items, financial institutions often make decisions outside the optimal environment envisioned by the Monti-Klein's theory.

On the other hand, Matz and Neu (2012) propose a methodology for determining the financing cost of a bank loan, which integrates both the interest rate risk and liquidity risk arising from the inherent mismatches in banking business.

The cash flows of the transaction must first be represented. The transfer price is then determined as the difference between the internal rate of return or the par rate with respect to the swap curve and the financing curve (swap curve modified by the liquidity premium for terms quoted by the financial institution).

The internal rate of return for the swap curve, see Figure 5.6, represents the transfer price paid by loan at the time of its origination to the ALM centre as the transfer price for interest rate risk (Matz and Neu, 2012).

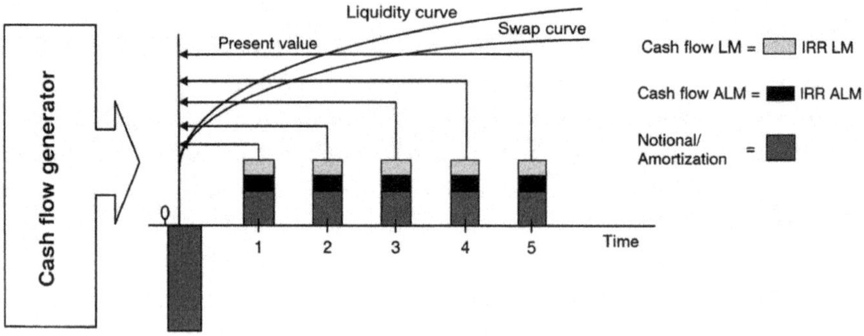

Figure 5.6: Example of Cash Flow Representation for a Credit Investment Operation.
Source: *Matz and Neu (2012).*

$$\sum_{t=1}^{T}(N_{t-1}{}^{*}IRR_{ALM}+A_t)^{*}e^{r^{t}swap^{*}t}=N_0\Rightarrow IRR_{ALM}$$

Where:

N_t = Outstanding notional amount of the loan in period t.
A_t = Amount amortised in period t-1 to t.
$r^t{}_{swap}$ = Swap interest rate in period t

Similarly, the IRR of the financial institution's funding curve is the transfer price for the interest rate and liquidity *mismatch*, which is reflected in the following formula:

$$\sum_{t=1}^{T}(N_{t-1}{}^{*}IRR_{ALM}+A_t)*e-{}^{(r^t}swap+BLS^t)*t=N_0\Rightarrow IRR_{ALM}$$

Where:

N_t = Notional amount outstanding in period t.
A_t = Amount amortised in the period t-1 to t.
$r^t{}_{swap}$ = Swap interest rate in period t.
BLS_t = Liquidity spread in each period t on the swap curve.

Therefore, the isolated liquidity cost due to the mismatch, which the ALM centre must pass on to the business unit at the of loan origination is calculated as follows (Matz and Neu, 2012):

$$Liquidity\ cost = IRR_{LM} - IRR_{ALM}$$

In addition, financial institutions face another form of liquidity risk in credit investment products, known as contingent liquidity risk. For the sake of simplicity, this is not a central element of this handbook and will limit itself to a brief discussion of the need for its measurement.

Contingent liquidity risk is intended to reward business units that provide liquidity and penalise those that consume it. Following the framework proposed by Matz and Neu (2012), contingent liquidity risk may arise – exclusively in relation to credit investment assets, liabilities and customer deposits – from:
1) Irrevocable commitments on the balance sheet, e.g., credit account provisions.
2) Unexpected withdrawal of deposits.

Matz and Neu (2012) argue that irrevocable balance sheet commitments should be managed at the portfolio level, by analysing the average utilisation of the credit account portfolio and quantifying the volatility in the use of available funds. The average utilisation of credit accounts should be financed until maturity and incorporated into the assessment of liquidity risk arising from maturity mismatches. In contrast, the volatility of the use of available funds would require short-term finance, necessitating the maintenance of liquidity buffers. The costs of these buffers must be allocated across the different credit lines and, therefore, included in the pricing of transactions. Consequently, there are ultimately three components that must be considered in credit account pricing:
1. Cost of the liquidity mismatch due to current utilisation.
2. Cost of liquidity mismatch due to expected utilisation.
3. Cost of the contingent liquidity to account for the volatility in the expected utilisation of available limits in credit accounts.

As an approximation for pricing purposes, Matz and Neu (2012) suggest that contingent liquidity costs could be estimated by passing on the yield spread between unsecured and secured assets, multiplied by the financial assets that must be held. This reflects the obligations of the entity to adopt a more conservative wholesale investment policy due to contingent liquidity risk, thereby capturing the costs implied by market liquidity risk.

Furthermore, these calculations should be adjusted to account for the valuation of any explicit or implicit options embedded in the products whose financing costs are being set (prepayments, etc.).

In summary, Dermine (2009), as well as Matz and Neu (2012), provide a framework for determining the cost of financing using market curves and incorporating a liquidity cost based on the institution's financing structure. To simplify the discussion, this handbook does not cover the additional costs to be added to the financing cost due to the implementation of liquidity risk metrics such as the LCR and NSFR.

After all that has been noted above, from a practitioner's point of view, it is clear that using market curves is highly beneficial, e.g., Euribor curves for short-term instruments and swap curve for longer maturities. In other geographical regions outside Europe, these curves should be adapted to the local markets. The use of market curves allows for the incorporation of so-called "structural risks", including IRRBB risk, liquidity risk and currency risk (the latter requiring adjustment of the curve with respect to the currency used).

When an ALM unit uses a swap rate to fix the cost of funding for an investment operation, it ensures that, in the event of interest rate movements, liabilities move with the same sensitivity as the assets. This mechanism partially mitigates situations such as those experienced by Silicon Valley Bank, since, if it had taken out the hedge and maintained it over time, it would have sensitised the assets in the same way as the liabilities, and the valuation of the different balance sheet items would have moved in tandem, and it would also have been able to pay the interest rates demanded by depositors.

Additionally, this approach addresses a common challenge faced by commercial banks, where the primary source of funding comes from retail deposits, which typically have an average short term (e.g., six months). By setting the variable leg of a swap, e.g., equal to the six-month Euribor, the ALM unit can ensure that the cost of funding to be factored into the pricing of investment operations aligns both with the rate payable to customers and the tenor of the deposits – up to the 6-month Euribor rate. This forms a first line of defence against liquidity risk and, as explained above, provides additional profitability as needed to respond to deposits outflows or the materialisation of funding liquidity risk, as it could pay the remuneration on all deposits up to the 6-month Euribor, which is its average term, and if the market became more strained due to systemic issues, it could withstand betas greater than 1 (i.e., pay above the 6-month Euribor) to the extent that it is able to maintain a sufficient amount of NMDs to offset that higher beta. Maintaining this alignment consistently over time is essential.

If a bank is able to remunerate deposits at a rate below the Euribor curve, this generates an extra benefit. However, there can also be periods – such as in Spain between 2011 and 2013 – when liquidity premiums on deposits were considerable. In such cases, a compensatory mechanism available to banks is to balance the mix between customer demand deposits and term deposits. Demand deposits can provide a profitability margin relative to the Euribor curve, which may help offset the higher liquidity premiums paid on term deposits.

Therefore, the cost of financing should be considered without including liquidity premiums based on the bank's financing structure for two reasons:

1. Firstly, as noted above, the aim is to analyse investment and financing business lines separately. This distinction is necessary to understand where value is created when setting prices at the time of origination or its evolution over time

based on the movement of interest rate curves, whether in investment or in financing, because the terms of each have a significant impact.

Example: Consider a bank offering a pool of 30-year fixed-rate mortgages priced at 2.1%, where the equivalent swap rate for sensitivity purposes is approximately 15 years at 2.75% (ignoring other pricing components). These mortgages are financed with retail deposits: 30% in non-maturing deposits at 0% and 70% in 6-month term deposits at 1%, while the 6-month Euribor stands at 2%. Although the bank shows a very positive profit, the source of value differs. Deposit-taking contributes positively to value (with "value" understood as an advantage relative to market rates), whereas lending reduces value, since lending rates are below the relevant reference rate.

From the above example, it is evident that separating the sources of profits is key to understanding how the bank is managed, as well as to assessing the financial risks it may face in the future.

2. Secondly, incorporating liquidity premiums into the pricing of long-term investment products exposes institutions to significant risk, as the duration of the premiums is typically shorter. Even attempts to mitigate this risk, such as averaging premiums over time, do not provide an optimal solution. As noted earlier, financial institutions must set interest rates for investment transactions at the time of origination, with no possibility of adjustment except through management of IRRBB. Liquidity premiums, however, are fixed at origination, introducing additional uncertainty into management decisions. Commercial banks do not generally fund themselves over very long terms; their primary source of financing is customer deposits, although they occasionally issue longer-term debt—typically in the form of 10-year covered bonds. For this reason, it is more effective for a bank to avoid blending liquidity premiums into investment pricing and instead pursue two distinct strategies—investment and financing—so as to separate pricing approaches and maximise the institution's overall value.

For all the reasons outlined above, it is proposed to use the following as the financing cost:[21]

$$\textit{Cost of funding} = \textit{Euribor}/\textit{swap}\ (\textit{adjusted for modied duration})$$

This means selecting the point on the Euribor or Swap market curve that corresponds to the interest rate risk sensitivity of the investment, as measured by its modified duration. This point may be adjusted further based on prepayment behaviour modelling, which can alter the effective interest rate sensitivity of the investment.

21 Optional adjustments such as prepayments, etc., are not included in order to simplify the presentation of concepts.

5.3.2 Operating costs

Operating costs are a key element of the cost structure that must be considered when setting the price of a product. As can be seen in Figure 5.3, these costs are an essential component of the income statement, the cascade of which is used to determine prices for both asset and liability operations. Linking these costs to the ALM function of a financial institution is not straightforward, as it requires cost-allocation systems to isolate costs directly linked to investment or lending activities from other cost expenses. However, because the ALM function is responsible for constructing FTPs for pricing purposes, it must collect the necessary input data for correct price formation, most likely in cooperation with relevant units, e.g., accounting, even though it is not responsible for building the cost-control and monitoring process.

Operating costs must include all overheads (personnel, administrative and depreciation) associated with investment operations, referred to as cost factors, and must be allocated as a percentage of the nominal value of the operation.

Once the different items comprising the operating costs have been identified, it is necessary to map the banking production processes. These can be broken down into three sub-processes: fund raising, fund placement, and other costs such as origination, servicing, etc. Each phase within these sub-processes, along their interdependencies, should be identified (Ibarrondo, 2002).

Next, the most appropriate cost-allocation criteria should be applied to allocate these cost factors to each sub-process or cost centre, specifying the units of measurement for cost allocation. There are different cost allocation methodologies in cost accounting, such as standard costs, activity-based costing (ABC), etc. It is important to note that, for pricing purposes, average costs should be used rather than marginal costs, as this better reflects the normal evolution of a bank's business development

For the sake of simplicity, the following formula is proposed:

$$Operating\ Cost = \frac{Total\ Operating\ Cost}{Total\ Assets + Total\ Liability + Total\ off\ Balance\ sheet\ Exposure}$$

The result obtained from this formula represents the yield that each monetary unit – whether lent, financed or exposed off-balance sheet – must generate periodically to cover the full cost structure of the financial institution.

Different weights can be applied by business area or other criteria to account for whether the management of balance sheet assets consumes more or fewer resources than liabilities. The primary purpose here is not to discuss these allocation criteria in detail, but to emphasise that the use of the average costs is the key principle for price construction.

5.3.3 Expected loss – credit risk

Depending on the governance structure of the ALM function within a financial institution, credit risk may or may not be fully integrated into ALM. However, at the pricing level, the ALM is responsible for constructing FTPs and must therefore obtain the relevant parameters from risk control areas. These parameters are essential for determining the level of credit risk both at the time of origination and throughout the life of the transaction.

Specifically, as already noted in Section 2.1.1, credit risk is factored in into the pricing process by using the expected loss, which can be obtained from the following formula:

$$Expected\,credit\,loss = PD \ast LGD \ast EAD$$

Where:

PD = Probability of default.
LGD = Loss given default.
EAD = Exposure at default.

In Section 3.1.2, one of the main challenges in measuring credit risk under IFRS 9 for new transactions was highlighted. For these transactions, the IFRS 9 standard required that the PD is calibrated based on expected defaults over a 12-month horizon. The reasons for using a lifetime PD instead were discussed in Section 3.1.2. Therefore, a robust pricing scheme should use the lifetime PD and assume that the total expected loss over the economic cycle is considered, as this more accurately reflects the actual cost of credit risk incurred by the bank.

5.3.4 Unexpected loss – capital

In addition to expected credit loss, financial institutions may also incur unexpected losses. Unexpected losses arise from the volatility of potential losses and must therefore be incorporated into the pricing of investments as an additional cost. Since regulatory frameworks require that unexpected losses are covered by capital, which belongs to the shareholders, pricing must also reflect the cost of remunerating shareholders for the capital held, which is commonly known as the cost of capital.

Prudential regulation determines the capital requirement for each transaction based on the various risks to which the transaction is exposed, including credit, operational and market risk -commonly referred to as Pillar 1 risks. Other risks, such as IRRBB, CSRBB and credit risk concentration, are addressed under the supervisory review process known as SREP (Pillar 2), which requires institutions to maintain a capital add-on in addition to the minimum Pillar 1 requirement. Therefore, the capital requirement to be factored in into the pricing process must account for both Pillar 1 and Pillar 2 risks.

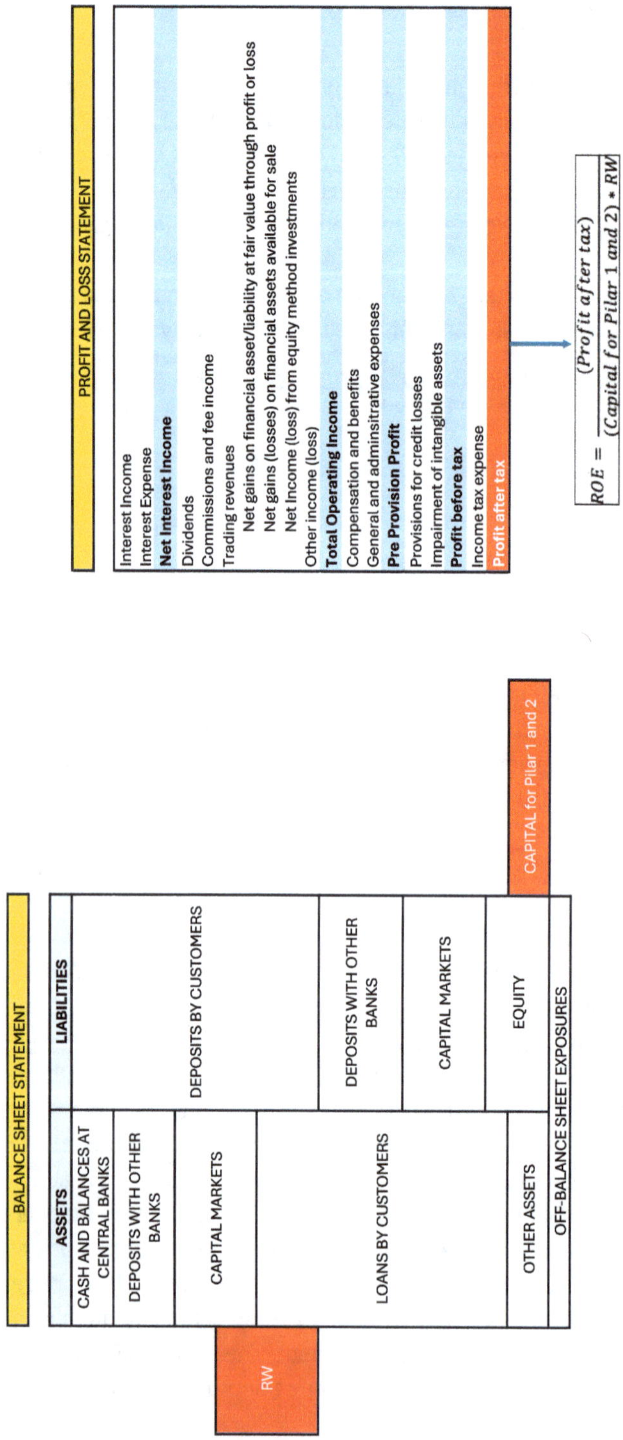

Figure 5.7: Calculation – Cost of Capital.
Source: Own elaboration.

To determine the cost of capital to be applied to investment transactions, the following inputs should be taken:

1. Credit risk risk-weight (RW) of the transaction, calculated for prudential purposes under the applicable regulatory framework (Basel or European standards, which allow both IRB and standardised approaches).
2. The capital required to the institution to cover both the risks under Pillar 1 and Pillar 2.
3. The return-on-equity (ROE) of the financial institution, which represents the remuneration expected by the shareholders.

The ROE and the cost of capital can be calculated using the following two formulas:

$$ROE = \frac{(Profit\ after\ tax)}{(Capital\ for\ pilar\ 1\ and\ 2) * RW}$$

$$Unexpected\ Loss = ROE * (Capital\ for\ Pilar\ 1\ y\ 2) * RW$$

It is important to note that the proposed ROE differs from the standard market metric, which relates net profit to total equity. In the proposed approach, capital requirements under Pillar 1 and Pillar 2 are used instead, as they more accurately reflect the portion of own funds that must be remunerated.

Accordingly, the price component needed to cover unexpected losses (expressed as a percentage) corresponds to an institution's required ROE – valued by the market based on the perceived risk of its business model – multiplied by the capital requirements of the investment, adjusted for its risk profile.

Example: Consumer Loan.

In August 2022, financial institution "X" grants an 8-year consumer loan for the purchase of a car. The bank has a total volume of €1 billion (total assets, liabilities and off-balance sheet items) and operating costs of €7 million. The institution's internal models, based on the customer's credit quality, show a PD LFT of 6% and, in the event of default, recovery would be 40%. For unexpected losses, the institution wants to maintain a sustainable ROE of 15%, with a target capital of 12.5% and a risk weighting of 75%.

On the day the loan is granted, the rates are as shown in Figure 5.8:

1.- Cost of funding

The point on the curve equivalent to the modified duration is taken. As this is a consumer loan with a French repayment system, the proxy where this duration is equal to the term divided by 2 is used.

Loan term = 8y -> Modified duration = 4y -> 4y swap rate = 2.23%

2.- Operating Cost

Average costs are used.

Operating costs = 7/1,000 = 0.70%

3.- Expected Loss

ECL LFT = 6% * (1-40%) = 3.6%. This expected loss is total for the economic cycle. The entity must ensure that the transaction price is charged at the price in accordance with its amortisation table. As it is a loan under the French amortisation system, the ECL LFT is divided by the modified duration.

The expected loss to be considered in the price would be equal to 3.6% / 4 = 0.9%.

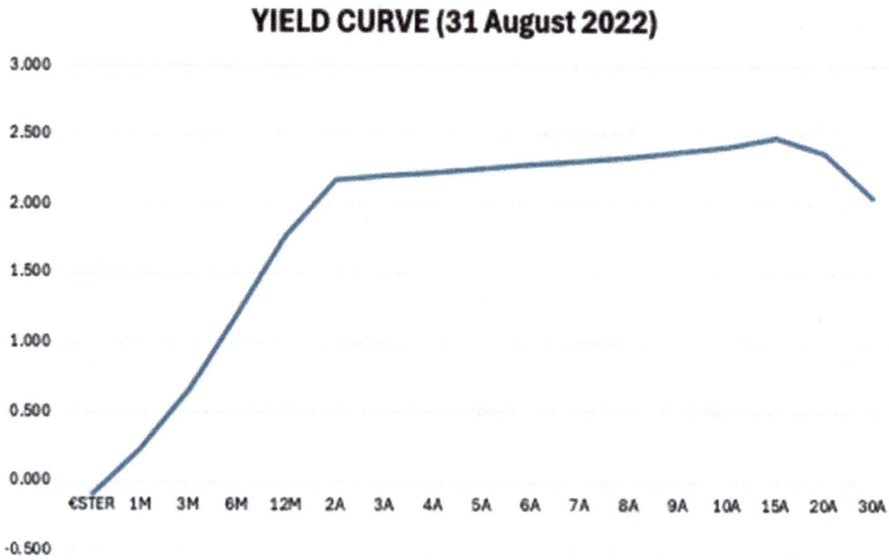

Figure 5.8: Yield Curve.
Source: Own elaboration based on data from Bloomberg.

4.- Unexpected Loss
UL = 15% * 12.5% * 75% = 1.41%

TOTAL PRICING = Cost of funding + Operating costs + Expected loss + Unexpected loss

TOTAL PRICING = 2.23% + 0.70% + 0.9% + 1.41% = 5.24%. This is the minimum at which the loan should be granted to cover all financial risks at the time of origination.

5.3.5 FTP for investment operations

In conclusion, the FTP to be determined – whose purpose is to set the minimum price for investment transactions – corresponds to the level at which the business unit begins to generate a positive margin in addition to covering the cost of capital, would be:

$$\textit{FTP Investment Operations} = \textit{Cost of Funding} + \textit{Operating Costs} + \textit{Expected Loss} + \textit{Unexpected Loss}$$

It should be noted that the FTPs for investment operations do not take into account any commissions that may be generated from cross-selling other products.

5.4 Construction of FTPs as pricing in financing operations

With regard to deposit pricing, when financial institutions determine the maximum rate they should be able to pay, the analysis must be performed on a marginal basis, assessing the use of the funds raised. These deposits are placed on the interbank market, as noted by Dermine (2009), for a term equivalent to the modified duration of the deposit, used as a measure of interest rate risk sensitivity. Since deposits are exposed to sudden liquidity outflows, they must be covered with liquid assets that protect against potential liquidity outflows, requiring the establishment of a liquidity reserve or buffer. Finally, deposit-taking activity incurs operating costs associated with the resources to originate, manage and maintain these products, which must be factored in into the deposit rates.

Therefore, given the above, the components to be taken into account when setting the maximum price for deposits would be:

- Marginal interest rate of investment
- Liquidity reserve
- Operating costs

5.4.1 Marginal interest rate on investment

As noted earlier, Dermine (2009), drawing on the theoretical banking model of Monti-Klein, provided an alternative and intuitive rationale for using the interbank market rate as the transfer price. If a business unit significantly expands its deposit base, the resulting balance sheet impact is an increase in positions in interbank loans or sovereign bonds. In such cases, transfer prices provide a signal indicating the optimal level of funding, based on the interest rates applied to the raised funds.

The appropriate interbank rate is obtained by breaking down the future flows of the deposit and following the procedure followed by Matz and Neu (2012), applying only the notional amount formula for micro-hedging (IRR_{ALM}) presented in Section 5.1.3.1, since no liquidity premium is required in this context. Obtaining IRR_{ALM} enables the ALM function to determine the notional micro-hedging transaction that isolated the interest rate risk of deposits.

However, customer deposits pose an additional challenge because certain products have no contractual maturity date. To obtain the future cash flows and interest rate risk measures needed to determine the appropriate interbank investment rate, modelling of deposit behaviour is required. One possible approach, suggested by Matz and Neu (2012), relies on approximation techniques similar to those used to quantify contingent liquidity risk. The modelling, based on a stochastic process, must be carried out on a product-by-product basis, aiming to estimate the balance that will remain available to customers over the defined time horizon. This estimated balance is treated as term financing. Subsequently, the drift and volatility of the stochastic process must be determined through statistical analysis and based on present and historical behaviour. The resulting outputs divide the current balance of non-maturing deposits into a core or stable component and a volatile balance, while also providing information on their duration. Based on these results, the same procedure used for maturing deposits is applied, using the IRR_{ALM} formula to obtain the relevant interbank market investment rate (Matz and Neu, 2012).

Therefore, the reference rates would be set as follows.

$$\textit{Marginal interest rate on investment} = \textit{Euribor/Swap}\ (\textit{adjusted for modified duration})$$

For reasons of prudence, all non-maturing deposits will be assigned the 6-month reference rate. Customer term deposits will be assigned a modified duration equal to their contractual maturity, as they involve no interim payments and are settled through a single bullet repayment at maturity.

5.4.2 Liquidity reserve

From the point of view of constructing FTPs for pricing purposes, deposits carry the risk of being withdrawn at any time. This liquidity risk – addressed under Basel standards through the compliance with the LCR requirement – necessitates holding a certain proportion of liquid assets to cover potential deposits withdrawals. This regulatory cost reduces the maximum rate that can be paid for a deposit.

For the sake of simplicity, it will not be taken into account in the subsequent sections of the manual. Choudhry, 2023, also supports this approach of not including it in the pricing exercise.

5.4.3 Operating costs

With regard to operating costs, the reasoning is identical to that set out in Section 5.1.3.2. on pricing for investment operations, therefore, reference is made to that section.

5.4.4 Conclusion

In conclusion, the FTP to be determined – whose purpose is to set the maximum rate for financing operations, above which business unit would obtain a positive margin – would be:

$$\textit{FTP Funding Operations} = \textit{Marginal interest rate on investment} - \textit{Operating Costs}$$

6 PRICING GAP: A new methodology

Prior to dealing with concept of pricing gaps, it is important to do a recollection of the main concepts discussed so far:

1. The business model of a commercial bank is to buy and sell money and as a complement also to provide a range of services for which it charges a commission.
2. In this process of buying and selling money, banks incur various risks, including IRRB, liquidity, currency and credit risks. Moreover, banks make decisions about the terms on which they carry out this intermediation work, decide to lend at one type of credit rate or another, borrow money at a fixed rate, lend at a variable rate and vice versa.
3. These risks banks incur can be seen as the production factors for financial institutions and should form the basis for pricing. It is important that these risks are correctly identified, measured, controlled and managed, with governance of these risks being a priority.
4. Banks have the capacity to measure these risks in expected terms, and when there is an unexpected development, such as a sudden increase in credit risk, etc., capital protects depositors and creditors from such unexpected events, maintaining confidence in the system and financial stability. Such capital is held by an institution's shareholders so that it has to be remunerated accordingly. Such remuneration also forms part of the costs to be factored in in price setting.
5. The regulatory response to past crises has been misguidedly focused on measures involving more and more capital without addressing the root causes of the problems.
6. Asset and liability management in financial institutions is a function that is responsible for looking at financial risks from a holistic perspective. Therefore, it has the capacity and vision to aggregate those risks, factor them into the pricing of products through the implementation of an FTP system. This FTP system discourages business units from making decisions that are contrary to profitability. The ALM unit becomes the nerve centre of financial institutions and must gain prominence in decision-making from both a tactical and strategic point of view.
7. In the commercial banking business model, several distortions can affect its future viability, including:
   a. Banking competition: Excessive efforts to increase market share can place downward pressure on pricing, potentially preventing it from covering all the financial risks to which financial institutions are exposed.
   b. Treatment of credit risk provisions – IFRS 9: Stage 1 provisions are calculated using a 12-month ECL, which can result in insufficient accumulation of provisions if the economic cycle deteriorates, thereby impacting banks' results.

Note: Note that this methodology applies to the entire balance sheet in Stages 1 and 2.

 | https://doi.org/10.1515/9783111328386-006

This issue is amplified when combined with the pricing pressures created by banking competition.

c. Distortions in accounting vision: The banking business model relies on pricing at the time of origination, which remains fixed over the life of the transaction, while underlying production factors (financial risks) are volatile. Consequently, financial analyses based solely on accounting information can provide only very limited insights.

The excerpt above highlights the flaws in pricing and its consequences, which can place banks in undesirable situations and jeopardise the financial stability of the banking system in question.

Even when the interest rates are set correctly at the time of granting, the temporary structure of interest rates, as well as the expectations of future implicit rates can "force" banks to take long-term fixed-rate positions. These positions have implications for balance sheet management and, over time, may contribute to potential destabilisation. In other words, a bank may correctly price instruments based on FTP; however, this does not mean that the bank is fully protected against long-term risks. Even when FTP is used for pricing, management may decide to grant fixed-rate loans, thereby exposing the bank to IRRBB risks, or the funding market conditions may deteriorate, which could negatively impact the institution's P&L.

Example:

Consider, for example, a financial institution or financial system that grants mortgage loans at 1% fixed-rate at the end of August 2019, using the yield curve shown in Figure 6.1 (with no hedging into a variable rate). This loan portfolio is financed with non-maturity deposits that carry a cost of 0%.

The "FTP investment operation" would be:

1. Cost of funding:
   a. Modified duration of the 30-year mortgage (30y) is approximately 15 years, assuming that the principal amount is amortised according to a French amortisation system.
   b. Then, the 15-year swap on 6-month Euribor is taken as the reference. This guarantees that the bank will be able to pay the 6-month Euribor on deposits.
   c. 15y swap = -0.06%. We take this swap that matches the modified duration of the loan.
2. Operating Cost:
   a. Assumed to be 0.50%. Depending on the efficiency ratio and the composition of assets and their profitability, this value may vary across banks or banking systems.
3. Expected Loss:
   a. PD Lifetime=2% and LGD=0.4% are assumed, which is reasonable for a mortgage market.
   b. ECL = PD Lt x LGD = 2% x 0.4% = 0.8% expected loss of the portfolio over the economic cycle.
   c. To factor the ECL into a price, the result of 0.8% must be divided by the modified duration of the transaction, as this step allows the ECL to be annualised within the loan amortisation table.
      i. 0.8%/15 = 0.0533%
4. Unexpected Loss:
   a. A target ROE of 11% is assumed.
   b. Capital requirement (Pillars 1 and 2) = 12%

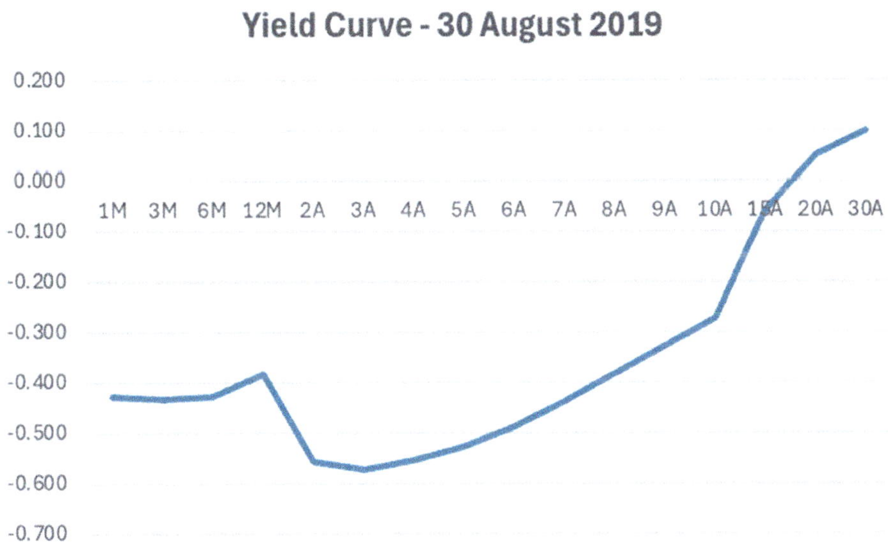

Figure 6.1: Yield Curve.
Source: Own elaboration based on data from Bloomberg

i. Pillar 1 = 8%
ii. Pillar 2 = 1.5%
iii. Combined buffer requirement = 2.5% (1.5% of capital conservation buffer and 1.0% of countercyclical buffer)

c. Risk Weight = 35%[22]
d. UL = 11% * 12% * 35% = 0.46%

FTP Investment Operations = Cost of funding + Operating Costs + Expected Loss + Unexpected Loss

$$\textit{FTP Investment Operations} = -0.06\% + 0.50\% + 0.05\% + 0.46\% = 0.95\%$$

This represents the minimum rate at which the mortgages should have been marketed. Since they were marketed at 1%, this means that the mortgages were correctly priced.

The "FTP funding operation" would be:

1. Marginal interest rate on investment
   a. A prudent approach is to assume that deposits are invested without modelling the behaviour of non-maturing deposits, in which case the marginal rate on investment would be equal to the 6-month Euribor:
      i. 6-month Euribor = -0.428%
2. Operating costs
   a. Assumed to be 0.50%. Depending on the efficiency ratio and the composition of assets and their profitability, this value may vary across banks or banking systems.

22 Standardised approach for mortgages with LTV ≤ 80%, according to Basel II standards.

$$FTP\ Funding\ Operations = -0.428\% - 0.50\% = -0.93\%$$

This represents the maximum rate at which non-maturing deposits should be remunerated. Logically, retail customers cannot be charged for these deposits, and the bank must therefore accept this limitation.

Given the term structure of interest rates and the indications from implied market rates,[23] the 6-month Euribor is not expected to reach 0% over the next 10 years. Considering that the FTP for investment operations (mortgages) is lower than the 1% rate at which they were offered, the bank's management decides to leave them at a fixed rate without any hedging. No additional actions are assumed regarding financing based on non-maturing deposits.

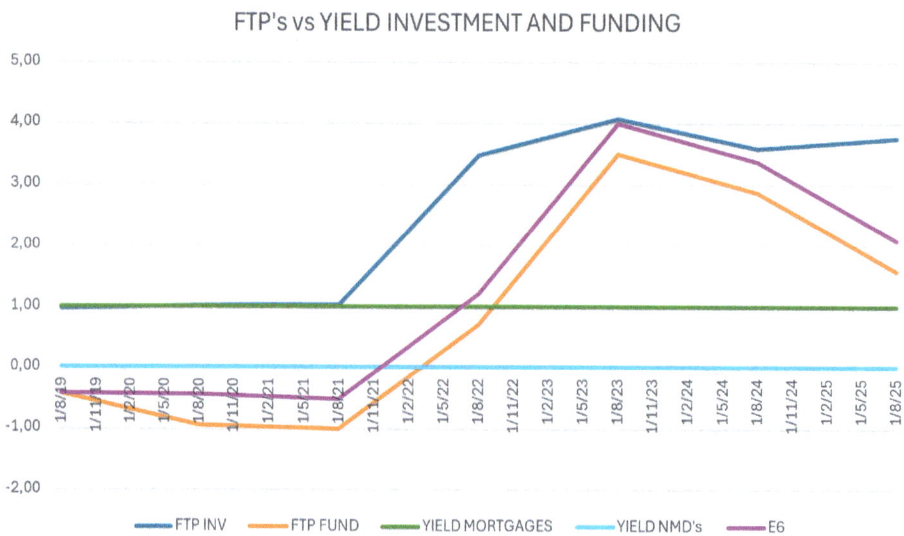

Figure 6.2: FTP vs. YIELD.
Source: *Own elaboration.*

Figure 6.2 shows that, until 2021, the bank in question was in a situation where its investments and the associated financial risks were correctly remunerated. From that date onwards, however the yield curve shifted, and the FTPs periodically calculated for the financial risks existing in each observation period indicate that the institution's loan portfolio now carries implicit risks that are no longer properly remunerated. At the same time, non-maturing deposits began to accrue significant value relative to their FTP, providing some compensation. Nevertheless, the open risk in the investments remains long-term, as the mortgages were granted for 30 years while the deposits are on demand and exhibit volatile behaviour.

From an accounting perspective, the financial institution continues to record the same earnings – loans at 1% and non-maturing deposits at 0% – which masks the underlying risks and limits the insights that can be drawn from the annual accounts.

How could these risks materialise? The root problem is a matter of IRRBB, stemming from the decision not to hedge the investment position (i.e., the mortgages). If non-maturing depositors decide to transfer their funds to term deposits, demanding remunerations at the market rate for the term (i.e., at the 6-

23 Implied market rates were estimated using forward rates.

month Euribor), the institution's first line of defence for managing liquidity risk would be weakened, as discussed earlier. In practical terms, this means having properly remunerated assets in order to be able to respond to customers' demand for a higher remuneration. If the bank is unable to do so, it would be forced to activate the second line of defence: selling or discounting HQLA at the central bank to cover deposit outflows (that cannot be remunerated due to insufficient profitability).

Had the mortgage portfolios been granted at a variable rate—using, for instance, the 6-month Euribor as the reference—the FTP for Investment Operations would now track the 6-month Euribor. Under this FTP, the bank would need to achieve a minimum spread of 1.01% to create value. Therefore, the FTP would be as follows:[24]

$$\text{FTP Investment Operations} = \text{Euribor 6M} + 1.01\%$$

Considering that the 6-month Euribor stands at -0.428%, the FTP for new operations should be at least 0.58%. Hedging the position at the outset would have been a reasonable solution to mitigate IRRBB risk; however, in this situation, managers may not have incentives to do so, given that the expectation for the next 10 years is that the 6-month Euribor will remain below 0%.

Another issue that may arise is credit risk. The assessment of this risk in the mortgage portfolio has been an EL of 0.8%, which translated into a periodic yield to be included in the price that was an increase of 0.05%. What would happen if the credit event occurred at the end of the second year after the loans were originated, or if a credit event occurred on that same date but was much higher than expected?

When a risk materialises within the expected loss (EL) range, the entity would have accumulated only a small portion of the EL. Without prudent provisioning—and under IFRS 9, where Stage 1 only allows 12-month provisions—the entity may need to adjust profits for an event that falls within the EL range. This underscores the importance of provisioning policies that adopt a lifetime perspective for Stage 1 assets, which IFRS 9 currently does not allow. For a credit event above the expected loss (EL), the loss is treated as unexpected (UL) and should be absorbed by profits or available regulatory capital.

6.1 Annual PRICING GAP (PGa)

For both supervisors and bank managers, one concept of vital importance is the "sustainability" of the banking business. This can be defined as the structural ability of a financial institution to maintain its profitability, reputation and compliance with regulatory requirements (e.g., capital, liquidity, etc.) over the long term, ensuring that its operating model generates a positive economic value in a manner consistent with prudent risk management, regulatory compliance and contribution to the sustainable development of the financial system. This concept is widely referenced in academic literature and extensive regulatory documentation. As noted in Chapter 3, the use of accounting information is not suitable for analysing the sustainability of financial institutions, due to its lack of a forward-looking perspective on risks.

Using the FTP concept noted in Chapter 5, the sustainability of a financial institution – specifically in the field of commercial banks – occurs when the financial risks on the balance sheet, arising from its core business of lending and borrowing, are

24 Operating Costs = 0.50% + Expected Loss = 0.05% + Unexpected Loss = 0.46% = 1.10%

properly remunerated under normal market conditions. To measure this, a novel metric is introduced: the Annual Pricing Gap (PGa). This metric allows the assessment of the sustainability of banks' business models over time by taking into account all costs and risks borne by banks. It is presented as follows:

$$\textbf{\textit{Margin on Investment}} = \textbf{\textit{Pricing on Balance sheet}} - \textbf{\textit{FTP Investment Operations}}$$

$$\textbf{\textit{Margin on Funding}} = \textbf{\textit{FTP Funding Operations}} - \textbf{\textit{Pricing Funding on Balance Sheet}}$$

$$\textbf{\textit{PRICING GAP ANNUAL (PGa)}} = \textbf{\textit{Margin on Investment}} + \textbf{\textit{Margin on Funding}} + \textbf{\textit{Fees}}$$

The FTP Investment Operations and FTP Funding Operations calculations are obtained using the same methodology presented in Chapter 5.

A PGa with a zero or positive indicates that the financial institution – or the banking system as a whole – has its risks correctly priced and can therefore be considered sustainable over time. Conversely, a negative PGa signals that financial risks are not fully covered by current pricing. For both positive and negative PGa, it is important to identify their origin. Therefore, it is essential to analyse the investment margin and the funding margin separately, ensuring that tactical and strategic decision-making accurately reflect where increases or decreases in PGa occur, both in management and in the decisions implemented.

Example:
For the case analysed in the previous point, the results would be as shown in Table 6.1.

Table 6.1: PGa Calculations.

	FTP INV	FTP FUND	Margin INV	Margin FUND	YIELD MORTGAGES	YIELD NMD's	PGa
29-08-2025	3.76	1.57	-2.76	1.57	1.00	0	-1.18
30-08-2024	3.59	2.86	-2.59	2.86	1.00	0	0.27
31-08-2023	4.07	3.49	-3.07	3.49	1.00	0	0.42
31-08-2022	3.48	0.70	-2.48	0.70	1.00	0	-1.78
31-08-2021	1.02	-1.02	-0.02	-1.02	1.00	0	-1.04
31-08-2020	1.02	-0.95	-0.02	-0.95	1.00	0	-0.96
30-08-2019	0.96	-0.93	0.04	-0.93	1.00	0	-0.89

Source: *Own elaboration.*

To obtain the FTP Investment Operations, only the point on the swap curve has been adjusted over time; the rest of the parameters have been assumed to be constant. As can be seen, the entity's exposure to IRRBB over time was mainly driven by a latent loss in the margin on investment as interest rates rose and it had exposure to fixed rates. Similarly, due to this same rise in interest rates, as the cost of financing has been maintained, the margin on funding has increased in value, acting as a counterbalance. It can be seen that in 2019 (Figure 6.3), the PGa was negative (-0.89) due to the financing structure and negative rates, and in 2025, the same balance sheet also shows a negative PGa (-1.18) but now motivated by main-

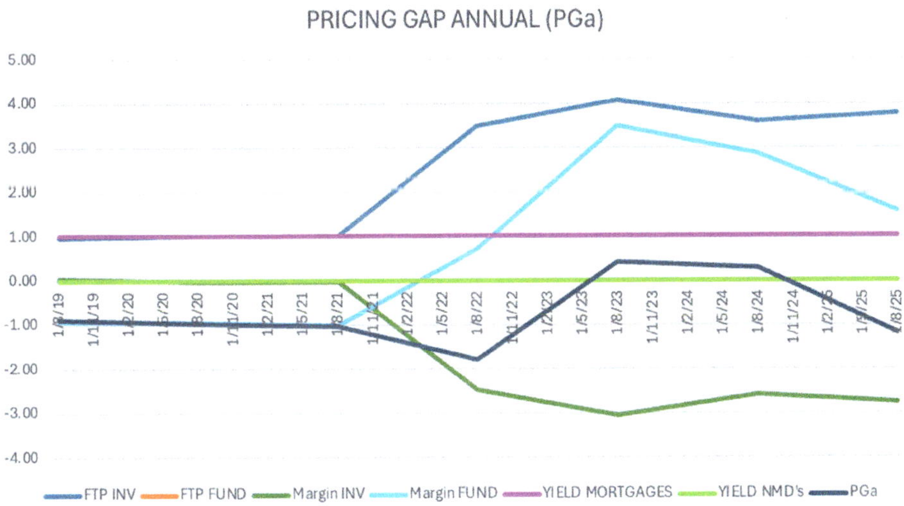

Figure 6.3: PGa Calculations.
Source: *Own elaboration.*

taining a fixed-rate investment with low rates given the market curve and partially offset by the value of liabilities represented by the margin on funding.

These calculations, which would be obtained in percentage terms if linked to balance sheet balances, help to quantify in monetary units the risks to which we are exposed without being properly remunerated, concluding how viable we are or are not.

Having this information at a granular level, as enabled by the methodology and bottom-up approach, facilitates aggregation by business unit, product type, geography, and other dimensions, providing significant value for the balance sheet management of financial institutions. Additionally, as illustrated in Table 6.2, tracking the evolution of the PGa metric at the level of the risk components allows attention to be focused on specific risk exposures that may lead the institution to situations where balance sheet risks that are not properly remunerated. A key advantage of the PGa metric[25] is its simplicity, which allows it to support both strategic and tactical decisions while providing flexibility and traceability in the analyses performed. It is closely aligned with the day-to-day management of a financial institution, as its results can be openly discussed by the Board of Directors, Management Committee or ALCO.

Finally, analysing the information resulting from the PGa by its time horizon provides significant insights when interpreting the results. For example, as mentioned above, this evolution is caused by the financial institution's exposure to IRRBB. Maintaining fixed-rate asset positions and deposits, which over time have managed to keep up with the rise in costs, has led to the current situation. In 2025, it presents a PGa of -1.18, but for a different reason than in 2019, namely that the fixed-rate investment position is accumulating profitability problems that are being financed with short-term positions, NMDs, as reflected in Tables 6.3 and 6.4.

25 Essentially, the PGa metric is equivalent to the aggregate managed in an ALM centre of an FTP system with a matched-maturity approach, but PGa provides much more value in management.

Table 6.2: PGa Calculations Detailed.

	CF	OC	EL	UL	FTP INV	YIELD MORTGAGES	Margin INV	INTERBANK	OC	FTP FUND	YIELD NMD's	Margin FUND	PGa
29-08-2025	2.74	0.50	0.05	0.46	3.76	1	-2.76	2.07	0.50	1.57	0.00	1.57	-1.18
30-08-2024	2.57	0.50	0.05	0.46	3.59	1	-2.59	3.36	0.50	2.86	0.00	2.86	0.27
31-08-2023	3.05	0.50	0.05	0.46	4.07	1	-3.07	3.99	0.50	3.49	0.00	3.49	0.42
31-08-2022	2.47	0.50	0.05	0.46	3.48	1	-2.48	1.20	0.50	0.70	0.00	0.70	-1.78
31-08-2021	0.16	0.50	0.05	0.46	1.02	1	-0.02	-0.52	0.50	-1.02	0.00	-1.02	-1.04
31-08-2020	0.03	0.50	0.05	0.46	1.02	1	-0.02	-0.45	0.50	-0.95	0.00	-0.95	-0.96
30-08-2019	-0.06	0.50	0.05	0.46	0.96	1	0.04	-0.43	0.50	-0.93	0.00	-0.93	-0.89

Source: Own elaboration.

Table 6.3: Temporal Structure – PGa – 30 August 2019.

	Until 1y	1y-3y	3y-5y	5y-10y	10y-15y	15y-20y	20y-25y	>25y
Margin INV								0.04
Margin FUND	-0.93							
PGa					-0.89			

Source: *Own elaboration.*

However, the data for August 2025 is already different. The value comes mainly from liabilities due to the lack of transfers to deposits and because the market is not paying customers the value of the curve. The negative aspect comes from fixed-rate positions, with IRRBB not being managed correctly in the long term, meaning that the PGa situation of -1.18 is not much higher than in 2019, but an analysis of the temporary structure of the margins indicates that the current situation is more negative.

Table 6.4: Temporal Structure – PGa – 30 August 2025.

	Until 1y	1y-3y	3y-5y	5y-10y	10y-15y	15y-20y	20y-25y	>25y
Margin INV								-2.76
Margin FUND	1.57							
PGa					-1.18			

Source: *Own elaboration.*

6.2 Total PRICING GAP (PGt)

The viability of the banking business can be defined as a financial institution's ability to withstand a stressful situation over a period of time, cushion it and continue to generate sufficient recurring income to cover its operating, financing, risk and capital costs in a business-as-usual environment, while maintaining compliance with regulatory requirements and the confidence of its depositors, investors and supervisors.

A bank's capacity is demonstrated by its level of usable buffering for extreme events. This cushion is measured by the adequacy of provisions, which are above those identified in the balance sheet for Stage 3 operations, to respond to expected losses with a lifetime view of Stage 1 operations in the balance sheet, and when it exceeds that level, to identify that there are sufficient capital buffers to cope with unexpected losses. There are other risk involved, for example, structural risks, which, if sustained over time or in extreme situations, may require the use of the buffer capacity.

This conflicts with IFRS 9, which only allows credit risk provisions for Stage 1 transactions with a 12-month PD. This, combined with the competitive environments already mentioned, compresses prices to such an extent that they do not recognise the risks on the balance sheet, preventing the generation of sufficient recurring financial income to absorb economic downturns that would be within a predictable framework, such as expected losses. The regulatory response has focused on the consequences of this phenomenon, which has resulted in significant losses in financial systems, by implementing additional capital regulations (macroprudential buffers, TLAC/MREL) that at least guarantee that countries' fiscal budgets will not be used to bail out financial institutions. However, the response is far from addressing the real problems at the root of the issue and is nothing more than a pricing deficiency in origination for competitive reasons, a problem in the definition of IFRS 9 in provisions for Stage 1 assets, and a lack of accumulation of provisions at least up to the expected losses of the economic cycle to respond to sudden negative economic events (COVID, etc.).

Addressing the above correctly would allow for a review of the current regulations, which place an excessive focus on capital, which has a high cost for institutions and whose use in times of uncertainty by institutions has already been shown to be practically nil, as it would mean a signal in financial markets affecting their share price.

To address this issue, another innovative metric called Total Pricing Gap (PGt) is proposed. Conceptually, it is the same as PGa with one difference: PGt incorporates the lifetime ECL for the entire investment portfolio, giving us a view of the impact of a sudden risk event on credit, numerically assessing how a given institution or financial system would fare.

PGt is presented as follows:

$$\textit{Margin on Investment}\,(LFT) = \textit{Pricing Investment on Balance Sheet} - \textit{FTP Investment Operations}(LFT)$$

$$\textit{Margin on Funding} = \textit{FTP Investment Operations} - \textit{Pricing Investment on Balance Sheet}$$

$$\textit{PRICING GAP TOTAL}(PGt-1st) = [(\textit{Margin on Investment}(LFT) + \textit{Margin on Funding}) + \textit{Fees}] + \textit{Provisions}$$

$$\textit{PRICING GAP TOTAL}(PGt-2nd) = (\textit{PRICING GAP TOTAL}(PGt-1st)) + \textit{capital}$$

$$\textit{Capital at Risk} = (\textit{PRICING GAP TOTAL}(PGt-1st))/\textit{Capital}$$

PGt-1st, or Total Pricing Gap with a first line of defence (this can be seen in Figure 6.4), provides us with an answer to the response capacity of the financial institution/system in the event of a credit risk event within the range of expected losses, including any deficiencies in the profitability of recurring business and how provisions are able to absorb this environment of deterioration. This can be seen clearly in Figure 6.1.

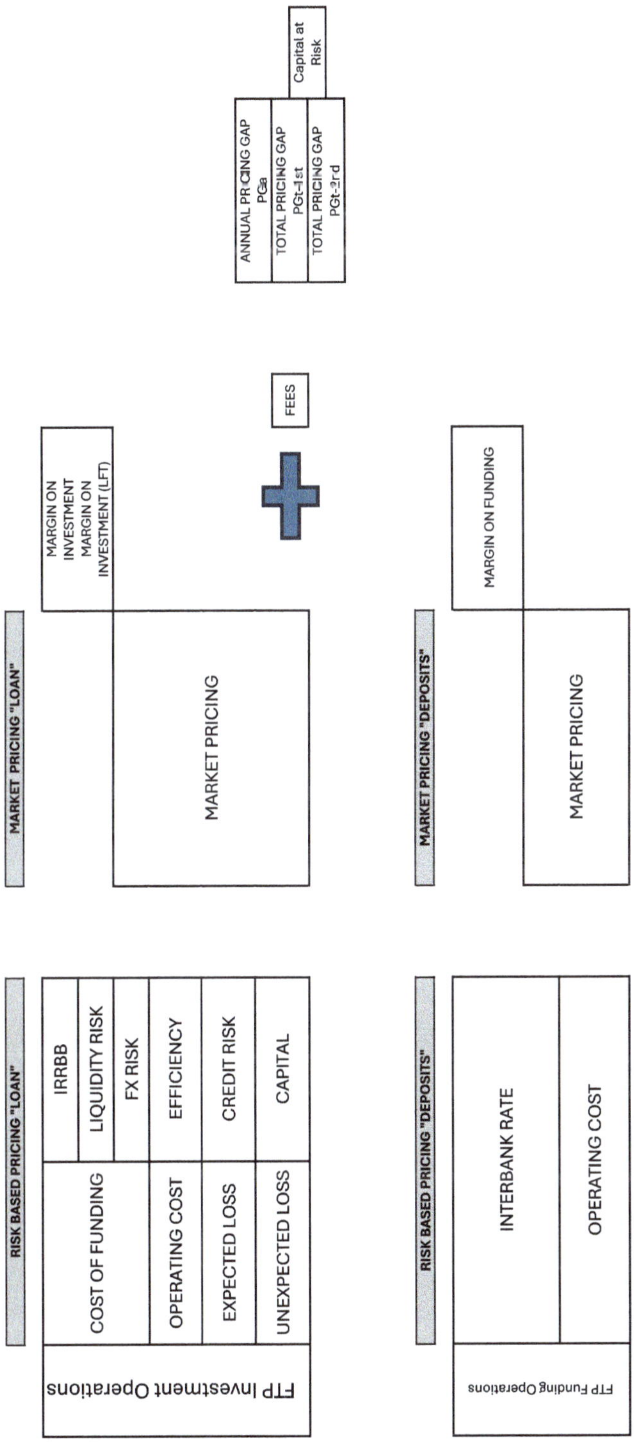

Figure 6.4: PRICING GAP ANNUAL/TOTAL.
Source: *Own elaboration.*

PGt-2nd, or Total Pricing Gap with a second line of defence, provides us with an answer to the response capacity of the financial institution/system in the event of a simulated credit risk or other extreme financial risk, or one resulting from stress tests, also including any deficiencies or lack of profitability in recurring business and, in this case, capital, in addition to the provisions that would also be incorporated to absorb the deterioration of an expected environment.

Capital at risk could be translated as the percentage of capital that would be consumed after absorbing the financial risks of the entity's business model, once the provisions established in PGt-1st have been applied.

Attention can be paid to the importance of this PGt-2nd metric, as it allows us to obtain the capital that would be used to absorb a stressed environment, providing guidance for supervisors for the quantification of capital buffers with full traceability of calculations, obtaining information on the origin of the problems, in which loan portfolios, in which geographies, which entities with their exposures are causing it, etc. This exercise is similar to the calculation performed by institutions to quantify capital under Pillar 2 guidance but avoids the accounting perspective that limits conclusions.

6.3 Multiple uses

These metrics have multiple potential uses in the management of financial institutions, as well as for regulators/supervisors. The following chapters will discuss how these analytical proposals can complement the work being done in different areas:

- Economic crises vs. banking crises:
  - Definition of macroprudential capital buffers.
  - Definition of an automatic stabilisation tool for the financial system.
- Business Model Analysis (BMA).
  - Definition of capital requirements after SREP.
- Stress testing exercises.
- Design of strategic plans.

7 Economic crisis, financial crisis and banking crisis. A possible solution to the problem. PRICING GAP toolkit

7.1 Economic and financial cycles

Comparative evidence suggests that the financial cycle, low-frequency and high-amplitude fluctuations in credit, leverage and asset prices, does not necessarily coincide with the short- and medium-term economic cycle, and that its peaks are often associated with episodes of systemic instability when the banking system enters a phase of vulnerability (Borio, 2014). In emerging economies, the combination of credit gap and housing prices tends to anticipate banking episodes with greater reliability (Chen & Svirydzenka, 2021). All of the above introduces a first methodological lesson: the diagnosis is multidimensional and cannot rely on a single indicator. Furthermore, evidence in a low-growth environment shows that credit-to-GDP is not providing adequate signals. Therefore, drawing on insights from the various studies, further efforts are required to enhance understanding of the different crises and their interrelationships.

In summary, the crisis development process initially follows a sequence of expansion, followed by a weakening of the environment that fragilises the system. Subsequently, a turning point occurs with the activation of one or more triggers, which push the economy into a process of deleveraging and credit contraction. Thus, a dynamic results in a crisis whose severity depends on the available buffers (capital, liquidity) and on the institutional architecture, as documented by various authors (Freixas, Laeven, & Peydró, 2015; Laeven & Valencia, 2018). The essential issue is how to safeguard the banking sector so that credit restrictions do not amplify the depth of systemic crisis.

7.2 Boom phase. Foundations on which the weakening of the system is based

In the expansionary phases of the economic cycle, there is usually a self-reinforcing combination of loose financial conditions and increased risk-taking. On the one hand, persistently low real interest rates, whether due to macroeconomic slack, a global environment of abundant savings or accommodative monetary policy stance, compress risk premiums and reduce the cost of financing leveraged positions.

On the other hand, abundant liquidity and the perception of lower volatility fuel the search for returns in both banks and non-bank intermediaries (Borio, 2014; ECB, 2021). Moreover, financial innovation (e.g., securitisation, daily liquidity investment

 | https://doi.org/10.1515/9783111328386-007

vehicles with less liquid assets, repo financing) facilitates the transformation of maturities and risks and broadens the scope of market intermediation, allowing the system to build up aggregate risk exposure, while risk measurement, based on "benign" historical data, falsely suggests a safe environment (ECB, 2021). In this context, lending standards tend to loosen noticeably: LTVs and DTIs/DSTIs increase, maturities are extended and *covenants* are relaxed; credit grows steadily above income and with sectoral concentration, especially in real estate and related activities, while financing structures become more fragile due to greater dependence on short-term liabilities and wholesale markets (Freixas, Laeven, and Peydró, 2015; ECB, 2021).

The literature to date shows that this pattern can be recognised through early warning frameworks:

1. The credit/GDP gap captures the decoupling of leverage from income-generating capacity, although this issue is not conclusive in all studies.
2. Housing prices in relation to fundamentals (income and rents) reveal misalignments that often precede episodes of correction.
3. The debt service ratio (DSR) of households and businesses provide information on their ability to face interest rate or income shocks. If interest rates rise suddenly, households with a high DSR will see their monthly payments increase, which may limit their consumption capacity.
4. Various market indicators (spread, low implied volatility, euphoria in issuance) point to tense valuations and compressed liquidity premiums (Chen & Svirydzenka, 2021; ESRB, 2021).

The literature also emphasises that these indicators gain strength when combined: risks are more likely to materialise when credit and housing deviate simultaneously, the DSR approaches stress thresholds and spreads remain abnormally compressed (Chen and Svirydzenka, 2021).

The most dangerous feature of the end of a credit boom is the "illusion of stability", i.e., prolonged periods of low volatility and observed losses reduce internal risk assessments, which implies a reduction in regulatory and economic capital just when the system increases leverage and homogenises portfolios without properly assessing the risk due to imitation and competitive pressure (Borio, 2014; Freixas, Laeven, & Peydró, 2015).

In this environment, small disturbances – e.g., a rate turnaround, an income shock, an idiosyncratic credit event – can trigger events that reveal the strong but previously concealed correlation between exposures, precipitating a deleveraging dynamic that feeds back into falling prices and credit tightening (ECB, 2021).

In short, "successful" financial expansions are, by design, a breeding ground for systemic vulnerabilities: the smoother they appear in the short term, the more fragile the system becomes in the face of shocks and the more intense the adjustment phase when complacency gives way (Borio, 2014; Freixas et al., 2015).

7.3 Market triggers

In practice, the triggers that precipitate the turn of the cycle tend to fall into three categories, but they share very similar transmission channels and quantitative effects:

1. Real shocks, such as a sharp rise in energy prices, persistent disruptions in supply chains or a pandemic, erode corporate cash flows and household disposable income, increase macroeconomic uncertainty and often suddenly deteriorate the relationship between debt servicing capacity and debt service. If, in addition, the real shock is accompanied by inflationary pressures, the deterioration in real income and the fall in corporate operating margins reduce borrowing capacity and collateral quality (e.g., commercial real estate), triggering defensive deleveraging processes (Borio, 2014; ECB, 2021).
2. Policy shifts, particularly a cycle of rate hikes or liquidity withdrawal (normalisation of central bank balance sheets), mechanically revalue all duration assets, as higher risk-free rates raise discount rates, depress long-duration bond and equity prices, and increase the cost of debt servicing for variable-rate loan borrowers or those subject to refinancing (ECB, 2021).
3. Breaches of confidence due to the disclosure of fraud, governance problems, unexpected losses in leveraged portfolios, or sovereign events (rating downgrades, selective defaults) trigger a flood of negative news. Investors and financiers cut back on their activity, raise haircuts and demand additional collateral, causing unwanted asset sales and contagion to connected counterparties (Freixas, Laeven, and Peydró, 2015; Laeven and Valencia, 2018).

Although the triggers are different, their common effect is an abrupt repricing of risk and illiquidity, manifested in a rise in risk premiums across the credit structure and in the financing markets (senior, subordinated, repos), an increase in the haircuts required on collateral, and a deterioration in the realisable value of eligible assets. At the same time, wholesale markets narrow in depth and, in the most fragile segments, may close to new issues or refinancing (ECB, 2021).

The result is accelerated deleveraging in banks and non-financial institutions. Funds with short-term financing liquidate positions to meet redemptions, banks accumulate high-quality liquid assets and slow down lending to protect ratios. Moreover, issuers with upcoming maturities face rollover risk on more onerous or, in extreme cases, impossible terms.

7.4 Banking crises

Systemic banking crises are a subset of financial crises in which the epicentre is located in the banking system, characterised by the insolvency or lack of liquidity of a significant number of institutions. These institutions require public support, face abrupt credit restrictions and risk contagion within the banking system. Financial literature shows that severe banking crises tend to coincide with deep and persistent recessions (Laeven and Valencia, 2018; Freixas et al., 2015).

Specifically, for the banking balance sheet, the **combined effect**[26] (ECB, 2021) could be as follows:

1. Mark-to-market losses in their ALCO portfolios.
2. Higher provisions for credit impairment when expected and observed delinquency increases.
   There is supervisory evidence comparing recent cycles and finding that internal estimates of expected loss (EL) tend to be overly optimistic at the end of expansions, particularly after periods of high ROA, amplifying the negative surprise and provisioning needs when the cycle turns (Birn et al. 2023).
3. Higher financing costs, including collateralised financing.

This triple squeeze erodes capital and liquidity, raises risk-weighted assets (Feixas et al., 2015), fuelling further credit tightening by increasing its procyclicality and accelerating macro-financial feedback via lower investment and consumption.

Bank deterioration feeds back into the real economy in a number of different ways (ECB, 2021):

- The bank lending channel: tightening of conditions, rationing and increased cost of credit.
- The balance sheet channel: companies and households with depreciated collateral and higher financial burdens reduce investment and durable consumption.
- Market channels: high volatility and rising spreads paralyse issuance and refinancing, forcing investment projects to be cancelled or postponed.
- The wealth effect: falls in housing and financial assets reduce aggregate demand.
- If the public response gets involved (guarantees, capital injections), the bank-sovereign loop appears, i.e., the sovereign premium rises, devaluing bank portfolios of public debt and reinforcing deleveraging (Laeven and Valencia, 2018; ECB, 2021).

The aggregate result tends to be a deeper and more persistent recession than those not associated with banking crises, with permanent losses in GDP due to hysteresis in investment and employment, leaving lasting effects on the shock, as investment and employment do not fully recover their pre-crisis trajectory.

The speed and intensity of this spiral depend on three factors:

26 The "combined effect" is the simultaneous squeeze of market losses, credit losses and more expensive financing, which weakens capital and liquidity at the same time and forces credit restrictions, thereby feeding back into the crisis.

1. Prior leverage and maturity mismatch. The higher and shorter, the greater the sensitivity.
2. Effective usability of buffers. If capital and liquidity are sufficient and releasable, the need to sell decreases. However, the use of releasable capital stigmatises institutions and is not providing the initially desired utility.
3. Public backstop capacity, i.e., central bank liquidity lines, guarantees, and resolution frameworks containing externalities, which can break the cascade of sales and stabilise the system before the damage becomes macroeconomically persistent (ECB, 2021; Leitner, Dvořák, Magi, & Zsámboki, 2023).

7.5 Regulatory response – post-crisis macroprudential framework

The position that regulators established in response to the problems focused on a macroprudential framework. This approach involved the development of tools and policies aimed at identifying and limiting systemic risks before they materialised, promoting the resilience of the financial system.

Three guiding principles have shaped the macroprudential regulation proposal (ECB, 2020; ECB, 2021):

- Temporal anticipation, activating measures before overheating becomes obvious.
- Instrumental parsimony, prioritising a few well-calibrated and well-communicated tools.
- Credibility and usability, so that releasable buffers are actually consumed in times of stress without regulatory or market friction.

This macroprudential framework aims to reduce procyclicality, limit systemic risk and contagion, and ensure the continuity of critical functions. To address this, Basel III standards established capital buffers, as well as another set of measures or tools, including those relating to borrowers (e.g., RWA floors, exposure limits based on LTV, etc.).

The capital buffers and their stabilising function can be summarised as follows:

- Capital conservation (CCoB): structural buffer to absorb losses without breaching minimums.
- Countercyclical buffer (CCyB): variable buffer depending on aggregate cyclical risk. It builds up in good times and is released in times of stress.
- Systemic buffers: for G-SIIs and O-SIIs (global systemically important institutions and other systemic institutions) and SyRB (structural or sectoral systemic risk).

The aim of this buffer structure is to give greater weight to buffers with countercyclical and sectoral components such as CCyB and SyRB, while maintaining a neutral positive CCyB under normal conditions to create room for immediate release in the event of unexpected shocks (ECB, 2020; ECB, 2021).

As for the measures on borrowers, they are intended to address real estate booms and episodes of household and corporate over-indebtedness because, in theory, they act ex ante as a new credit production. Unlike capital requirements, which strengthen bank resilience, these tools reduce the probability of default and the expected loss on the borrower base by limiting leverage at the time of origination. These measures are the following:

- Loan to Value (LTV): This ratio is the relationship between the loan and the value of the collateral. It acts as a limit on the loan and attempts to moderate the impact on loss given default (LGD).
- Debt to Income/Debt Service to Income (DTI/DSTI): These ratios generally relate debt to income, and the limits that may be imposed are intended to reduce PD levels in the event of income shocks or interest rate rises.
- Term limits and repayment structure: This consists of placing limits on the contractual maturity period at the time of origination or on grace periods, thereby mainly limiting the duration of the risk.

Other measures not associated with borrowers include the establishment of limits on large exposures, sectoral requirements and systemic buffers (sectoral SyRB, which are generally combined).

7.6 Brief reflection on macroprudential policy

This handbook does not reflect on the use and coordination of macroprudential policy in times of economic boom and stress, nor will it discuss the market's perception of the use of buffers as a sign of weakness. Nor will it discuss the problems posed by the restrictions imposed by maintaining the leverage ratio at the time of releasing buffers, etc.

What is of interest for the purpose of this handbook is to understand how the choice of capital-focused instruments came about and how the calibration of these capital buffers was performed. It should be noted that the establishment of these buffers is the result of a prudential regulation focused primarily on capital, the quantification of which is primarily based on the fiscal impacts of previous crises (Laeven and Valencia; 2013), resulting in a considerable increase in the capital cost for financial institutions.

For the CCyB, the credit-to-GDP gap analysis is used as a benchmark indicator, since as actual crisis cases show, the gestation of the crisis due to the credit boom always went hand in hand with excessive credit above GDP. Now, given the capital surcharges, it is unlikely that prolonged periods of such credit growth. Furthermore, the credit-to-GDP gap reacts very slowly to structural changes in credit and can send out misleading signals in episodes such as COVID, where GDP falls sharply and credit grows due to government support measures.

Additionally, through this metric, there was weak evidence between its results and its translation into capital requirements to cover unexpected losses.[27] The calibration of the CCyB has evolved towards a guided-discretion approach, using a structured scorecard and transparent supervisory judgement, without relying on automatic triggers and with the principle that this buffer should be positive in normal times.

The CCoB is the result of a series of empirical studies on probabilities of crises and their cost-benefit analysis, but its ultimate justification is simply that it provides a static reserve of additional structural loss-absorbing capacity.

The calibration of the SyRB is justified in terms of structural or sectoral risk and does not fit well with other macroprudential tools.[28] Its calibration depends on the definition of sectoral risk subsets that depend on three dimensions: type of debtor, type of exposure and type of collateral. These subsets must first be evaluated for systemic significance and then calibrated. Although the guidelines do not impose a fixed rule, they generally rely on stress tests that project segment-level losses and compare them with available absorption capacity. Past crises are also analysed, and buffers can be established based on past experience. Finally, they are complemented by tools associated with origination policies such as the establishment of LTV, DTI/DSTI and term limits, which reinforce each other.

As can be seen, these buffers are not being calibrated based on the endogenous behaviour of financial institutions in a highly competitive environment that may distort the pricing process.

Reflection on this information may raise questions that need to be addressed in an interesting debate:

- From an economic, non-regulatory point of view, if the CCoB has a structural level of 2.5% and is not intended to operate countercyclically during periods of stress, why is not incorporated into the Pillar 1 requirements the CCoB?
- Within the current CCyB and SyRB calibration frameworks, is there scope for improvement in identifying and quantifying the intrinsic vulnerabilities of the banking sector and in measuring countercyclical capacity so as to enhance the allocation process?
- Are the measures affecting origination policies really effective? What is better for the stability of the system – restrictive measures based on capital or certainty that origination prices reflect the risks that are being installed in banks' balance sheets?

27 Drehmann and Tsatsaronis (2014); Committee on the Global Financial System (2012).

28 The SyRB was created for "underlying" systemic risks (structural or specific to certain sectors) and its calibration reflects this nature. By design, it does not replace (nor is it a suitable substitute for) cyclical tools (CCyB), microprudential tools (Pillar 2) or risk-weighted measures/Art. 458 CRR, although it must be coordinated with them to cover gaps without duplicating burdens.

Three issues are clear from the above:

1. Boom phase: All banks' vulnerabilities cannot be remediated via capital-based measures.[29] Banking supervision needs to focus on the sustainability of the banking business. As noted above, in such phases, business models deteriorate and the aforementioned illusion of stability occurs. A capital buffer based on credit-to-GDP plus a dashboard of indicators does not seem an optimal option for mitigating the effects of a crisis.
2. A policy of keeping prices aligned with balance-sheet risks helps ensure—over the economic cycle, in the case of credit risk—that the banking sector earns returns sufficient to generate the resources needed to provision appropriately throughout the cycle. It also supports an asset-profitability structure and liability mix that enable banks to remunerate customer deposits in line with market curves without undermining the profitability required to sustain other activities. Using the Annual Pricing Gap (PGa) as a prudential management tool can be helpful, as it would allow for the establishment of a system that would encourage proper balance sheet management through the ALM function and the implementation of a business model with an economic cycle perspective.
3. Detonation phase: This phase essentially involves analysing the impacts of events that lead to risk repricing and illiquidity situations. The instruments established for this phase must be traceable to the instruments proposed in the boom phase. The Total Pricing Gap (PGt) metric provides continuity with what was established in the boom phase, helps us to assess the impacts of the onset of crises and also provides the information necessary for establishing an automatic stabilisation mechanism for the banking system.

The following sections present a simulation exercise for the Spanish financial system that analyses its behaviour during the 2009 financial crisis from a pricing perspective. The exercise also explores what information can be extracted to assess whether there are additional ways to design macroprudential policies more closely associated with the endogenous behaviour of financial institutions.

Based on the above results, Section 7.8 proposes an automatic mechanism to stabilise the banking system. The aim is to establish a direct relationship between the quantification of vulnerabilities within the banking system and the implementation of macroprudential measures—a link that is difficult to identify under the calibration of the current regulatory framework. The proposal seeks to provide banks with clear incentives: institutions that demonstrate sound governance in balance-sheet management, set prices appropriately, and maintain profitability consistent with the risks

29 European Central Bank. (2023). Assessment of the European Central Bank's Supervisory Review and Evaluation Process: Report by the Expert Group to the Chair of the Supervisory Board of the ECB (Annex). https://www.bankingsupervision.europa.eu/ecb/pub/pdf/annex/ssm.pr230417_annex.en.pdf

they assume would be rewarded with more efficient capital management through lower capital requirements. This approach also enhances traceability between the boom-and-bust phases of financial crises.

7.7 Simulation exercise for the Spanish case

This simulation exercise,[30] with an ALM perspective, seeks to present the distortion in pricing in both asset and liability operations of commercial banks in the resident, non-resident and public sectors of the Spanish financial system, represented through the PGa (Annual Pricing Gap) and PGt (Total Pricing Gap) metrics. This innovative approach can be a valuable tool for macroprudential decision-making during credit booms, and even without the need for excessive credit growth, acting as a barometer of the health of the banking system.

The data has been extracted from the Bank of Spain's statistical bulletin[31] and Bloomberg. A time horizon from 1999 to 2015 with quarterly data will be used.

It is important that the calculations are conducted over periods of crisis. To this end, the crisis episodes identified in Laeven and Valencia (2012) and Lo Duca (2017) are used, which as applied to the Spanish case by Castro, C. et al. (2016).

Based on the above, the period from 2009Q2 to 2013Q4 is identified as a period of crisis. Emphasis is placed on the results of the PGt metric during the detonation phase, as this metric is key to assessing the viability of the banking sector. In addition, to analyse the behaviour of the PGa metric in earlier periods, the 16 quarters preceding the onset of a crisis are examined to determine whether the metric provides information that can serve as an early warning signal, allowing anticipatory measures to be taken during the boom phase, when the sustainability of the banking business model is of particular importance.

To develop the simulation, we will adapt the principles explained in the Chapter 6 on PGa and PGt, where we will make some adjustments and assume working hypotheses based on the information obtained.

7.7.1 Model hypothesis

The objective is to construct the two visions outlined in the handbook, sustainability and viability of the banking business, but applied to a banking system, taking into account the limitations of existing data, and therefore, making the necessary adjustments.

---

30 The model presented here is taken from the author's unpublished and evolved doctoral thesis. However, the variables used are reflected in the appendix.
https://repositorio.uam.es/entities/publication/7ed27d57-c8f8-4cd0-8eb3-d16c275d7ff0

31 https://www.bde.es/webbde/es/estadis/infoest/bolest.html

ANNUAL PRICING GAP

$$\textit{Margin on Investment} = \textit{Pricing Investment on Balance Sheet} - \textit{FTP Investment Operations}$$

$$\textit{Margin on Funding} = \textit{FTP Funding Operations} - \textit{Pricing Funding on Balance Sheet}$$

$$\textit{PRICING GAP ANNUAL}(PGa) = \textit{Margin on Investment} + \textit{Margin on Funding} + \textit{Fees}$$

PRICING GAP TOTAL

$$\textit{Margin on Investment }(LFT) = \textit{Pricing Investment on Balance Sheet} - \textit{FTP Investment Operations}(LFT)$$

$$\textit{Margin on Funding} = \textit{FTP Funding Operations} - \textit{Pricing Funding on Balance Sheet}$$

$$\textit{PRICING GAP TOTAL }(PGt-1st) = [(\textit{Margin on Investment}(LFT) + \textit{Margin on Funding} + \textit{Fees})] + \textit{Provisions}$$

$$\textit{PRICING GAP TOTAL}(PGt-2nd) = (\textit{PRICING GAP TOTAL}(PGt-1st)) + \textit{Capital}$$

$$\textit{Capital at Risk} = (\textit{PRICING GAP TOTAL}(PGt-1st))/\textit{Capital}$$

Pricing Investment on Balance Sheet

The interest rate recorded on the balance sheets of financial institutions are taken from the financial income information (not including the interbank market) obtained from the Bank of Spain's statistical bulletin.

The information obtained corresponds to the current interest rate on credit investments recorded on the balance sheet. However, the available data do not allow for a distinction between the interest rate applied to outstanding loans and that applied to newly originated loans.

FTP Investment Operations

Cost of funding

Two options are used for the funding cost:

1. Hypothesis 1: All loans are fixed rate, and the cost of funding is derived from the swap curve rate corresponding to the modified duration of investments, see Table 7.1. The modified duration is obtained through assumptions about the average terms of the transactions in the different credit investment categories. For the conversion to modified duration, it is assumed that all transactions follow a French amortisation payment scheme, so the modified duration is approximated by dividing the term of the transaction by 2.

2. Hypothesis 2: All loans are granted at variable interest rates. The 6-month Euribor is set as the cost of funding.

Table.7.1: Hypothesis Calculation of Operation's Terms and RW.

	TERM	RISK WEIGHT
DEPOSIT-TAKING INSTITUTIONS. OSR. Commercial credit	1	1
DEPOSIT-TAKING INSTITUTIONS. OSR. Debtors	=0.7*20+0.3*10	=0.7*0.4+0.3*0.7
DEPOSIT-TAKING INSTITUTIONS. OSR. Term debtors. Total	5	=0.7*100%+0.3*75%
DEPOSIT-TAKING INSTITUTIONS. OSR. Demand debtors	=7/365	1
DEPOSIT-TAKING INSTITUTIONS. OSR. Finance leases	5	1
DEPOSIT-TAKING INSTITUTIONS. OSR. Non-performing loans	1	1.5

Source: Own elaboration

Operating Cost

This is obtained by allocating the general expenses identified in the statistical series across loan portfolios and deposits, including wholesale banking.

Expected Loss

As already mentioned, one of the major distortions in the banking business model was the treatment of Stage 1 assets, where the provision requirement resulting from the expected loss calculation was made using the 12-month PD.

For the simulation exercise, the delinquency rate is used (in different versions, quarterly, the average for the cycle, etc.)[32] as a proxy for lifetime PD. The default rate is the accounting reflection of credit risk throughout the economic cycle. Although institutions tend to manage Stage 3 by selling portfolios, which may imply even higher default rates, the limited availability of data at this level makes this approach the most feasible option. LGD are assumed to be 50%, which is the current market average rate.[33]

Unexpected Loss

Conceptually, unexpected losses should reflect what the proposed model gets wrong about expected losses. Another function is to cushion extreme business situations involving other risks, such as paying well above the interbank curve for customer deposits on a sustained basis over time and not having this correctly recognised in the income model in the pricing of investments or in the funding strategy.

The formula already identified in the previous chapter is used:

32 Taking the data on doubtful assets from deposit institutions, the doubtful loan ratio is obtained by dividing them by the credit investment that includes the public administration, other resident sectors and non-residents. From the point calculation, the cycle average is obtained (from March 1992 to December 2016). The data on the non-performing loan ratio used as a proxy for lifetime PD is multiplied by the LGD of 50%.
33 Based on data obtained from the EBA risk dashboard. https://www.eba.europa.eu/risk-and-data-analysis/risk-analysis/risk-monitoring/risk-dashboard

$$Unexpected\ Loss = ROE^{*}\,(Capital\,for\,Pilar\,1\,y\,2)^{*}\,RW$$

As ROE, we will take the average for the cycle from the existing data,[34] which is 9.53%, finally setting it at 10% in line with the results of various studies on the cost of capital for financial institutions. We will use 12% as the average level required of financial institutions for capital. Risk weights (Table 7.1) are obtained on a quarterly basis under assumptions for transactions in the different credit investment categories, to which average levels resulting from industry practices have been applied using standard methodology.

FTP Funding Operations

Marginal Interest Rate on Investment

Two assumptions are made for the calculation of the FTP with a pricing perspective:

1.- All deposits are remunerated at the 6-month Euribor.

2.- 50% of deposits are considered demand deposits and are remunerated at 0%, while the other 50% are term deposits and are remunerated at 6-month Euribor.

Operating Cost

The same treatment is applied as for the FTP Investment Operations.

Fees

Net fees have been taken from the Bank of Spain's statistical bulletin and expressed in relative terms as a percentage of total lending.

Provisions

The credit investment provisions reported in the statistical bulletin will be used. Existing provisions are assumed to correspond to Stage 3, or doubtful, assets; therefore, only provisions exceeding the total level of Stage 3 assets will be considered as absorption capacity.

When provisions in the historical series are below the level of doubtful assets, this shortfall will not be recorded as a provision deficit. Instead, it will be reflected as the value of collateral backing Stage 3 assets.

In expected losses, current provisions are enough to cover current defaults; the issue is the capacity that must be considered for retaining profits to cushion new provisions resulting from the evolution of specific expected losses or cycle averages.

Capital

34 Data is taken from March 1992 to December 2016. To calculate the specific ROE, the annualised profit for each quarter is divided by the average capital and reserves for the last 12 months. Finally, the average for the entire observation period is calculated to obtain the figure of 9.53%.

Within the statistical series, the stock of capital and reserves of the banking system will be used as absorption capacity, with a portion of these designated as a buffer. In the study, it is referred to as capital at risk.

7.7.2 Results

Sustainability of the Banking Business – Key to the boom phase in banking crises
At the end of 2000, the ECB set rates at 4.75%. From 2001, with the dot-com crash combined with 9/11, and especially from 2002 and 2003, the ECB cut rates to 2%, keeping them low until 2005. The Euribor curve moved in line with the ECB's official rates, settling at around 2-3% from 2003 onwards.

From 2005 onwards, the economic landscape changed. The eurozone economy recovered, inflationary pressures began to appear, and the ECB began a cycle of increases from 2% in December 2005 to 4% in 2007.

The Spanish economy showed strong growth compared to the EMU, driven by:
- A fall in real interest rates with the introduction of the euro.
- Very dynamic domestic demand, especially in consumption and investment in housing.
- Intense job creation.

Inflation was higher than the European Union average, but rates were the same for all eurozone countries, so the real rate in Spain was even lower, fuelling credit and investment, especially in construction.

The banking sector was undergoing a transition to low rates and a change of currency. There was an explosion in mortgage lending, as can be seen in Figure 7.1,[35] specifically from 2005 to approximately 2008. During this period, variable-rate mortgages at very low prices further stimulated demand for credit. To compensate for the fall in interest rates and supported by the situation in the real estate sector, financial institutions managed to maintain significant year-on-year growth in quarterly financial income. This can even be considered explosive, as interest rates began to rise in line with the evolution of credit around 2005–2006.

This growth was financed (Figure 7.2) through greater dependence on capital markets and is reflected in the loan-to-deposit ratio, which peaked in 2007 at 130% for the sector.

35 In the graphs, the blue band identifies 16 quarters before the start of a crisis. The grey band identifies the crisis period identified in the works of Laeven and Valencia (2012) and Lo Duca (2017).

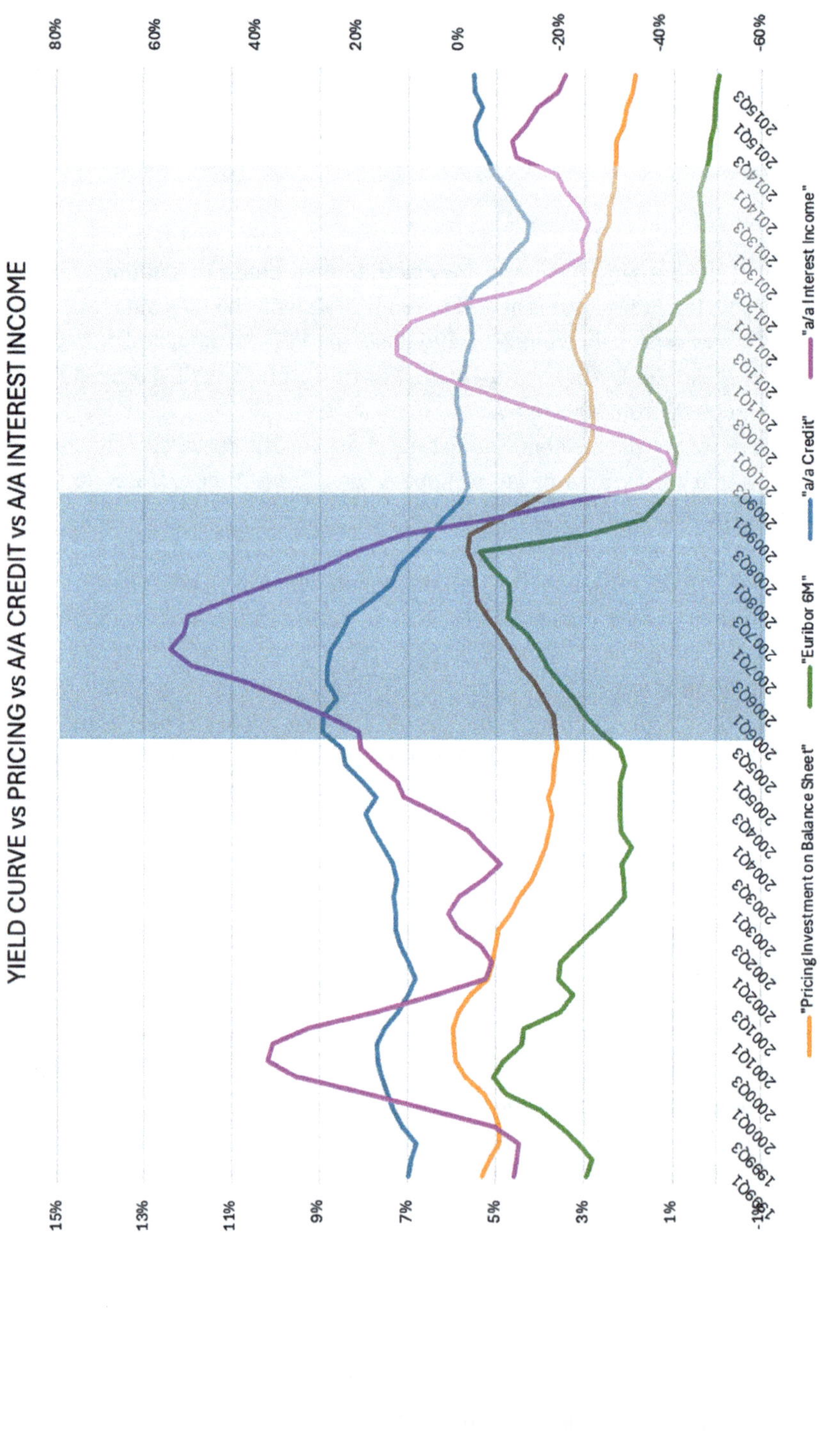

Figure 7.1: Spanish Banking Sector Evolution – Credit Investment.
Source: Own elaboration based on data from the Statistical Bulletin of the Bank of Spain.

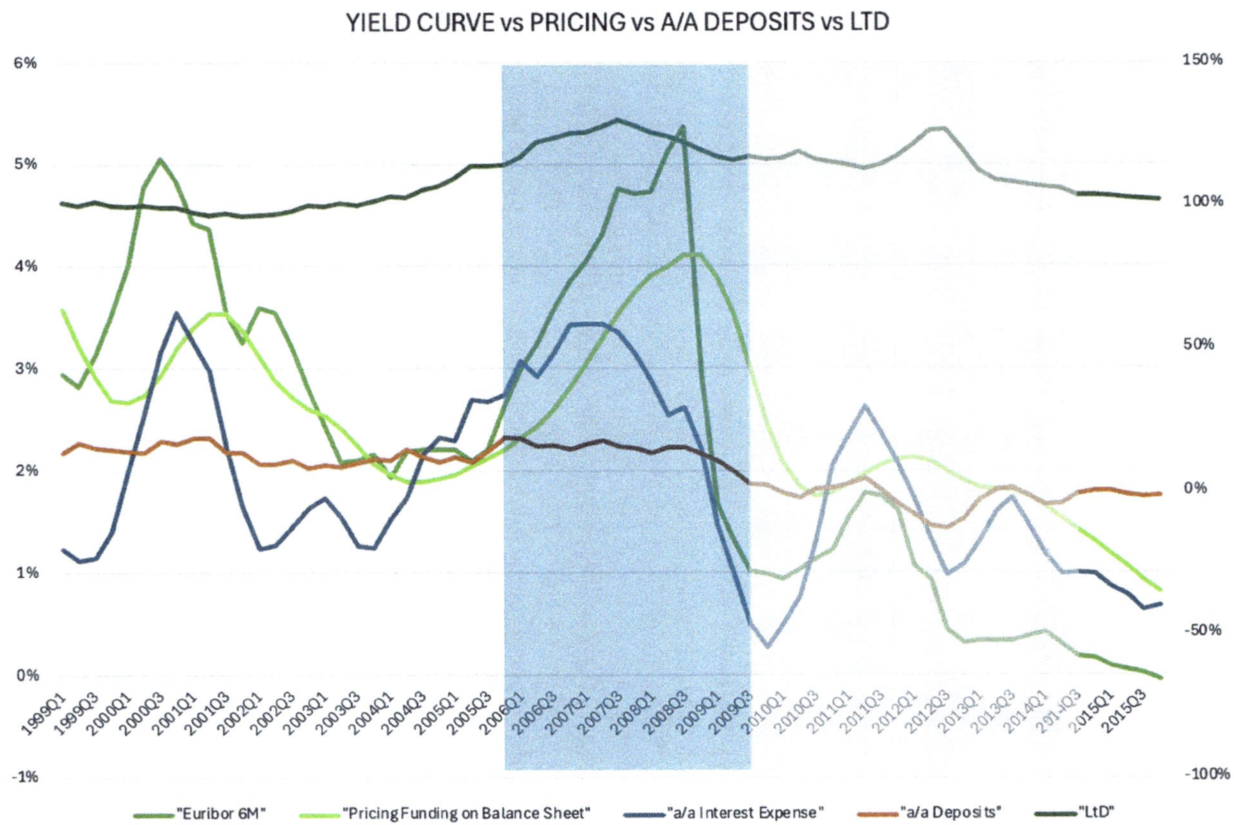

Figure 7.2: Spanish Banking Sector Evolution – Funding.
Source: Own elaboration based on data from the Statistical Bulletin of the Bank of Spain.

Interest expenses during 2011 and 2012 exhibit a year-on-year evolution in quarterly data with a beta[36] well above 1, reflecting the financing difficulties faced by the financial system in an uncertain environment and the challenges Spanish banks encountered in renewing wholesale funding.

This is simply an accounting view of the evolution of credit, deposits, income and costs, etc. A supervisor may be particularly interested in assessing whether investment and financing interest rates are appropriate in such an environment and whether the business model of financial institutions is sustainable. This assessment is especially important during the boom phase of a crisis.

To address this question, it is useful to rely on the Annual Pricing Gap (PGa) metric, which allows for an assessment of whether loan interest rates adequately cover the financial risks on the balance sheet, ensuring both for the proper development of the business, as well as the sustainability of the financial institution.

Figure 7.3 reveals some interesting issues. The Margin on Investment[37] (right axis), which provides an overview of how sustainable the retail credit investment business is, remains negative for much of the time horizon. It is noteworthy that during the expansion period, which is within the 16 quarters at the start of the financial crisis (blue band zone), the margin on investment begins a significant downward trend. It can be seen that balance sheet prices are not adequately reflecting the rise in the curve. Overhead costs with the volume effect are falling, but this does not justify the misalignment of prices on the balance sheet. Furthermore, it should be borne in mind that these price deficiencies are occurring despite very low levels of late payments due to the excessive growth of credit, i.e., prices were becoming unbalanced without any forward-looking perspective. From 2005 to approximately 2008, there were clear signs that the financial system was growing in an unbalanced manner, as prices were not reflecting the financial risks embedded in the balance sheet and unexpected losses, UL, are completely absorbed by the negative margin on investment.

Added to this is the fact that the expected loss[38] is valued on a spot basis, and as a good management practice, prices should reflect an average expected loss over the economic cycle, in order to accumulate profits and create provision buffers that can respond in times of economic downturn, making the financial system less procyclical. This is the manifestation of the phenomenon known as the illusion of stability: historically, results appear in the accounts, but from an ALM perspective, the reading is different. As discussed in the previous chapter, banking competition and the failures in

36 In this case, beta is defined as the percentage above the interest rate curve that is paid as interest on deposits. If we have 6-month deposits paying 2% with a 6-month Euribor at 1%, then we would have a beta equal to 1.

37 The financial cost selected is the 6-month Euribor, given that the vast majority of credit investment in the Spanish financial system was variable. The calculations made using the modified duration of the estimated portfolio would further exacerbate the negative levels of the margin on investment.

38 The LGD used is 50%.

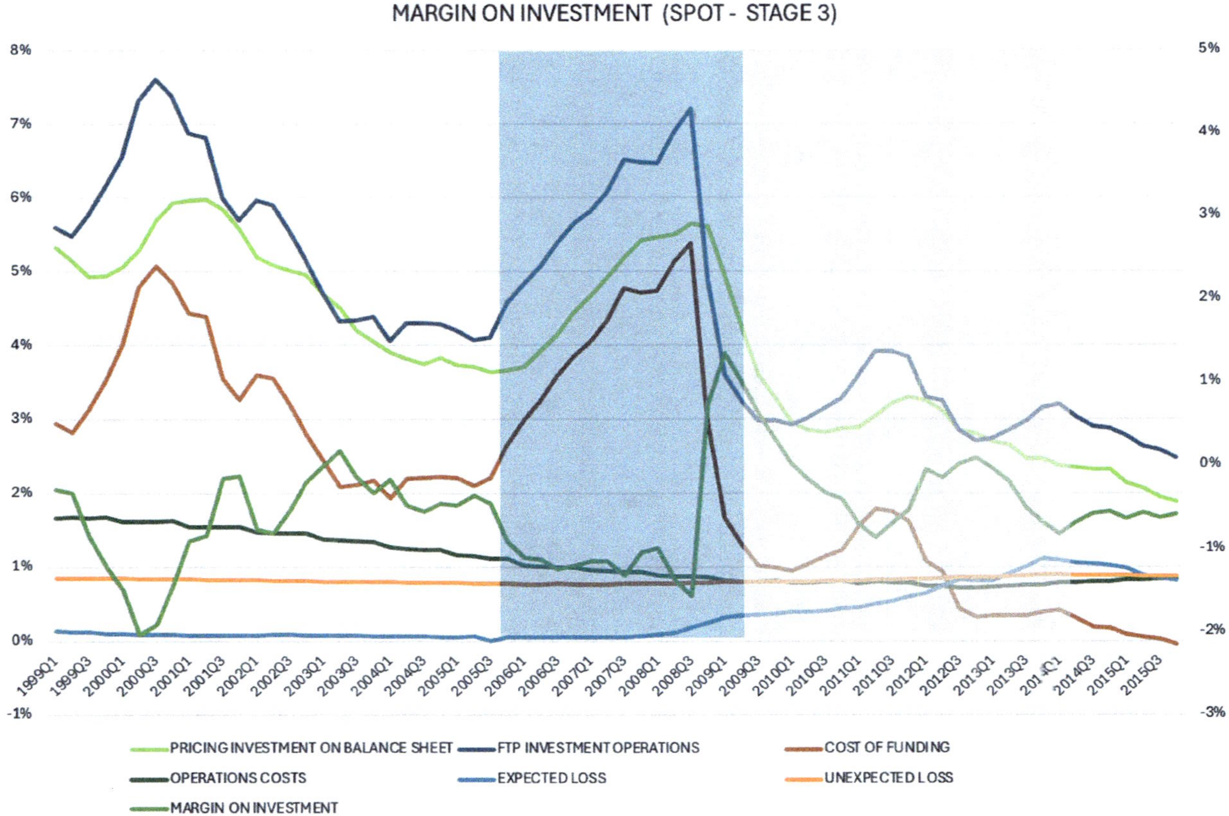

Figure 7.3: Margin on Investment (Spot – Stage 3).
Source: Own elaboration based on data from the Statistical Bulletin of the Bank of Spain.

the credit risk provisioning model for impaired assets are part of this identified problem.

It can also be seen that, following the sharp fall in interest rates in 2008 with the onset of the subprime crisis, the margin on investment became very positive as the yield curve falls sharply and loans remain fixed at higher rates. This is a temporary effect of loan rates being adjusted due to the delay in their repricing. If this positive effect is not accompanied symmetrically by financing, it is only a temporary effect of the balance sheet's interest rate risk sensitivity structure.

If profitability were assessed by taking into account the average expected loss over the economic cycle,[39] the resulting system would exhibit less procyclicality in pricing during periods of volatility. Moreover, adopting this perspective would reduce part of the negative investment margin associated with expected spot losses, although in the time horizon the sustainability of the business is supported by the unexpected loss or cost of capital, that is, the profit that in theory should be obtained is absorbed by the pricing deficit to contemplate the financial risks of the operations, as can be seen in Figure 7.4.

Maintaining an appropriate return on credit investment must be measured by incorporating the average expected loss over the economic cycle into the pricing exercise. The institution must ensure that it has the capacity to generate a return that at least covers the average risks of the economic cycle. Figure 7.4 shows the two margins on investment resulting from applying the expected spot loss to one and the average expected loss of the cycle to the other. It can be seen that until approximately 2009, using the average value, the margin on investment sends early signals that there is a business model that, with average cycle parameters, is not generating sufficient financial income to subsequently, if regulation allows, provision the necessary amount to absorb losses when the economic cycle deteriorates and obviously remunerate the rest of the risks incorporated in the commercial banking business, that is, a sustainable banking business.

From 2009/2010 onwards, as the default rate increases and reaches average cycle levels, the two margins on investment become practically equal. These practices would allow for less procyclicality in credit supply, as banks would be more robust in times of uncertainty.

Until we arrive at an overall view of the pricing scheme through the Annual Pricing Gap (PGa), we will analyse the behaviour of retail financing over the time horizon under study through the margin on funding.

The main conclusion that can be drawn from Figure 7.5 is that, since the outbreak of the crisis in 2009, the margin on funding has fallen to very negative levels due to

39 The average Stage 3 rate since 1992 is 4.01% and an LGD of 50% is applied.

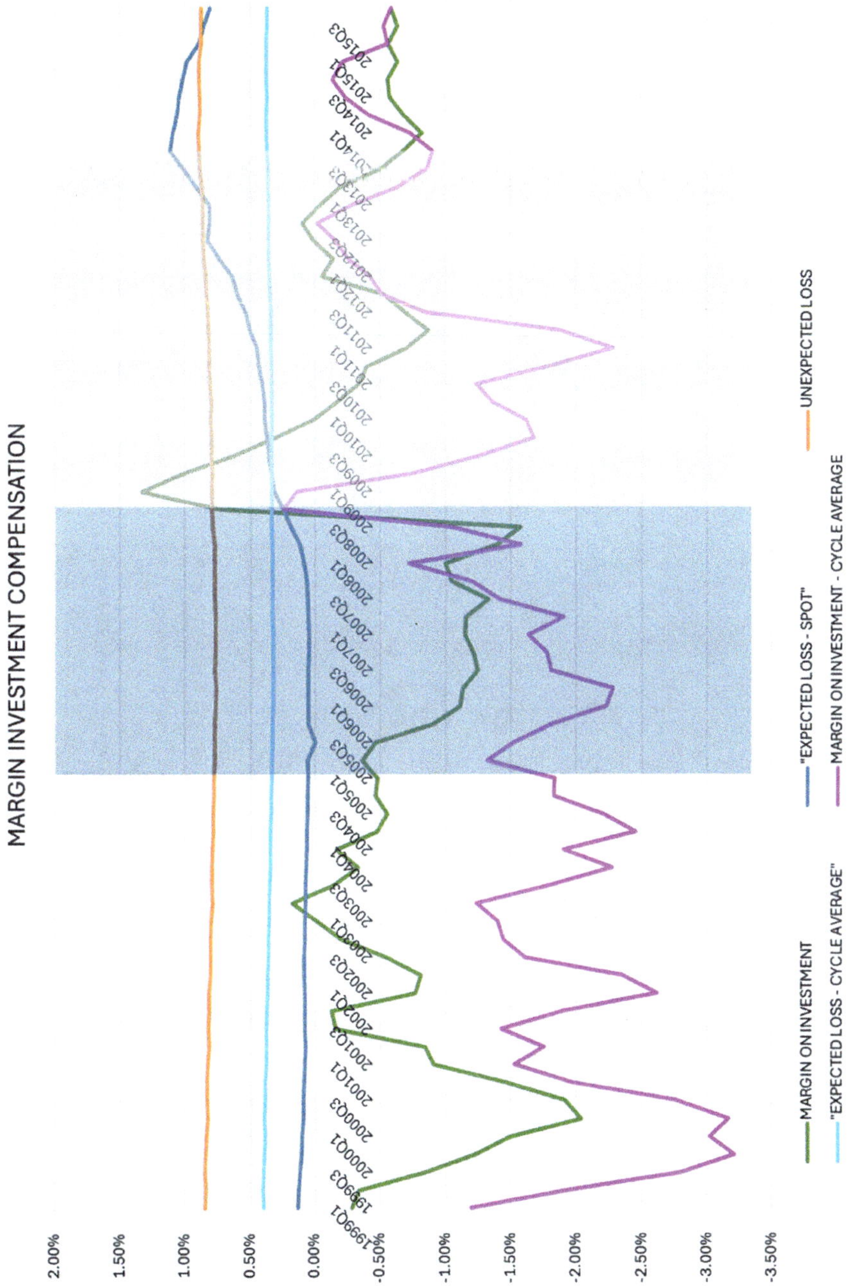

Figure 7.4: Margin Investment Compensation.
Source: Own elaboration based on data from the Statistical Bulletin of the Bank of Spain.

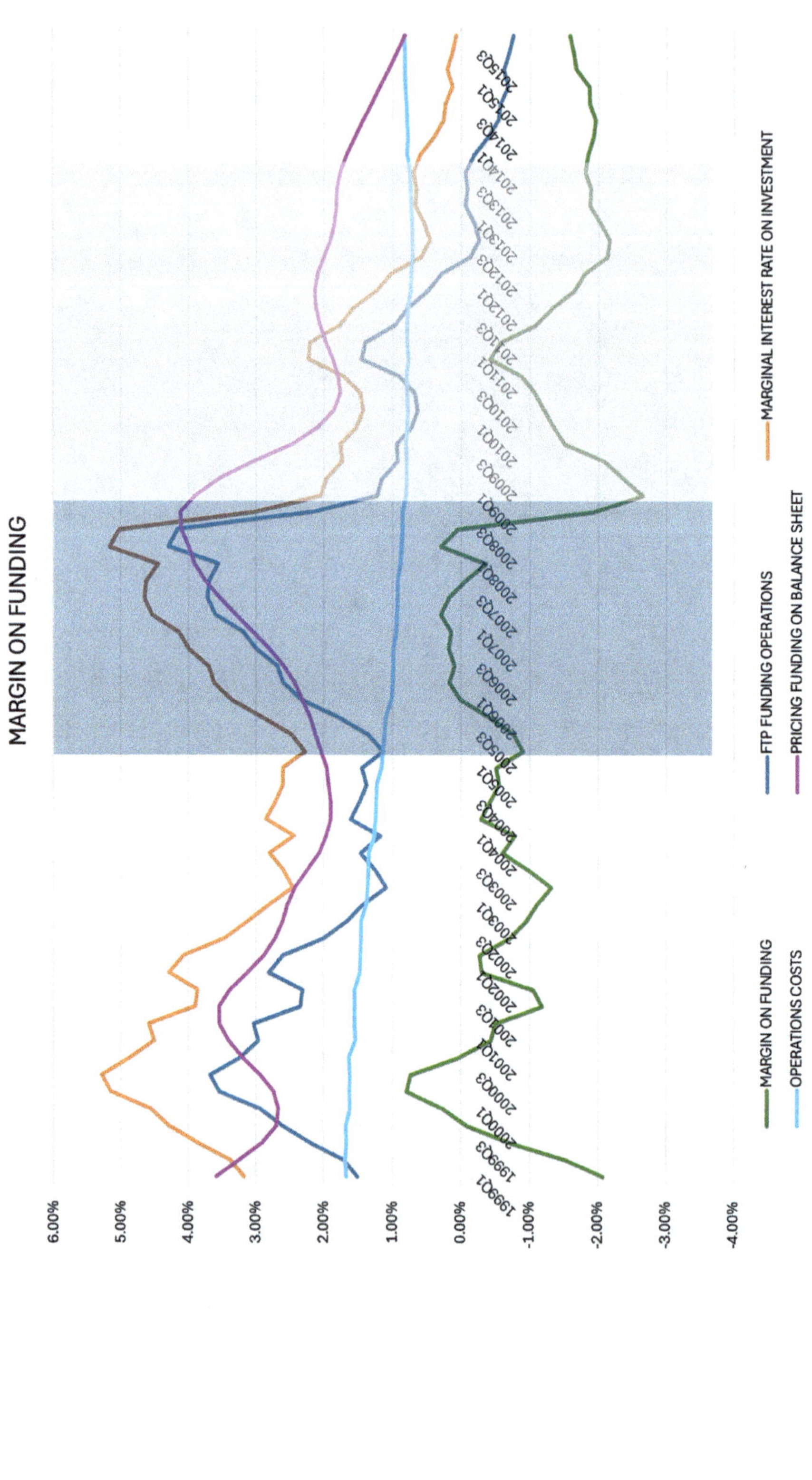

Figure 7.5: Margin on Funding.
Source: Own elaboration based on data from the Statistical Bulletin of the Bank of Spain.

tensions in the capital markets and the battle for deposits that took place in the Spanish financial system, leading to the introduction of price control measures.[40]

A very negative margin on funding may affect the sustainability of the banking business when crises arise, particularly from a liquidity risk perspective, as institutions may be required to remunerate deposits at rates well above the term structure of interest rates. This does not imply that financial institutions should price assets under extreme market conditions in a business-as-usual environment. However, prudence is required to ensure that investments offer a return profile consistent with interest rate risk—that is, prices should be set in line with the prevailing market curve and their modified duration. This helps ensure that, in the event of a sharp shift from non-maturing deposits to term deposits, institutions retain sufficient financial income to partially absorb such shocks.

In addition, from a liability composition perspective, a prudent growth strategy helps maintain a structure in which the weight of NMD offsets periods when deposit remuneration may lie well above the term curve. In such cases, the spread paid above the curve can be mitigated by the share of NMD, which are remunerated at 0%.

It is important to know how to interpret the combined view of margin on investment and margin on funding. Margin on investment must be viewed in the context of previous developments prior to the onset of any financial crisis. With regard to margin on funding, its evolution before the onset of any financial crisis must also be analysed, but above all, lessons must be learned from its behaviour during the development phases of financial crises, because it provides insight into the prudence that must be maintained in the composition of liabilities and the speed of investment growth that will affect the future sustainability of the banking business via financing.

Figure 7.6 shows that during the 16 quarters prior to the onset of the crisis, the system maintained a negative PGa[41,42] caused by strong growth in credit investment with prices not adjusted to their risk profile. This dynamic was largely driven by competition, as credit growth intensified and pricing imbalances widened. This imbalance could not be offset by the funding structure prevailing at the time. As shown, both the structure of liabilities and their remuneration further undermined the sustainability of the banking business from the onset of the crisis in 2009. Resources theoretically allocated to absorb unexpected losses proved insufficient to correct the underlying sustainability imbalances of the business model or to sustain double-digit returns on equity during that period (based on accounting data)—a weakness that has also been

40 Real Decreto 771/2011 of 3 June discouraged the "liability war" without setting legal caps, thereby increasing the contributions to the Deposit Guarantee Fund (FGD) for financial institutions that paid out on deposits exceeding certain reference thresholds based on the term of the deposit.

41 The middle of the economic cycle is being considered: 4.01%.

42 The margin on funding is adjusted to calculate PGa with the LtD so that the percentages are homogeneous and in the same dimension as the credit investment.

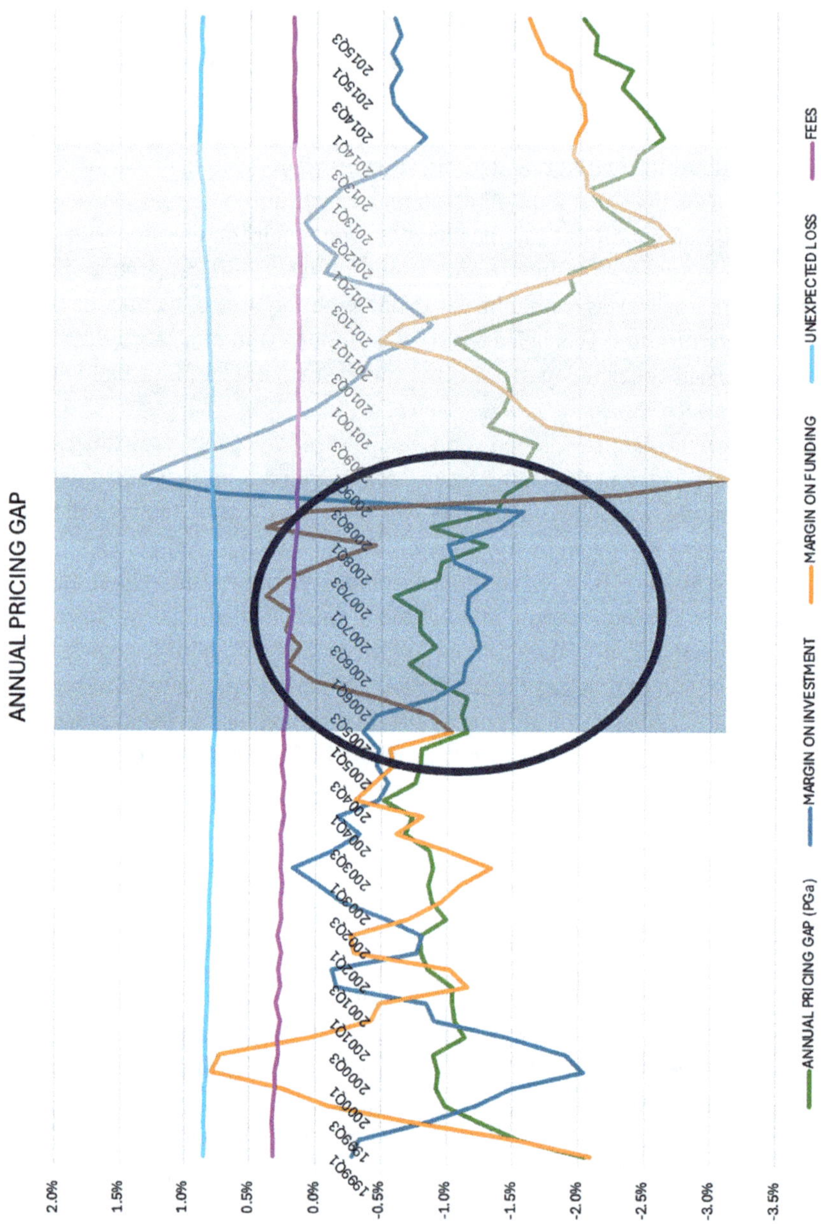

Figure 7.6: Annual Pricing Gap.
Source: Own elaboration based on data from the Statistical Bulletin of the Bank of Spain.

highlighted in analyses of banking business models, particularly under conditions of heightened uncertainty.

Moreover, during the 2005–2006 financial years and thereafter, compensation within the PGa metric for the funding component relied on margins generated by short-term lending, while the investment margin—associated with very long-term operations—was negative. This mismatch constitutes an additional early warning indicator. Finally, the fee and commission incomes were notably flat and did not function as an active management tool in customer negotiations. As investment margins came under pressure, fee and commission were not increased to offset the deterioration in customer profitability management.

Therefore, it can be concluded that PGa presents an opportunity as a complementary analysis to the methodologies developed by supervisors to assess the sustainability of the banking business, which is key to establishing early warning indicators in the boom phases prior to the detonation phases of systemic crises.

Banking business viability – key in the detonation phases of banking crises

Once a crisis begins, attention must shift to the viability of the banking business. In this context, Total Pricing Gap – PGt is considered a very useful tool for this purpose. Unlike the PGa metric, PGt incorporates expected loss in its entirety. Conceptually, it is equivalent to simulating the immediate materialisation of a financial crisis and assessing its impact, including the absorption capacity provided by existing provisions and the amount of capital that would be required to absorb the losses not covered by those provisions. In addition, PGt accounts for how credit risk may increase or decrease depending on the financing structure and remuneration scheme.

For the period analysed for the Spanish financial system, the results of a simulation using the spot expected loss can be seen in Figure 7.7.

This graph shows, through the margin on investment, that if the same expected loss of Stage 3 spot for each period were to be repeated on the Stage 1 portfolio, it would reflect the financial situation of the banks in the event that the risks on the balance sheet were to materialise, in addition to the aforementioned credit risk.

It can also be observed that the margin on funding was also negative, especially after the onset of the crisis, and was insufficient to offset the profitability deficit for the risks assumed. In other words, 16 quarters before the onset of the 2009 crisis, the financial system only had the capacity to deal with the specific defaults it had at that time if they were to be repeated for the Stage 1 portfolio, without having the capacity to apply a forward-looking perspective in risk management.

Provisions fell significantly from 2005 onwards, due to the transition to new accounting standards (CBE 4/2004). In addition, during the period of strongest credit growth, the weight of provisions did not increase to take advantage of this boom, which left the system more vulnerable.

Fees were obviously too low to absorb the observed levels of profitability deficits.

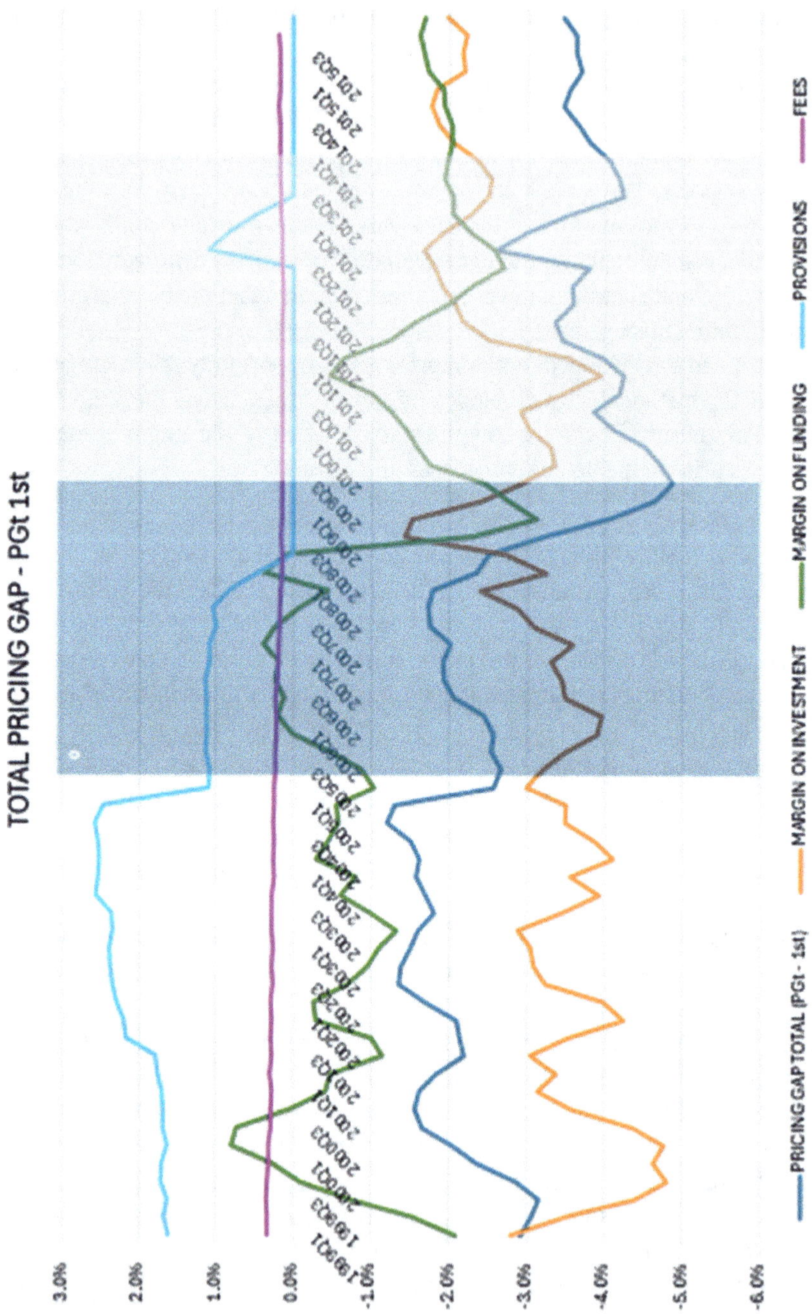

Figure 7.7: Total Pricing Gap – PGt 1st.
Source: Own elaboration based on data from the Statistical Bulletin of the Bank of Spain.

Figure 7.8 shows the evolution of the PGt-2nd and its main components that help explain it. Firstly, it should be remembered that this metric shows us what the capital level of the banking system would be in the event of average economic cycle losses, as well as incorrect asset pricing according to their modified duration, which would be a problem if the margin on funding were to be consistently negative. A negative margin on funding in the short term, for fixed-rate balance sheets on the asset side and financed with deposits, would be a problem if that negative level were greater than the slope of rates between the modified duration of assets and liabilities. Logically, the evolution of PGt-2nd over time depends on PGt-1st (with average expected loss over the economic cycle or LFT), which has remained negative since the beginning of the series and has worsened since approximately 2008. The most negative PGt-1st level, from 2008 onwards, comes hand in hand with the fall in market rates and the maintenance of the deposit remuneration policy in order to preserve liquidity levels in a banking system such as Spain's, which is highly dependent on capital markets due to its real estate boom. This whole issue can be seen through the margin on funding from the 2008/2009 financial year onwards.

The assessment of the potential impacts on capital, in the event of the risks materialising, is reflected in the capital at risk metric. In general terms, the evolution of capital at risk is determined by the pricing deficit in the asset, which is correctly identified through the margin on investment. It is like a thermometer in terms of the level of capital on the risks on the balance sheet that are not correctly remunerated. Its sharp fall in 2009 goes hand in hand with the decline in capital levels on banks' balance sheets at the same time, and its recovery coincides with the recapitalisation of the Spanish banking system around 2012.

The fall in capital since 2009, as can be seen in the graph, goes hand in hand with a sharp rise in the expected spot loss, which, as can be seen, exceeds the average levels of the system since 2009, together with a need to maintain a remuneration of deposits above the yield curve as a result of the war on liabilities during the financial crisis. The impact on capital could have been mitigated through the implementation of a dynamic provisioning model, as will be seen below.

It should be emphasised that the accuracy of the simulation exercise would increase substantially with access to credit bureau data. Such information would make it possible to model transactions at the individual level, generating significantly greater analytical value. A rich, bottom-up perspective would then be available, enabling the development of a real-time monitoring framework capable of identifying herd behaviour within the financial system. Moreover, the mere existence of a supervisory instrument based on this approach is likely to induce self-regulation, as market participants adjust their behaviour in response to enhanced oversight.

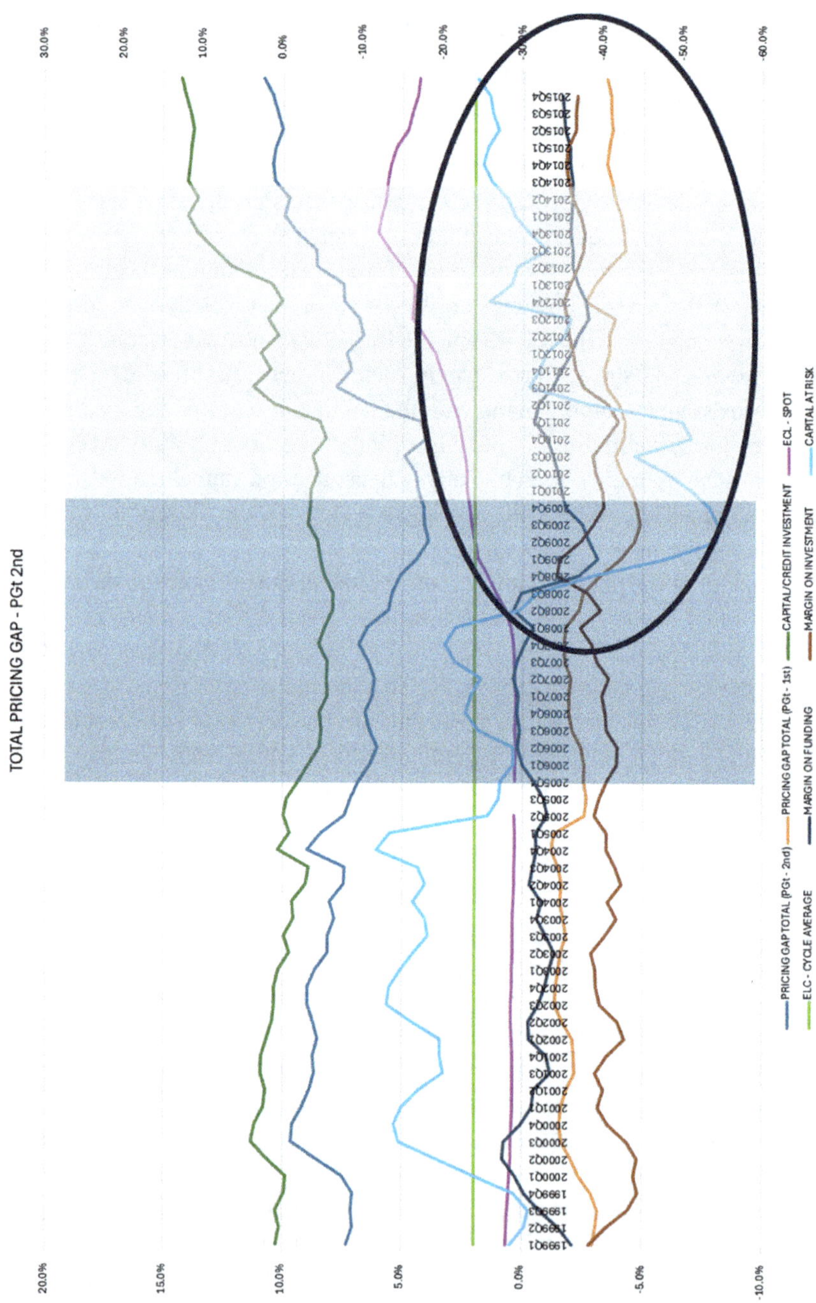

Figure 7.8: Total Pricing Gap – PGt 2nd.
Source: Own elaboration based on data from the Statistical Bulletin of the Bank of Spain.

7.7.3 Conclusions

The conclusions that can be drawn from the simulation exercise are:

- Entities must maintain orthodoxy in keeping balance sheet profitability levels in line with financial risks. In the boom phases prior to the onset of systemic crises, the PGa metric can provide value as an early warning indicator and for monitoring the banking sector, providing a more complete assessment than that provided by accounting information.
  - Focus on structural risks:
    - Correct pricing in line with the modified duration of assets (plus the other well-established pricing components) ensures that term deposits can be remunerated at curve levels and that the liquidity premiums payable on those deposits at times of maximum volatility in the system can be balanced against the weight of NMDs which, due to their remuneration, generally at 0%, offset that liquidity premium for term deposits.
    - As long as there are long-term fixed-rate risks with a profitability deficit, greater weight and discipline must be maintained in the financing structure and its remuneration, since, although a long-term profitability deficit is being financed with short-term structures, at least that discipline must not be lost.
- Macroprudential measures for the boom phase, such as limits on LTV and DTI, are not sufficient. They can be established, but if prices continue to be set poorly due to competition issues, the problem still remains. If there are doubts, for example, about real estate valuations, it is sufficient to establish modifications in the LGD of the pricing model. If the doubts are about laxity in admission policies regarding payment capacity, it is sufficient to ensure that the appropriate PDs are being recognised for the risk profile of borrowers.
- Risk premium setting policies should be established with a forward-looking vision, at least with the average of the economic cycle, to ensure a profitability model that makes the banking business model sustainable and less procyclical.
- At the macroprudential level, for the detonation phase of systemic crises, a countercyclical framework should be established, based on provisions that are capable of mitigating the harmful effects of a financial crisis such as that of 2009 and that are also capable, in the event of low growth, of guaranteeing a financial system with a sustainable business model and allowing for traceability with early warning systems for boom phases. If we combine this with proper price maintenance in balance with the market curve at any given time based on the modified duration, and work in that direction, these are key factors for the viability of the financial system. The PGt metric would help to implement this macroprudential vision, as it provides the information needed to construct the automatic banking system stability mechanism presented below.

7.8 Automatic mechanism for stabilising the banking system: A proposal

When designing or proposing a mechanism to safeguard financial stability in periods of credit expansion —and even in the absence of excessive credit growth when economic conditions may still pose future risks to the banking system—a two-pronged approach is required:

1. Ensure that the financial system maintains an appropriate balance between profitability, risk, provisioning and capital, both for new lending and for existing exposures. This objective underpins the sustainability of the banking business model and can be supported through the application of the Annual Pricing Gap (PGa) metric, which provides an assessment of the extent to which balance sheets are appropriately remunerated relative to the risks undertaken.

   At the macro level, this vision has been explored through a simulation exercise, and a potential implementation path has been outlined. At the micro level—on an institution-by-institution basis—it can be operationalised through the Supervisory Review and Evaluation Process (SREP), which is discussed in detail in the following chapter.

2. Ensure that the financial system has the capacity to respond effectively to systemic credit events, such as those experienced during the 2009 financial crisis. This capacity should be implemented through instruments other than traditional macroprudential buffers, whose activation may be constrained by the stigma associated with their signalling effects on financial institutions' valuations in capital markets. Such instruments should be governed by clear and transparent rules for both accumulation and activation.

Figure 7.6 clearly shows how, through the correct measurement of the PGa, correct pricing can be guaranteed both in times of strong credit growth and without it, providing more information than that provided by the classic view of accounting. Therefore, this would be the first step.

The second step would be to design a countercyclical mechanism for accumulation and activation mechanism of provisions capable of absorbing systemic shocks. Such a mechanism would aim to decouple banking crises from broader economic downturns by preventing contagion through the measures described above. This objective can be achieved by maintaining a banking system whose business model ensures that profitability accurately reflects the financial risks embedded in its balance sheet, alongside a dedicated mechanism to absorb sudden systemic crises in which the materialisation of financial risks exceeds their average level over the economic cycle.

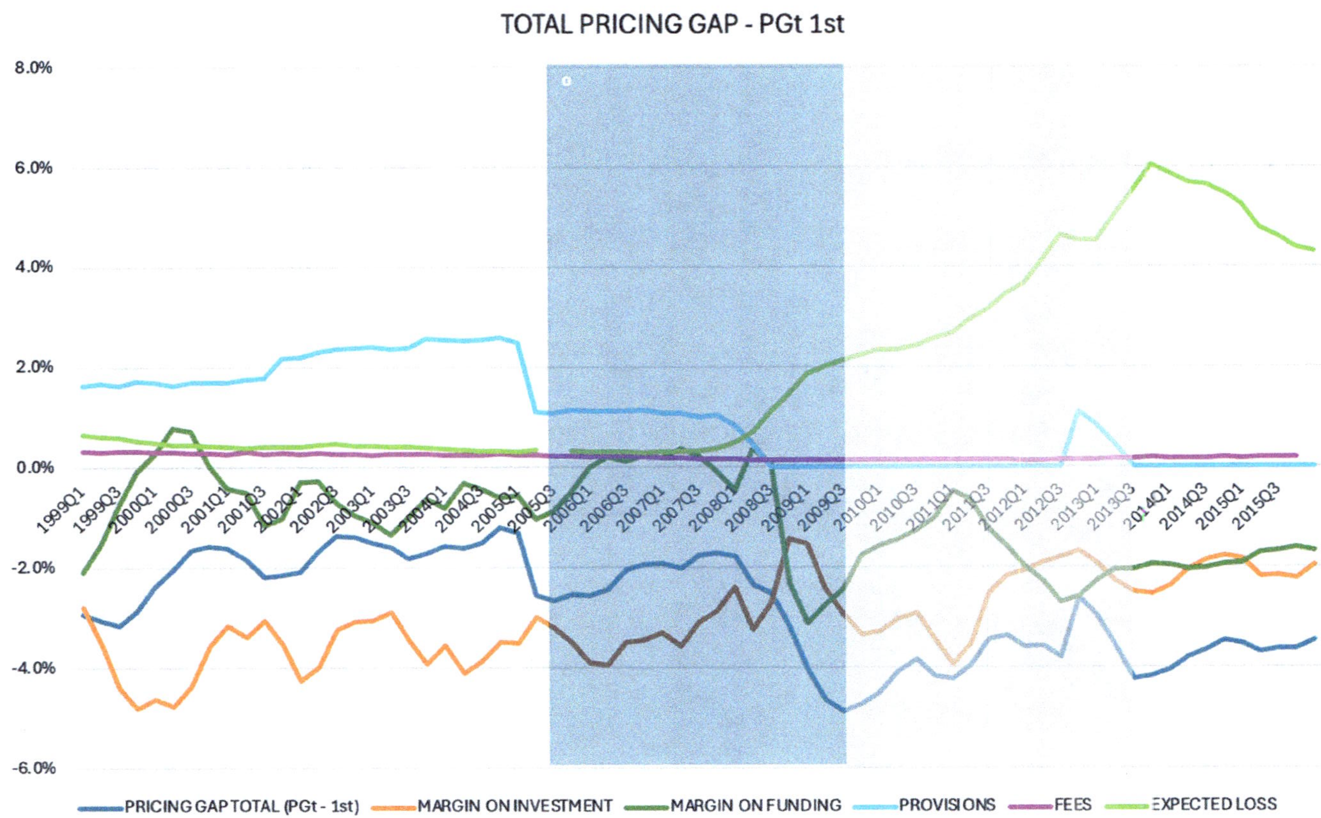

Figure 7.9: Total Pricing Gap – PGt 1st (Spot Expected Loss).
Source: Own elaboration based on data from the Statistical Bulletin of the Bank of Spain.

Clearly, the macroprudential instrument must be a buffer of provisions.[43] Based on historical experience, Figure 7.9 shows that the deterioration was not only significant but was driven almost entirely by expected losses. This experience is well documented and measurable. While it is clearly impossible to predict future developments with certainty, recent history suggests that maintaining a banking system equipped with a dynamically accumulated provisioning mechanism—calibrated to an average level over the economic cycle—may represent an optimal solution.

The next step, therefore, is to propose a framework governing the accumulation and use (activation) of such a mechanism, see Figure 7.10.

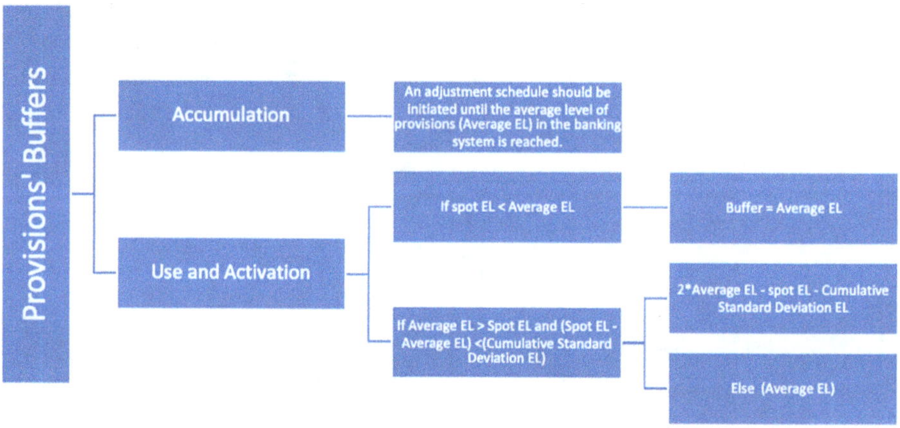

Figure 7.10: PROVISIONS' BUFFER RULES.
Source: Own elaboration.

In essence, the automatic mechanism would aim—through a predefined transition path—to ensure that the system accumulates countercyclical provisions equivalent to the average level of expected losses over the economic cycle. These provisions would be activated only when the increase in expected losses exceeds the cyclical average by one standard deviation (or a higher threshold, depending on the assessment of the system's profitability, as certain credit events may occur without a liquidity crisis and may be absorbed through other sources of earnings). Activation would continue until the accumulated provisions are fully deployed to cushion the impact of the shock.

Graphically, the automatic mechanism for using the provision buffer would appear as shown in Figure 7.11.

It can be seen that the level of the buffer is equal to the average expected loss for the cycle, and, for example, in the case of Spain, the expected loss tripled that level in

43 The legal and operational framework, including its gradual implementation, warrants intense debate within the financial and regulatory communities, etc.

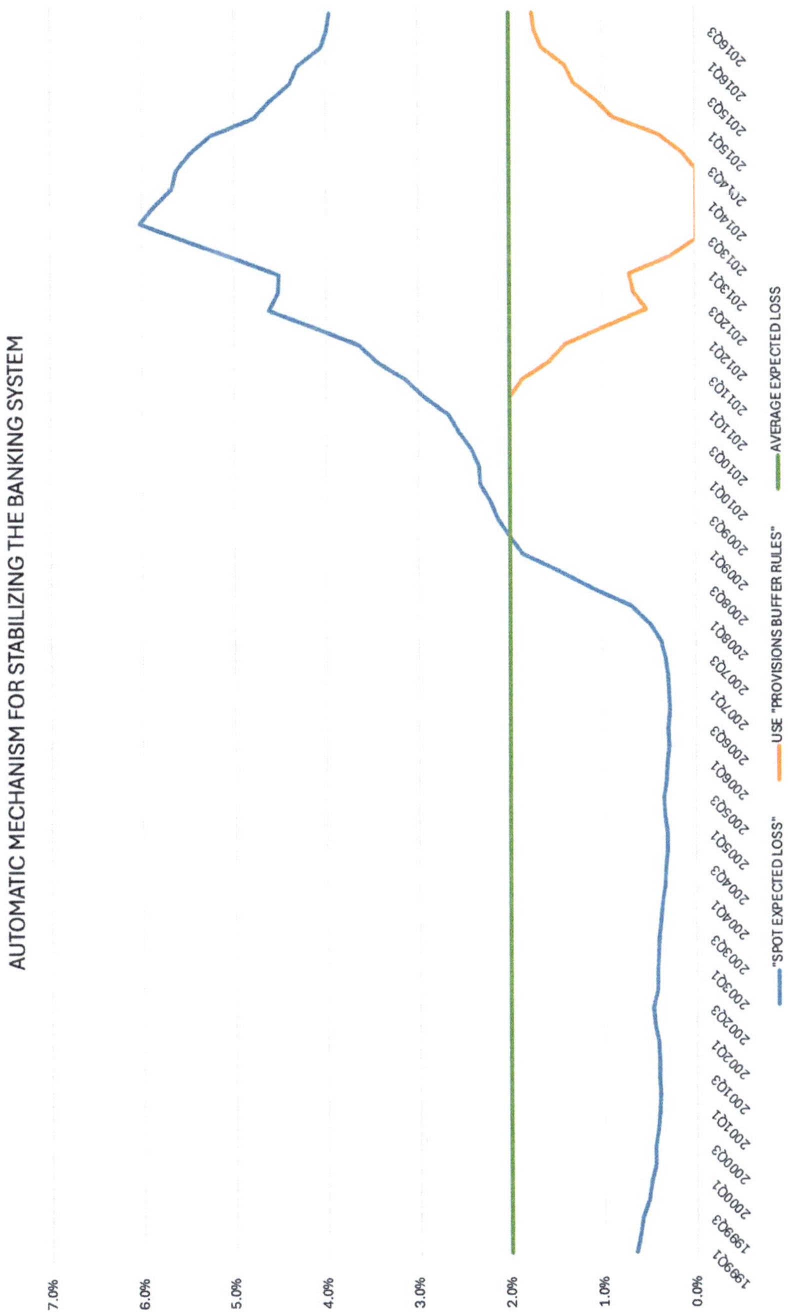

Figure 7.11: Automatic Mechanism for Stabilising the Banking System.
Source: Own elaboration.

the simulation exercise. It should be emphasised that the key to the automatic mechanism is not based exclusively on the level of the buffer, but on the incentive scheme generated in the management of banks by requiring its maintenance over time as institutions grow organically and inorganically. If a banking system grows significantly, it has to accumulate provisions for the buffer (within the established time frame), which would imply a significant retention of profits and, therefore, a lower capacity for growth with organically generated capital. Only those financial institutions that have accumulated larger buffers in the past will be able to grow somewhat faster than their competitors, and this will only be possible with the correct application of prices in the business model that remunerate the risks to which they are exposed or, in other words, maintaining proper PGa discipline and/or developing complementary activities in the banking business that increase profitability, such as cross-selling through the banking-insurance business, investment funds, pension plans, ALCO portfolios, structural efficiencies, etc.

Discussing macroprudential LTV and DTI policies under this working model does not make much sense either, as the only thing that matters is ensuring that the system is setting and maintaining prices (although they may be complementary measures, nevertheless, with the pricing policy prevailing) in line with the PDs and LGDs inferred from the macro situation in terms of accepted collateral and the micro situation in terms of customer credit quality.

Finally, this proposed model could be debatable and is obviously incompatible with the current system of macroprudential buffers through capital instruments, which should be eliminated[44] as well as with a structure of MREL requirements, which, with the potential integration of an automatic mechanism such as the one presented here, should be gradually reduced due to their reduced necessity and current high cost for financial institutions, leading to a simplification of prudential regulation for financial institutions in the sector.

44 In future chapters, we will see that the pricing gap methodology will address these issues at the micro level through the SREP process and stress test exercises.

8 PRICING GAP: A regulatory view. An assessment tool of banking business risk

The purpose of this chapter is to introduce the Annual Pricing Gap (PGa) and Total Pricing Gap (PGt) metrics as instruments that can be used in the current Supervisory Review and Evaluation Process (SREP) and, more specifically, in the Business Model Analysis (BMA). To this end, the latest available information of interest to the value-added proposal will be reviewed and its process and possibilities for integration will be discussed.

The value of integration into the SREP process, and within it, into the BMA process, is very important, as it allows for traceability between the macro view discussed in Chapter 7 and the micro view discussed in the SREP procedure.[45] More specifically, this chapter presents how the issue of the sustainability and viability of the business model of financial institutions can be integrated into the quantification of P2R and P2G.

8.1 Regulatory framework and evolution of the SREP

The regulatory framework of the SREP (Supervisory Review and Evaluation Process) has its origins in the second pillar of the Basel II capital agreement (Pillar 2), which introduced the supervisory review as a complement to the minimum capital requirements of Pillar 1. Pillar 2 establishes two main components:

a. Banks must internally assess their risks and capital needs (through the ICAAP (Internal Capital Adequacy Assessment Process) and the ILAAP (Internal Liquidity Adequacy Assessment Process).
b. Supervisors must comprehensively review and assess each institution and may require additional capital or other measures depending on the risk profile observed. This second component is precisely the SREP, whose key purpose is to ensure that each bank has robust corporate governance and risk management systems in place, as well as sufficient capital and liquidity to cover all its present and future risks.

In the European Union, the SREP was legally established by Directive 2013/36/EU, which in Article 97 requires competent authorities to carry out, at least annually, a supervisory review and evaluation of each institution. This legal requirement is maintained in subsequent revisions of the directive (CRD V and CRD VI proposals), with

45 European Banking Authority. (2022). Guidelines on common procedures and methodologies for the supervisory review and evaluation process (SREP) and supervisory stress testing (EBA/GL/2022/03).

 | https://doi.org/10.1515/9783111328386-008

additions on the treatment of certain risks and coordination between supervisors. CRD IV also empowered supervisors to impose Pillar 2 measures, including additional capital requirements, restrictions or improvements to internal processes, and a capital guidance (P2G), which constitutes a capital expectation rather than a requirement, as a breach does not trigger any MDA restrictions.

To achieve uniformity in the application of Pillar 2 across the various EU countries, in 2014 the EBA issued guidelines on common procedures and methodologies for the SREP (EBA/GL/2014/13). These guidelines provided, for the first time, a common framework for all supervisors (whether national authorities or, in the euro area, the SSM through the ECB) to assess certain elements in a consistent manner: the sustainability and viability of the business model, the adequacy of internal governance and controls, risks affecting capital and risks affecting liquidity.

The guidelines established a harmonised scoring system from 1 to 4 for the different areas and for the overall assessment, criteria for determining capital surcharges, and principles of proportionality according to the size and complexity of the institutions. When the European Central Bank assumed direct supervision of significant institutions in the euro area in 2014 (Single Supervisory Mechanism), it adopted these EBA guidelines and integrated them into its own SREP methodology, known for its structured approach and categories of institutions.

Since their introduction, the EBA's SREP guidelines have been updated several times to incorporate new regulatory developments and improve methodological aspects. An important milestone was the conceptual separation between the Pillar 2 Requirement (P2R), which is binding and computable in capital requirements, and Pillar 2 Guidance (P2G), which is non-binding, clarified after the 2018 edition of the SREP guidelines. Elements such as the specific assessment of excess leverage risk (introducing P2R-LR and P2G-LR for the leverage ratio), cooperation between prudential and anti-money laundering (AML) supervisors, and qualitative considerations such as environmental, social and governance (ESG) risks have also been incorporated. The most recent version under development (draft 2025) updates the SREP to align it with CRD V/VI, Basel III final and the lessons learned from its implementation, including a review of the P2G methodology (given the experience of stress tests).

It is worth mentioning that, in addition to the EBA guidelines, there are specific complementary guidelines that develop particular aspects of the SREP. For example, the EBA has issued guidelines on interest rate risk assessment in the banking book (IRRBB), on technological/ICT risk assessment in the SREP, on concentration risk management, among others. All of these fall under the umbrella of Pillar 2 and are intended to ensure that supervisors comprehensively assess all the idiosyncratic risks faced by an institution.

8.2 SREP architecture and the role of the BMA

The SREP process is structured into four thematic blocks or "pillars" of assessment, covering all critical areas of an institution's risk and solvency profile. These four elements are analysed both separately and jointly to form an overall supervisory view of each bank. The pillars of the SREP and a brief description of their scope are listed below:

- Block 1: Business Model Analysis (BMA). Assesses the viability and sustainability of the institution's business model and strategy. It includes an analysis of the institution's competitive position, sources of income and expenditure, ability to generate risk-adjusted returns, consistency of its strategic plan with the resources and risks assumed, and potential vulnerabilities (e.g., excessive concentrations, dependence on certain markets or products, etc.). It is both a retrospective (current and past performance) and prospective (future projections) analysis, incorporating micro- and macro-prudential considerations. This pillar answers the question: Is the bank's business model sound and sustainable, and can it survive over time by creating value within a reasonable level of risk?
- Block 2: Assessment of Internal Governance and Controls. This examines the quality of the institution's corporate governance and the effectiveness of its control functions at an overall level. It includes the organisational structure and suitability of the Board of Directors and senior management, the risk and conduct culture, remuneration policies, the functioning of internal control units (risk management, internal audit, compliance), the existence of a robust risk management framework (risk identification, measurement, control and monitoring) and risk data aggregation capacity, as well as specific aspects such as technology risk management (ICT), cybersecurity, money laundering (ML/TF) risks insofar as they affect prudential risk, and crisis recovery planning. Poor governance and internal control are often a catalyst for financial problems, so this pillar is essential for assessing confidence in the bank's management and its risk control systems.
- Block 3: Capital Risk Assessment (Capital Adequacy). It analyses in detail the main quantifiable risks that consume regulatory capital, as well as the adequacy of the institution's own funds in relation to those risks. It typically covers credit and counterparty risk (including credit concentrations), market risk, operational risk (and operational loss events, including technological ones), and interest rate risk in the banking book (IRRBB), among other relevant risks depending on the bank's profile.

For each risk category, the supervisor assesses the bank's inherent exposure, the effectiveness of its management/controls to mitigate it, and the resulting residual risk. This forms a view of the bank's internal capital adequacy (ICAAP) and determines whether the minimum Pillar 1 requirements are sufficient or whether Pillar 2 capital surcharges are needed to adequately cover those risks. This quantitative pillar is central to the determination of P2R, discussed below. In short, it answers the questions: What are the bank's most significant financial risks, and does it have sufficient capital to absorb unexpected losses associated with them?

- Block 4: Assessment of Liquidity and Funding Risks (Liquidity Adequacy). Reviews the bank's liquidity position and its resilience to liquidity shocks or funding difficulties. It includes the assessment of intrinsic liquidity risk (e.g., asset/liability maturity structure, concentration of funding sources, deposit stability), liquidity risk management (e.g. quality of the ILAAP framework, liquidity contingency plans, liquid asset buffers) and stable funding risk (dependence on wholesale funding, etc.).

Supervisors check compliance with regulatory ratios (LCR, NSFR) but go further, assessing internal liquidity scenarios and possible outflows of funds in stress situations. If they detect significant weaknesses, they may require corrective measures or even additional liquidity requirements (e.g., maintaining a certain level of quality liquid assets or reducing funding gaps). This pillar answers the question: Can the bank meet its liquidity obligations and needs even under adverse scenarios, and is its long-term funding strategy adequate?

Each of these four pillars typically receives a supervisory score ranging from 1 (low risk or concern) to 4 (high risk or concern) based on the supervisor's findings. The supervisor then prepares an overall assessment of the bank, often reflected in a composite or overall score that determines the institution's supervisory category, which influences the intensity of future supervision.

The SREP assessment culminates in a comprehensive supervisory decision, which sets out the measures to be implemented by the institution. Among the most important measures are additional capital requirements (Pillar 2 Required, P2R), expressed as a percentage of risk-weighted assets that the bank must maintain above the Pillar 1 minimums. Alongside these, from 2016-2018, capital guidance (Pillar 2 Guidance, P2G) is also communicated, indicating a recommended level of capital to withstand severe stress conditions, although non-compliance does not automatically trigger supervisory measures. In addition to capital, the SREP may involve qualitative measures: for example, requiring improvements in internal controls, limiting certain operations or exposures until deficiencies are corrected, strengthening management bodies, among others. It may also set additional liquidity requirements, such as maintaining a certain liquidity coverage ratio (LCR) above the legal 100%, etc. All these measures are set out in the formal SREP Decision that the supervisor communicates to banks each year.

A crucial aspect of the methodology is proportionality. Not all banks are analysed with the same depth or frequency in each area; rather, the scope of the SREP is adjusted to the systemic importance, size, complexity and risk profile of the institution.

In conclusion, the overall SREP methodology combines quantitative and qualitative analysis, retrospective and prospective approaches, and a holistic view of the bank. The end result is a comprehensive assessment of the institution's current and future viability. The SREP provides the supervisor with an informed diagnosis for action. If the diagnosis is favourable, it can maintain a normal monitoring approach; if it identifies weaknesses, it may activate closer monitoring, corrective measures or require extra capital or liquidity, as appropriate; if it discovers severe risks to viability, it can even escalate actions to early intervention measures or coordinate with resolution authorities.

8.3 Critical aspects in business model analysis

Business Model Analysis (BMA) is the first pillar of the SREP and aims to provide a comprehensive view of the bank's business strategy, its short-term viability and its medium- to long-term sustainability. It is based on the premise, supported by historical experience, that many banking crises cannot be explained solely by unexpected external shocks, but rather by pre-existing structural vulnerabilities in the institution's own business model. Typical vulnerabilities include uncontrolled excessive growth strategies, shifts towards high-risk segments without adequate management capacity, strategic plans based on overly optimistic assumptions, or poor execution of well-conceived plans. The BMA therefore enables the supervisor to identify these root weaknesses before they manifest themselves in losses or solvency problems, enabling more forward-looking and preventive supervision.

The ultimate purpose of the BMA is to assess whether the bank can generate sustainable and sufficient returns, commensurate with its risks, both in the immediate term (next 12 months, concept of viability) and over a broader strategic horizon (3 years or more, concept of sustainability). According to the definition adopted by the ECB's SSM and reflected in EBA guidelines, the viability of the business model refers to the institution's ability to generate acceptable returns in the coming year (usually measured in terms of return on equity (ROE) above the cost of capital, among other indicators), given its current situation, its revenue and cost drivers, and the environment in which it operates. Business model sustainability, on the other hand, refers to the bank's ability to maintain that acceptable profitability over at least three years and through a complete economic cycle, considering the expected evolution of its business environment and the execution of its strategic plan. In short, viability is a short-term concept (one year) and sustainability is a medium-term concept (three years or more), both from the perspective of a supervisor who judges whether the benefits are acceptable and proportionate to the risk assumed.

To reach such an assessment, the supervisor must gain a comprehensive understanding of the bank's business model and strategy. This encompasses multiple facets: How does the institution generate profits? What are its main lines of business, products or geographical markets, and how much does each contribute to income and expenses? What competitive advantages or disadvantages does it have? What macroeconomic or market assumptions underpin its business plan? Does it have the necessary resources (financial, human, technological) to execute its strategy? What are the external conditions (regulatory, technological, competitive) that could favour or threaten its future success? The BMA seeks to answer these questions by combining quantitative analysis (e.g., financial indicators, projections) with expert qualitative judgement on less tangible elements (quality of management, credibility of the plan, strategic positioning, etc.).

The sources of data and information for the BMA are varied. The EBA's SREP guidelines and ECB practices explicitly identify a number of minimum inputs that supervisors should consider:

- The institution's strategic plan, including multi-year financial projections and underlying economic assumptions.
- Financial statements and regulatory reports: financial information (balance sheets, income statements) and prudential reports (COREP, FINREP) to analyse the balance sheet structure, profitability, capital levels and other current and past quantitative indicators.
- Internal management information: analytical accounting by business unit, geography, etc. This granular information provides a better understanding of which activities or segments generate profits or losses.
- Recovery plans: as they contain stress scenario analyses and strategic options for extreme situations, they can reveal vulnerabilities in the business model.
- Resolution plans and resolvability assessments: the conclusions of the resolution authority.
- Bank plans for ESG risks: in accordance with Article 76(2) of CRD IV, institutions must plan how to manage environmental risks.
- Third-party reports: external audits, analyses by rating agencies or financial analysts, which can provide an independent perspective on the bank's situation.
- Macroprudential studies: reports from the IMF, the central bank or other institutions on the economic environment, markets or financial stability, to provide context for the bank's operations.

With this broad information base, the supervisor proceeds to carry out the analysis in several stages or areas of assessment within the BMA. These areas can be summarised in three blocks:

1. Quantitative analysis of the current situation.
2. Qualitative analysis of structural factors.
3. Prospective analysis of strategy and future projections.

8.3.1 Current quantitative analysis

The supervisor examines the bank's recent financial results to assess its ability to generate acceptable profits in the short term. Here, the drivers of profitability are evaluated: the result is broken down into its main components (interest margin, commissions, results from financial operations, operating expenses, cost of credit through provisions, etc.).

It is important to distinguish between recurring and stable sources of income and exceptional or volatile elements. Historical trends are analysed, such as whether income and margins are increasing or decreasing, and how efficient the bank is (cost/income ratio).

Key indicators such as ROE, ROA, net interest margin on assets, cost of risk and cost to income are compared with peer groups. The aim is to determine whether the bank is intrinsically capable of covering its costs and generating a return above its cost of capital, without relying on extraordinary factors.

At the same time, the balance sheet structure and capital situation are analysed: the mix of assets (loans, securities portfolio, others) and liabilities (deposits, wholesale debt, capital), the growth of risk-weighted assets and equity through retained earnings or issues.

The aim is to identify possible imbalances or concentrations: for example, excessive dependence on one type of financing, a high concentration of loans in one sector or geography, etc., which could compromise income stability or involve high risks.

Indicators such as return on assets or return on capital are considered in relation to the risks assumed (measured by capital ratios). In short, this quantitative part answers the questions: Is the bank making sufficient profits today and how sensitive are those profits to identifiable risk factors?

8.3.2 Qualitative analysis of structural factors

On the one hand, the supervisor analyses the external business environment. It examines the economic and market landscape in the main areas where the bank operates, as well as the competitive, regulatory and technological conditions that affect it. Assessing the environment allows threats or opportunities for the bank's model to be identified (e.g., structural changes such as banking digitalisation or the ecological transition may require the bank to adapt its model).

On the other hand, key internal or external dependencies for the bank are identified. For example, a bank may be heavily dependent on a costly physical distribution network or, conversely, on a technological platform. It may have a large base of loyal customers (strength) or depend on a few corporate customers (weakness). The franchise and competitive advantages are also assessed: the institution's reputation, the strength of its brand, relationships with customers and suppliers, and any areas where it has an advantage over competitors (e.g., specialisation in a profitable niche, economies of scale). This indicates how defensible its market position is.

Finally, the support of technology for the business is assessed. Is the bank's technological and digital infrastructure aligned with its strategy, enabling it to operate efficiently and offer new products, or is it rather an obstacle (obsolete systems that increase costs or make it difficult to compete online)? IT deficiencies can prevent adaptation to trends such as digital banking and thus threaten sustainability.

All this qualitative analysis allows the supervisor to understand the potential success or failure factors of the business model beyond the numbers.

8.3.3 Prospective analysis. Strategic plan and projections

This is the phase in which the supervisor evaluates the strategic objectives declared by the institution and its main drivers of success, assessing how realistic and well-founded the strategy is. The gap between the current business model and the one to be achieved ("target model") is examined, as well as how plausible the actions to close that gap are.

A critical task is to assess the credibility of the bank's financial projections. The macroeconomic (GDP growth, interest rates, inflation) and market (credit growth, margin trends, credit quality) assumptions underlying the plan are compared with reasonable scenarios or independent forecasts. If the bank uses overly optimistic assumptions, the supervisor will note this as an execution risk. The internal consistency of the plan is checked to ensure that the various objectives are not contradictory (e.g., growing market share and improving margins) and that they are backed up by concrete actions.

The bank's execution capacity is also considered. Its track record in delivering on previous plans, the quality of its management, and the resources available to implement the strategy. A useful element is to review how accurate its past plans were. If it systematically overestimated its earnings or underestimated its costs, this is a sign of bias in planning. An assessment is made of whether the entity's structure (staff, systems, culture) is adequate for what it intends to do.

As part of this forward-looking assessment, the supervisor may conduct its own analyses: idiosyncratic stress tests on projections, peer comparisons of assumptions, and questions such as "Are you projecting much faster growth than your peers without justification?" The supervisor may even engage in direct interactions with the bank to discuss its plans. In fact, it is good practice for the supervisory team to meet with the bank's senior management to question and understand the premises of the plan in an exercise of constructive challenge. These discussions provide clarity and also allow the supervisor to exert influence if it detects unrealistic approaches.

As part of the forward-looking analysis, specific issues relating to future profitability are also examined: whether the bank has a robust business cost allocation framework that allows it to know where it is making or losing money, whether its internal funds transfer pricing (FTP) system is adequate to correctly reflect liquidity costs in each unit, or whether its governance in loan pricing is sound. These technical aspects matter because if a bank lacks good methods for measuring profitability by product or customer, it could be taking on business that may appear profitable but is not once all the factors involved in transforming maturities are considered. For international banking groups, even how results are shared among different entities within the group is reviewed.

Another emerging point in prospective assessment is the incorporation of very long-term sustainability factors, such as environmental and climate change risks. Recent EBA guidelines urge supervisors to consider horizons of up to 10 years for certain ESG risks, assessing whether the bank has analysed climate transition scenarios and their impact on the business model. If the bank operates in sectors highly exposed to transition (e.g., financing fossil fuel companies), it would be expected to have strategies in place to reorient its business in line with regulatory and market changes linked to environmental sustainability.

8.3.4 BMA conclusions

Following the analysis, the supervisor summarises its BMA conclusions in three key areas:

- Main vulnerabilities of the business model: Identifies inherent weaknesses or risks that could compromise the bank, such as excessive concentrations, dependence on a few products, undifferentiated strategy, execution deficiencies, etc.
- Current viability of the model: An assessment of whether the bank's current business model is viable in the short term (12 months), considering its recent quantitative performance in terms of profitability, its risk appetite, its financial structure and current environmental conditions. If current profitability is very low or negative and there are no signs of immediate improvement, viability could be called into question.
- Sustainability of the strategy: An assessment of whether the stated strategy and medium-term projections are credible and sufficient to keep the bank afloat in the coming years, given what is known about its vulnerabilities, the environment and its execution capacity. This includes consideration of factors such as operational resilience (the institution's ability to adapt to operational or technological shocks), adaptation to megatrends (digitalisation, geopolitical disruptions, innovation in financial services, etc.), and the integration of emerging risks (e.g., crypto-asset risks, if the bank is exposed to that niche).

Finally, all these findings are reflected in a summary of conclusions and a score for the business model pillar, which forms part of the overall SREP rating.

- Rating “1”. The business model and strategy pose a low level of risk to the entity's viability.
  - The institution has a robust model, a solid competitive position and sustained returns clearly above the cost of capital, credible strategy and projections, without excessive dependencies or problematic concentrations.

- Score “2”. The business model and strategy pose a medium-low level of risk to the institution’s viability.
  - The entity has identified challenges, but profitability and execution are reasonable; vulnerabilities are limited and the strategic plan is plausible in the medium term.
- Rating “3”. The business model and strategy pose a medium-high level of risk to the entity’s viability.
  - The institution has clear weaknesses in the model or its execution; weak or volatile profitability (often below the cost of equity), competitive or funding pressures, and doubts about the bank’s ability to correct them with its current plan.
- Rating “4”. The business model and strategy pose a high level of risk to the institution’s viability.
  - There are serious doubts about the continuity of the institution’s model, either due to losses or a chronic inability to cover the cost of equity, an unrealistic or poorly executed strategy; immediate supervisory measures are usually required.

In summary, business model assessment is a deep and multidimensional process that requires both hard data analysis and qualitative judgement and dialogue with the supervised entity. An effective BMA allows the supervisor to anticipate problems that could later materialise in losses or capital shortfalls, providing the opportunity to intervene early. As noted in the BIS-FSI literature, a comprehensive BMA strengthens supervision by making it more proactive and forward-looking, addressing root causes rather than just financial symptoms. It can also have macroprudential implications, since if many banks share model vulnerabilities, the aggregate findings of the BMA can guide structural policies or early warnings at the systemic level.

8.4 Determination of P2R

P2R is defined as a bank-specific capital requirement that supplements the minimum regulatory requirements of Pillar 1 and covers risks that are underestimated or not covered by Pillar 1 requirements. In other words, if the SREP analysis concludes that the institution faces certain risks that are not adequately reflected in the minimum capital ratios (e.g., credit concentration risk, long-term interest rate risk, poor governance risk, etc.), the supervisor will impose an additional capital percentage (on risk-weighted assets, RWA) to cover those residual risks. The P2R is part of the Total SREP Capital Requirement (TSCR), adding to Pillar 1 and any applicable macroprudential buffer requirements. Compliance is mandatory if a bank falls below its TSCR (Pillar 1 + P2R), triggering automatic restrictions on distributions (dividends, bonuses), and may lead to immediate supervisory action.

The methodology for determining P2R typically follows a four-step structured approach.

8.4.1 Initial determination of P2R

First, a holistic assessment of the overall risk profile is carried out by the supervisory team to select an initial P2R level. This assessment is based on:
- SREP Pillar 1 results: Business Model Analysis
- SREP Pillar 2 results: Governance
- Results of Pillar 3 of the SREP: Capital Risks

These results are reflected in the ratings and qualitative assessments of each area, i.e. the bank's overall risk profile is examined.

Using predefined weightings by risk type, based on these scores and applying expert judgement, the supervisor chooses an initial P2R value from a possible range. This initial P2R is a holistic starting point, not a definitive one, which summarises the bank's overall risk in a single capital figure. This initial result, which already takes into account the quality of the ICAAP, can be adjusted in subsequent steps.

8.4.2 Breakdown by risk type

The supervisor breaks down the initial P2R into surcharges attributable to each major Pillar 2 risk category. In other words, that initial percentage is distributed among contributions from, for example, risk inherent in the business model/strategy, risk due to governance/control deficiencies, credit risk, market risk, operational risk, IRRBB risk, etc. The aim is to have a baseline of initial surcharges by risk type that serves as a working hypothesis. To make this allocation, the supervisor considers quantitative information (e.g., how much internal capital the bank estimates it needs for each risk in its ICAAP, or how much Pillar 1 capital already covers certain risks) and qualitative information (severity of deficiencies in each area).

An important principle is to avoid double counting: risks that are already fully covered by Pillar 1 should not be added again in Pillar 2 (concentration risk or model risk, for example).

Additionally, if the bank's ICAAP provides internal risk-based capital estimates, the supervisor may use them as a reference, albeit with caution due to the diversity of practices – the supervisor is given discretion to reflect the quality of the ICAAP in the final composition of the P2R.

The result of step 2 is a table of provisional surcharges, which lays the foundation for reviewing each component in the future.

8.4.3 Checks and adjustments

The supervisor performs a thorough check of the initial risk-type add-ons obtained in step 2, comparing them against various sources of information and performing horizontal benchmarking.

Multiple inputs are incorporated here:

- Key risk indicators, such as default ratios, concentration, and interest rate sensitivity, which could indicate that a certain risk warrants more capital.
- Results of the bank's own ICAAP, which compares internal capital estimates and the degree of reliability.
- Peer group analysis, the aim of which is to identify the capital surcharges of comparable banks.
- Findings from recent on-site inspections or specific in-depth reviews.

To facilitate this "consistency test", supervisors often use internal tools and models that consolidate data from many institutions and allow them to see outliers and verify the consistency of capital surcharge allocations based on quantitative indicators.

Step 3 also incorporates, to the extent possible, macroeconomic or systemic risk considerations that may affect the bank. Although these are usually addressed more in P2G, a supervisor could, for example, decide in a very adverse macro environment to maintain a slightly higher P2R as a buffer. However, formally, P2R covers idiosyncratic risks or risks poorly captured by Pillar 1, while adverse macro scenarios are covered by P2G.

8.4.4 Final decision and supervisory judgement

At this stage, the supervisor determines the final add-ons by risk type and the total P2R applicable to the institution, using its expert judgement to adjust any necessary elements.

Once decided, the final P2R is expressed as a percentage of risk-weighted assets. In Europe, P2R is typically required to be composed with high-quality capital, in general terms.[46] This P2R comes into effect with the formal SREP decision and must be maintained continuously. Failure to comply would trigger automatic restrictions via supervisory measures. However, if P2R is breached, this also implies a breach of the CBR, meaning that MDA restrictions would already have been activated before the

46 Pillar 2 Requirement (P2R) can be met with "Total" regulatory capital (CET1 + AT1 + T2), respecting the same minimum composition as in Pillar 1:

- ≥ 56.25% in CET1 of the P2R (equivalent to 4.5/8).
- ≥ 75% in Tier 1 (CET1 + AT1) of P2R (equivalent to 6/8).
- The remainder can be covered by Tier 2.

P2R breach. The SREP decision communicated to the bank usually breaks down the main reasons for the P2R: for example, it may indicate which risks or deficiencies have led to the size of the surcharge. This is done to provide transparency and guide the bank on where it needs to improve in order to reduce that extra capital in the future.

Finally, it should be noted that the P2R is not static; it is recalibrated in each SREP cycle, usually annually, or may be modified if the bank's risks change substantially.

8.5 Determination of P2G

P2G (Pillar 2 Guidance) was introduced as a component of Pillar 2 following the 2016 stress tests, with the aim of indicating to banks an "expected" capital buffer that they should maintain in order to survive severe adverse macroeconomic scenarios. Unlike P2R, P2G is not legally binding and failure to comply does not immediately result in automatic sanctions; however, supervisors attach great importance to it and expect institutions to comply. The methodology for determining P2G is closely linked to the results of supervisory stress tests.[47] In essence, P2G answers the question: How much additional capital does the bank need so that, under an extreme adverse scenario, it does not fall below the minimum requirements?

The process is as follows:

- An adverse macroeconomic scenario is considered for the future (normally 2-3 years ahead) and the impact on the bank's accounts (credit losses, fall in income, etc.) is projected using stress test models, either at European level (test coordinated by the EBA) or at national/supervisory level.
- The quantitative results show the evolution of the bank's CET1 capital ratio during the adverse scenario. Of particular interest is the minimum CET1 ratio that the bank would have at the worst point of the adverse scenario.
- The P2G is calibrated so that the bank, at the beginning of the scenario, has a sufficient buffer so that even at the worst point of the adverse scenario, it does not exceed its minimum capital requirement (TSCR). In other words, the P2G covers the difference between the initial ratio and that projected adverse minimum, adjusted for requirements. In other words, it "protects against the potential capital shortfall in an adverse scenario".

In practice, the stress tests used may be the EBA's periodic exercises (which generally occur every two years) for large banks, or local supervisory tests for smaller banks or in intermediate years. The EBA guidelines allow, on a proportional basis, simplified forms of stress testing to be used for non-systemic banks (e.g., applying shocks to cer-

47 These stress tests will be analysed in the following chapter.

tain parameters in the ICAAP, or extrapolating stress results from comparable banks). The important thing is that at least every 1-2 years, the P2G is reassessed after some significant stress exercise. In fact, it is usually established that after an EBA test (every two years), P2G is adjusted if necessary, and in the intermediate year without a stress test, the supervisor reviews whether the risks have changed materially and decides whether to keep P2G the same.

The finer calibration of P2G involves several additional technical steps:

- First, calculate the maximum stress impact on CET1: this is the percentage difference between the initial CET1 ratio and the lowest CET1 ratio in the adverse scenario (including the effects on RWA). For example, if a bank starts with CET1 at 14% and in the worst year of the scenario it falls to 9%, the stress impact is -5 percentage points.
- Next, consider the relationship between that impact and the requirements: if the bank's TSCR (Pillar 1 + P2R) is, say, 8%, falling to 9% does not exceed the TSCR (it remains 1% above). However, if it fell to 7%, it would be 1 point below the TSCR – in that case, at least 1% of P2G would be necessary.
- The EBA guidelines indicate that P2G must cover at least the maximum expected stress impact. In the example of a 5 pp impact, in principle P2G should be 5%. However, it is adjusted for existing mitigation factors: mainly, the capital conservation buffer (CCB), which already stands at 2.5% (in Europe), functionally overlaps with P2G, as both serve to absorb losses in stress. Therefore, the CCB is usually subtracted from the impact so as not to duplicate. Also, if there are other activated macro buffers (e.g., CCB, systemic) that cover similar risks, these could be considered, although the guidance explicitly mentions compensating with the CCB in particular. In the example, impact 5% minus CCB 2.5% = 2.5% net would be the base P2G.
- In addition, technical adjustments can be made. For example, if the stress test assumes a static balance sheet over three years and the bank is actually reducing risks at present, the real impact might be lower; or conversely, if there were changes between the date of the stress test and the setting of P2G (increased risks, acquisitions, etc.), these can be incorporated. The supervisor has some leeway to refine the calculation and avoid temporary inconsistencies.
- From that starting point (e.g., 2.5% base P2G), a bucket scheme can be applied. The guidelines suggest that, to promote consistency, supervisors could classify banks into impact ranges and assign them P2G within fixed ranges. For example, all banks with a net impact between 2% and 3% could receive P2G = 2.5%. However, it also allows for case-by-case exceptions to reflect particular situations and avoid sharp jumps between buckets (overlapping ranges if necessary).
- Finally, when deciding on the final P2G, the supervisor must consider additional qualitative factors:
  - In which year of the scenario does the largest capital decline occur? It matters whether it occurs at the end or the beginning of the horizon.

- Does the bank have reliable internal stress tests that may show higher or lower risk? (If internal tests are more adverse, P2G could be increased).
- Have there been any material changes since the stress test, such as portfolio sales or capital raising? This could mitigate some of the risk.
- Is there significant uncertainty about the bank's actual sensitivity to stress due to an atypical business model, etc.? In this case, P2G may be increased for prudence.
- What is the quality of the bank's available capital at the worst moment of stress?

Finally, after considering all of the above, P2G is set as a percentage of RWA and communicated to the bank. By convention, the bank is expected to maintain this extra level above its OCR (Overall Capital Requirement, which includes Pillar 1 + P2R + mandatory buffers) under normal conditions. Many authorities, including the ECB, indicate that banks should maintain P2G mainly in the form of CET1 (in fact, P2G is usually expected to be covered entirely with the highest quality capital).

Although P2G is not binding, supervisors monitor it. If a bank fails to meet its P2G, a supervisory dialogue is initiated to understand why, and the bank is usually required to submit plans to restore it. If the bank persists in not maintaining sufficient capital to cover P2G, the supervisor may decide to translate part of that guidance into a P2R requirement in the next cycle, making what was previously indicative binding. The EBA guidance suggests that if the P2G gap is not corrected within a maximum of two years, the supervisor should take measures to incorporate that deficit into P2R. This puts pressure on banks to treat P2G with almost the same seriousness as P2R.

8.6 How can PRICING GAP metrics help the SREP process?

Firstly, it should be remembered that within the SREP process, the Business Analysis Model is key. Through it, the authorities form a complete picture of the bank's business strategy, both in terms of its viability and sustainability.

These authorities have also made it clear that it is not only external shocks that explain banking crises, but that there are also structural vulnerabilities in the business model that can help explain such crises, such as excessive growth, excessive concentration, etc., hence the importance of the BMA.

The ultimate goal of the BMA is to assess the viability and sustainability of the banking business. Among its main drawbacks, two can be pointed out:

- In quantitative terms, accounting information is predominantly used to analyse profitability and subsequently make decisions. Previous chapters have already highlighted how, in the banking business, accounting information has serious limitations when it comes to drawing conclusions about the present and future situation of a financial institution in order to assess the viability and sustainability of its business model. Furthermore, accounting information does not accurately identify the sources of profitability in a financial institution or the risks to which it is exposed, and other types of complementary analysis are necessary.

– On the qualitative side, there is excessive reliance on expert judgement to make assessments and obtain capital requirement calibrations. In addition, the use of peer group analysis carries significant risks. A financial system may have financial institutions with gregarious behaviour and clear strategies to increase market share, sacrificing profitability and jeopardising financial stability. If all institutions as a whole imitate this behaviour in the face of the threat, any institution that lags behind may fare poorly in performance comparisons, which is not a correct conclusion.

The BMA is a key input for determining P2R and P2G, which, as identified above, rely too heavily on holistic assessments and expert judgements for their calibration.

The PGa and PGt metrics can help enrich this process by providing objective assessments of profitability and its sources, which contribute value in a very precise manner in determining the viability and sustainability of the banking business.

From a conceptual point of view, it has already been stated that the main activity of a commercial bank and its mission is the purchase and sale of money, where it also provides a series of services for which it charges a series of commissions. In this process of buying and selling money, prices are set to cover the financial risks to which financial institutions are exposed in the course of their activity. The key for a bank is both to originate transactions at appropriate prices based on the risks assumed and to maintain these transactions on the balance sheet at a level of profitability that is adequate and sufficient to cover the risks involved, which have been evolving over time, hence the importance of ALM in this entire process. The problem for financial institutions is not the risks themselves and their management, but rather their pricing, since an institution may have the best models for identifying, measuring and controlling risks, but if it does not price them correctly when buying and selling money, it may jeopardise the viability and sustainability of the banking business.

The sustainability of the banking business was understood as the structural capacity of a financial institution to maintain its profitability, solvency and reputation in the long term, ensuring that its operating model generates economic value in a manner consistent with prudent risk management, regulatory compliance and contribution to the sustainable development of the financial system. If we are reasonably certain that an institution's risks are correctly priced, we can conclude that that institution is sustainable over time. The Annual Pricing Gap (PGa) metric gives us an assessment of how sustainable or unsustainable a financial institution's business model is.

Viability has been defined as a financial institution's ability to withstand a stressful situation over a period of time, cushion it and continue to generate sufficient recurring income to cover its operating, financing, risk and capital costs in a business-as

-usual environment, while maintaining compliance with regulatory requirements and the confidence of its depositors, investors and supervisors. The Total Pricing Gap (PGt) metric has the ability to quantify this concept numerically, so both PGa for sustainability and PGt for viability can become two key elements in the BMA assessment within the SREP process and serve as an objective tool for calculating the need or otherwise for capital under Pillar 2 (it does not have to be capital; if the profitability shortfalls are due to credit risk issues, the predominant approach should be through provisions, as already justified in Chapter 7), eliminating the dependence on accounting information to conclude on the assessment of a bank's profitability and on expert judgements and holistic assessments.

In addition, the PGa and PGt methodology has a bottom-up approach and can help to carry out assessments by business units, geographies, etc., providing significant flexibility for the analysis of structural vulnerabilities within financial institutions.

A practical case study will be presented in which certain assumptions will be made for the sake of simplification to illustrate the proposal to integrate PGa and PGt into the SREP process to enrich the BMA.

8.6.1 Case study

We start with the assumption of a financial institution with the following balance sheet (Figure 8.1):

In addition to the balance sheet structure, a series of data (Table 8.1) is presented on the risk profile of investment operations, the duration structure of assets and liabilities, risk weight, and other parameters necessary to calculate the PGa and PGt metrics.

This bank's balance sheet is as of the end of August 2022, when the following interest rate curve existed (Figure 8.2).

In addition, for certain types of interest, the forward interest rate levels are presented (Table 8.2).

A constant balance hypothesis is assumed, i.e., all maturities are renegotiated with the same fixed and variable interest rate at the maturity of each loan instalment. This hypothesis also assumes identical terms and durations over the time horizon. Term deposits are for 1 year and are paid with a beta of 0.5 (i.e., 50% of the Euribor for the term). NMDs and their modelling provide a modified duration of 4 years and account for 11% of total deposits.

The accounting view would give us a very positive P&L (simplified average investment and financing rates have been calculated using the spot curve and applying the forward curve for the following years) (Table 8.3). Under IFRS 9, as all provisions are already in place, no additional provisioning is required. Only Stage 1 and 2 transactions are of interest, which is the picture presented here; Stage 3 transactions are as-

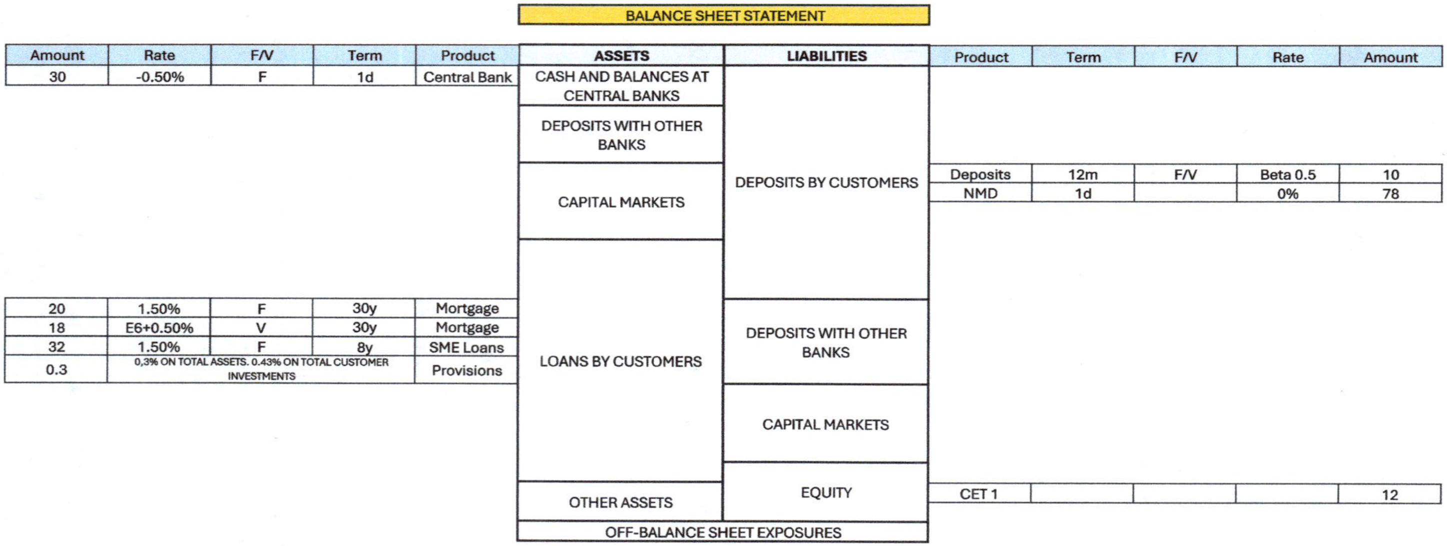

Figure 8.1: Balance Sheet Statement.
Source: Own elaboration.

Table 8.1: Balance Sheet Data Tape.

BALANCE SHEET DATA TAPE													
Product	**Amount**	**Rate**	**Fee**	**F/V**	**Term**	**Duration**	**PD LFT**	**LGD**	**OC**	**Provisions**	**RW**	**ROE**	**CAPITAL**
Mortgage	20	1.50%		F	30y	15	2%	40%	0.5%	0.2	35%		
Mortgage	18	E6+0.50%		V	30y	0.5	2%	40%	0.5%	0.2	35%		12%
SME Loans	32	1.50%		F	8y	4	6%	60%	0.50%	0.7	75%	10%	
Deposits ECB	30	€STER	0.30%		1d	0.0			0.50%	0	0%		
Deposits	10	Beta 0.5		F/V	12m	1							
NMD	78	0%			1d	0.5							
Equity	12	0%				10							

Source: Own elaboration.

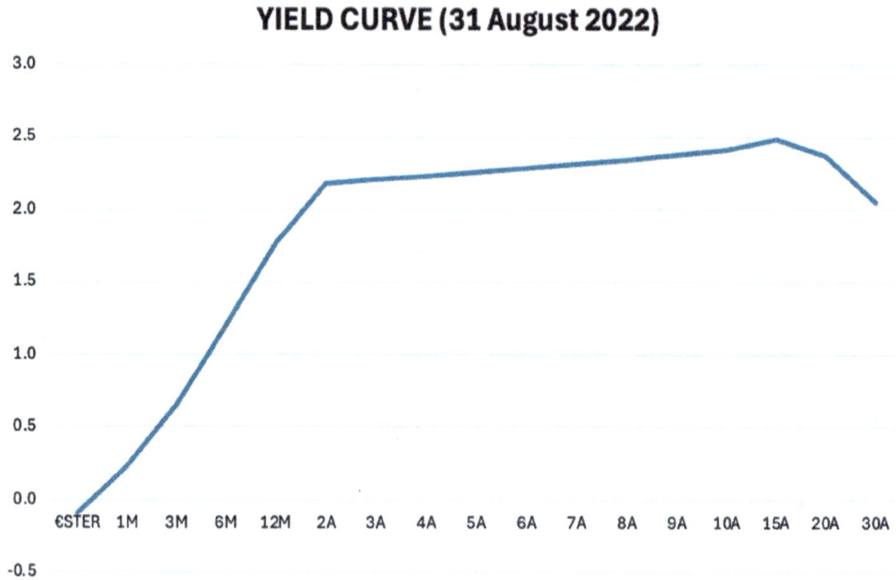

Figure 8.2: Yield Curve.
Source: Own elaboration.

Table 8.2: Forward Rate.

	SPOT RATE	FORWARD RATE		
		1Y	2Y	3Y
€STER	2.274	1.778	2.59	2.274
EURIBOR 6M	2.284	2.373	2.246	2.284
EURIBOR 12M	2.309	2.59	2.274	2.309
SWAP 4Y	2.402	2.389	2.35	2.402
SWAP 10Y	2.545	2.504	2.505	2.545
SWAP15Y	2.472	2.52	2.485	2.472

Source: Own elaboration (in %).

sumed to be 100% provisioned. No market liquidity stress is considered in the financial planning.

Under the SREP approach, within the quantitative analysis in which an assessment is made of current profitability compared to its peer group (based on the assumption that this entity compares well), the financial institution has no doubts about its ability to generate adequate returns.

Under the forward-looking analysis, seeing that it is an institution without excessive growth ambitions in times of rising interest rates, with stable funding and an LtD ratio of 0.8, it can be said that it is profitable from an accounting perspective.

Table 8.3: Profit and Loss Statement.

	P&L			
	22	23	24	25
YIELD INVESTMENT	1.57	2.34	2.56	2.47
YIELD FUNDING	0.10	1.55	1.36	1.39
NII	**1.47**	**0.79**	**1.20**	**1.09**
FEE	0.30	0.30	0.30	0.30
TOTAL OPERATING INCOME	**1.77**	**1.09**	**1.50**	**1.39**
OC	0.50	0.50	0.50	0.50
PRE-PROVISION PROFIT	**1.27**	**0.59**	**1.00**	**0.89**
PROVISION FOR CREDIT LOSS	1.46	0.00	0.00	0.00
PROFIT BEFORE TAX	**-0.18**	**0.59**	**1.00**	**0.89**

Source: Own elaboration.

The above information indicates to supervisors that the BMA's conclusions do not reveal any vulnerabilities in the business model. It does not have excessive concentrations, an undifferentiated strategy, etc. It can be considered a viable business as it has reasonable 12-month profitability and no excessive risk appetite. In addition, its financial structure is adequate. In terms of sustainability, it presents credible projections that allow for improving the entity's profitability, etc. In conclusion, under its strategic plan for the next three years, there is no doubt that it has a problem with the sustainability of its banking business. It will be necessary to see, based on qualitative aspects, whether for governance reasons, etc., some type of capital buffer is required, but initially the quantitative/accounting part does not present any tensions whatsoever in a BaU environment; therefore, it could be concluded that it is a sustainable business from the perspective of current regulations.

How can the PRICING GAP methodology help the BMA process?

Firstly, the main metrics are obtained to calculate the PGa and PGt metrics (Table 8.4), which help us to determine the sustainability and viability of this bank's business.

As of 31 August 2022, the picture is as follows:

Under this approach, the conclusion regarding profitability is no longer as comfortable as in the accounting view.

Although PGa is positive, when the components are analysed, it can be seen that investment operations have a profitability below what is necessary to correctly remunerate the risks installed in the balance sheet, and this is all reflected in the margin on investment (-1.09), all under current market conditions on the valuation date.

These fixed-rate transactions need to take into account, at market conditions, a cost of funding of 2.49, plus operating costs of 0.5, an expected loss for PGa of 0.05 and an unexpected loss of 0.42. All of this is necessary and results in an FTP investment operation of 3.46, minus 1.25 from on-balance sheet transactions, results in a margin

Table 8.4: PRICING GAP Metrics.

	AMOUNT	CF	OC	EL	EL (LFT)	UL	FTP INV	FTP INV LFT	YIELD	Margin INV	Margin INV LFT
Mortgage	20	2.49	0.50	0.05	0.80	0.42	3.46	4.21	1.25	-2.21	-2.96
Mortgage	18	1.20	0.50	0.05	0.80	0.42	2.18	2.92	1.703	-0.47	-1.22
SME Loans	32	2.23	0.50	0.90	3.60	0.90	4.53	7.23	3.25	-1.28	-3.98
ECB Deposits	30	-0.09	0.50				0.41	0.41	-0.091	-0.50	-0.50
	AMOUNT	**INTERBANK**	**OC**	**FTP FUND**	**YIELD**	**Margin FUND**					
Deposits	10	1.78	0.50	1.28	0.89	0.39					
NMD	78	2.23	0.50	1.73	0.00	1.73					
Equity	12	2.42	0.50	1.92	0.00	1.92					
	Margin INV	**Margin INV LFT**	**Margin FUND**	**Fee**	**PGa**	**Provisions**	**PGt-1st**	**Capital**	**Capital at Risk**	**PGt-2nd**	**UL**
	-1.09	-2.24	1.63	0.30	0.84	0.30	-0.01	12	0%	11.99	0.45

Source: Own elaboration.

on investment of – 2.21. The level of profitability established by the FTP investment operations protects the entity from a possible complete transfer of NMDs to term deposits and a beta of 1 for the 6-month Euribor for all deposits, hence the need to set the duration of all investments at market conditions. Additionally, it allows for the accumulation of a return for the average expected loss of the cycle of these operations, as well as paying the cost structure of the operations and providing a margin in line with their risk profile.

With regard to potential transfers, it is important to take into account the market situation, its current position, the structure of the financing mix in the cycle and its direction at times of maximum volatility in order to assess, to a greater or lesser extent, the risk of deposit transfers and remuneration with beta 1. This is the main problem that the institution could face if this situation were to continue, as it would not have the financial capacity to meet the other costs (for example, if it coincided with a sudden increase in non-performing loans) and would have to be subsidised with other balance sheet items, in the best-case scenario. However, in reality, banks would be protected even in payment environments with betas greater than 1 on term deposits. In practice, complete transfers to term deposits do not usually occur, so by counterbalancing with the NMD structure, this type of situation could be managed appropriately. This granular information is valuable for determining banks' funding strategies and is key to further developing future business plans.

Furthermore, the information in Table 8.4 shows that these long-term, fixed-rate transactions, with an EL of 0.05 and a UL of 0.42 with a Margin on Investment of -2.21, would be insufficient to cope with a higher return on deposits (even without considering credit risk and even with zero profit). This provides valuable information to define new business strategies for the future or at least focus on limiting these situations.

What can also be seen is that for variable-rate mortgages, the spread established in the balance sheet is lower than the sum of operating costs (OC), expected loss and unexpected loss, so cross-selling strategies will have to be developed to help offset these differences. With fees of 0.30, these are considered insufficient to compensate for the deficiencies in the identified Pricing Gaps.

The manifestation of this higher beta (Table 8.5) and transfer of deposits (e.g., 40% in MNDs and paying a beta equal to 1 for term deposits) could increase the problem of sustainability and viability of the banking business, since, if combined with a problematic sudden increase in expected loss above the cycle average in the first year, there would not be sufficient provisions to cover the expected loss of the average portfolio in the economic cycle of 1.46. The accumulated provisions would be 0.30 (of total assets), which is much lower, as can be seen, highlighting the problem of defining provisions under IFRS 9. The capital at risk would be 9%, which would absorb all impacts, including balance sheet risks.

A more in-depth analysis shows that after encapsulating the credit problem, the focus would be on the profitability issues arising from the transfer and remuneration

Table 8.5: PRICING GAP Metrics.

	AMOUNT	CF	OC	EL	EL (LFT)	UL	FTP INV	FTP INV LFT	YIELD	Margin INV	Margin INV LFT
Mortgage	20	2.49	0.50	0.05	0.80	0.42	3.46	4.21	1.25	-2.21	-2.96
Mortgage	18	1.20	0.50	0.05	0.80	0.42	2.18	2.92	1.703	-0.47	-1.22
SME Loans	32	2.23	0.50	0.90	3.60	0.90	4.53	7.23	3.25	-1.28	-3.98
ECB Deposits	30	-0.09	0.50				0.41	0.41	-0.091	-0.50	-0.50

	AMOUNT	INTERBANK	OC	FTP FUND	YIELD	Margin FUND
Deposits	53	1.78	0.50	1.28	1.78	-0.50
NMD	35	2.23	0.50	1.73	0.00	1.73
Equity	12	2.42	0.50	1.92	0.00	1.92

	Margin INV	Margin INV LFT	Margin FUND	Fee	PGa	Provisions	PGt-1st	Capital	Capital at Risk	PGt-2nd	UL
	-1.09	-2.24	0.58	0.30	-0.21	0.30	-1.06	12	-9%	10.94	0.45

Source: Own elaboration.

mentioned above, and fees of 0.30 would work with a PGa of -0.21, which means that the profitability model is not sufficient for the risks still on the balance sheet. Now, with the transfer to liabilities, although this mass continues to subsidise part of the pricing structure as seen by the Margin on Funding, which is equal to 0.58, it would be insufficient. Finally, with an unexpected loss (UL) greater than the negative PGa of -0.21, the model would not be sustainable over time with an adequate return on capital, but at least it would not incur losses.

The negative level of PGa is an issue that needs to be assessed because, from a supervisory point of view, it should influence the interpretation of strategic plans and the pillars on which the new business of financial institutions is based.

Dependence on the sustainability of certain balance sheet items or others and on a particular time frame (Table 8.5) helps to identify future sources of risk and should help to determine business strategy.

Returning to the starting point, in the case under analysis, in August 2022, the situation was as is shown in Table 8.6.

Table 8.6: PRICING GAP – Temporary scheme.

	Until 1y	**1y-3y**	**3y-5y**	**5y-10y**	**10y-15y**	**15y-20y**	**20y-25y**	**>25y**
Margin INV	-0.15			-0.41				-0.53
Margin FUND	0.04		1.36		0.23			
PGa – Buckets	**-0.11**	**0.00**	**1.36**	**-0.41**	**0.23**	**0**	**0.00**	**-0.53**
Fees					0.30			
PGa					**0.84**			

Source: Own elaboration.

It can be seen that the margin on investment shows very negative values across all maturities, particularly in the long and medium terms, and that these values derive mainly from fixed-rate transactions. The balance is found on the funding side and in shorter-term buckets, which is why close monitoring of funding policies and the stability of funding deposits is required, as well as of systemic events that could reverse this situation. In this regard, it should be remembered that the entity works on the assumption of NMD modelling, which extends the modified duration of these deposits to four years. This methodology can be used to quantify the impact on profitability of assuming that these deposits change from a four-year duration to six months, even though they are not remunerated when valued using the PGa and PGt approach.

This valuation exercise could be assumed to be an approximate quantification of the "model risk" of demand deposits (Table 8.7). In the case study, the PGa would go from 0.84 to 0.03, which implies a strong impact on maintaining this hypothesis, which is very likely to occur in periods of maximum stress. This fall in PGa occurs when the modified duration of NMDs is changed from the 4 years assumed by internal models to the 6 months granted to such deposits in more volatile environments.

Table 8.7: PRICING GAP Metrics.

	AMOUNT	CF	OC	EL	EL (LFT)	UL	FTP INV	FTP INV LFT	YIELD	Margin INV	Margin INV LFT
Mortgage	20	2.49	0.50	0.05	0.80	0.42	3.46	4.21	1.25	-2.21	-2.96
Mortgage	18	1.20	0.50	0.05	0.80	0.42	2.18	2.92	1.703	-0.47	-1.22
SME Loans	32	2.23	0.50	0.90	3.60	0.90	4.53	7.23	3.25	-1.28	-3.98
ECB Deposits	30	-0.09	0.50				0.41	0.41	-0.091	-0.50	-0.50
	AMOUNT	**INTERBANK**	**OC**	**FTP FUND**	**YIELD**	**Margin FUND**					
Deposits	10	1.78	0.50	1.28	0.89	0.39					
NMD	78	1.20	0.50	0.70	0.00	0.70					
Equity	12	2.42	0.50	1.92	0.00	1.92					
	Margin INV	**Margin INV LFT**	**Margin FUND**	**Fee**	**PGa**	**Provisions**	**PGt-1st**	**Capital**	**Capital at Risk**	**PGt-2nd**	**UL**
	-1.09	-2.24	0.82	0.30	0.03	0.30	-0.82	12	-7%	11.18	0.45

Source: Own elaboration.

The market curve gives us a 4-year swap of 2.23%, while the 6-month swap is trading at 1.20%. This difference in rates, multiplied by the amount of NMDs, is what reflects the fall in margin on funding and, therefore, lower PGa.

Now, returning to the beginning of the assumption, and based on the PGt metric, we can conclude the following:

Table 8.8: PRICING GAP Metrics.

Margin INV	Margin INV LFT	Margin FUND	Fee	PGa	Provisions	PGt-1st	Capital	Capital at Risk	PGt-2nd	UL
-1.09	-2.24	1.63	0.30	0.84	0.30	-0.01	12	0%	11.99	0.45

Source: Own elaboration.

PGt quantifies the impacts in the event of an immediate financial crisis with a credit event at average levels of the economic cycle (or with the credit risk scenarios to be simulated), together with the balance sheet structure with an already established business model and its financial risks and returns. The capital/provision requirements detected through this metric under normal conditions could be equated to the P2R of the SREP process.

The results show that, in the normal course of its business, knowing that the other parameters do not deviate from the business-as-usual environment, the entity has an EL (LFT) of 1.456,[48] with provisions of 0.30. This leads to a PGt-1st of -0.01 (Table 8.8), which in this case is a virtually neutral capital requirement. This situation shows a lack of mid-cycle provisions, which, due to the subsidy received by the liability structure, does not affect capital levels. This means that for P2R, in the event of a mid-cycle credit event, capital requirements would not be necessary from a Pricing Gap perspective as a starting point. However, as the origin is mainly due to a credit event, an improvement in the provisioning policy would be proposed to address a business environment identified with the occurrence of a credit event as defined in the scenario. Finally, due to the dependence on the liability structure, a different qualitative management approach would be required in the strategic plan to minimise subsidies.

Considering stress exercises, which will be detailed further in the next chapter, may help institutions to equate the results obtained from the PGt as an objective quantification of the P2G of the SREP process.

In this regard, and as an example, authorities may be interested in evaluating a stress exercise quantifying the impacts for their decision-making. It could be a scenario in which credit risk manifests itself with average cycle levels (other much

48 It is the weighted average of the EL (LFT) identified in the case.

higher scenarios are possible) and there is also an instant transfer of NMD to term deposits where they would be remunerated at beta equal to 1 (40% in NMD and 60% in term deposits), where NMD, due to the volatile situation, would not be considered equally stable, so it is assumed that their value is taken based on the 6-month Euribor. In addition, a forward-looking approach is applied (working with a constant balance sheet and applying forward curves), looking at the year-on-year impacts for the next three financial years. This could be done gradually, but for simplicity's sake, all simulation scenarios are applied from the starting financial year.

The Table 8.9 to 8.13, provides the results year by year, showing the different balance sheet items with the components needed to obtain the Pricing Gap metrics (PGa, PGt-1st and PGt-2nd) as well as the levels of capital at risk.

The worst year is 2022 (Table 8.9), and the authorities (to whom it may concern) could establish the need to increase provisions by 1.16 with a specific timetable and set a capital level of 0.27, which would be equal to capital at risk of 2.25%. However, as a weighted average return for unexpected losses of 0.45 on investments (the use of which would imply a profit equal to 0), the minimum capital requirement could be zero in P2G, at least as an initial assessment in a quantitative approximation under the Pricing Gap approach, but subject to the implementation of the dynamic provision buffer considered essential to address the average expected credit risk of the economic cycle.

Conclusions:

- The Pricing Gap methodology allows for an assessment of the sustainability and viability of a bank's business model, enabling a comprehensive quantification exercise that can serve as a quantitative tool for the BMA exercise and as an objective assessment tool for Pillar 2 capital requirements.
  - PGa provides a quantification of the sustainability of the banking business and, through the analysis of its factors, allows for an in-depth review of vulnerabilities that can be used to propose improvements in the governance of the entity, as well as challenge exercises with entities regarding the approach of different strategic plans.
  - Through PGt with an economic cycle view and without stressing parameters, it can be used as a quantification of provision/capital requirements adjusted to the SREP model. Similarly, PGt with a bottom-up perspective, subject to a coherent stress strategy, can help to quantify scenarios that identify capital/provision needs and serve as a quantitative basis for defining P2G requirements under the SREP process.
- Integrating the methodology with a bottom-up approach allows for a great deal of flexibility when identifying the focus of problems and value creation niches within financial institutions.

Financial year 2022

Table 8.9: PRICING GAP Metrics and Temporary scheme (2022).

	AMOUNT	CF	OC	EL	EL (LFT)	UL	FTP INV	FTP INV LFT	YIELD	Margin INV	Margin INV LFT
Mortgage	20	2.49	0.50	0.05	0.80	0.42	3.46	4.21	1.25	-2.21	-2.96
Mortgage	18	1.20	0.50	0.05	0.80	0.42	2.18	2.92	1.703	-0.47	-1.22
SME Loans	32	2.23	0.50	0.90	3.60	0.90	4.53	7.23	3.25	-1.28	-3.98
Deposits ECB	30	-0.09	0.50				0.41	0.41	-0.091	-0.50	-0.50
	AMOUNT	**INTERBANK**	**OC**	**FTP FUND**	**YIELD**	**Margin FUND**					
Deposits	53	1.78	0.50	1.28	1.78	-0.50					
NMD	35	1.20	0.50	0.70	0.00	0.70					
Equity	12	2.42	0.50	1.92	0.00	1.92					
	Margin INV	**Margin INV LFT**	**Margin FUND**	**Fee**	**PGa**	**Provisions**	**PGt-1st**	**Capital**	**Capital at Risk**	**PGt-2nd**	**UL**
	-1.09	-2.24	0.21	0.30	-0.57	0.30	-1.42	12	-12%	10.58	0.45
	Hasta 1y	**1y-3y**	**3y-5y**	**5y-10y**	**10y-15y**	**15y-20y**	**20y-25y**	**>25y**			
Margin INV	-0.15			-0.41				-0.53			
Margin FUND	-0.02		0.00		0.23						
PGa – Buckets	**-0.17**	**0.00**	**0.00**	**-0.41**	**0.23**	**0**	**0.00**	**-0.53**			
Fees				0.30							
PGa				**-0.57**							

Source: Own elaboration.

Financial year 2023

Table 8.10: PRICING GAP Metrics and Temporary scheme (2023).

	AMOUNT	CF	OC	EL	EL (LFT)	UL	FTP INV	FTP INV LFT	YIELD	Margin INV	Margin INV LFT
Mortgage	20	2.52	0.50	0.05	0.80	0.42	3.49	4.24	1.25	-2.24	-2.99
Mortgage	18	2.37	0.50	0.05	0.80	0.42	3.35	4.09	2.873	-0.47	-1.22
SME Loans	32	2.39	0.50	0.90	3.60	0.90	4.69	7.39	3.25	-1.44	-4.14
Deposits ECB	30	1.78	0.50				2.28	2.28	1.778	-0.50	-0.50
	AMOUNT	**INTERBANK**	**OC**	**FTP FUND**	**YIELD**	**Margin FUND**					
Deposits	53	2.59	0.50	2.09	2.59	-0.50					
NMD	35	2.37	0.50	1.87	0.00	1.87					
Equity	12	2.50	0.50	2.00	0.00	2.00					
	Margin INV	**Margin INV LFT**	**Margin FUND**	**Fee**	**PGa**	**Provisions**	**PGt-1st**	**Capital**	**Capital at Risk**	**PGt-2nd**	**UL**
	-1.14	-2.29	0.64	0.30	-0.21	0.30	-1.06	12	-9%	10.94	0.45
	Hasta 1y	**1y-3y**	**3y-5y**	**5y-10y**	**10y-15y**	**15y-20y**	**20y-25y**	**>25y**			
Margin INV	-0.15			-0.46				-0.53			
Margin FUND	0.40		0.00		0.24						
PGa – Buckets	**0.25**	**0.00**	**0.00**	**-0.46**	**0.24**	**0**	**0.00**	**-0.53**			
Fees				0.30							
PGa				**-0.21**							

Source: Own elaboration.

Financial year 2024

Table 8.11: PRICING GAP Metrics and Temporary scheme (2024).

	AMOUNT	**CF**	**OC**	**EL**	**EL (LFT)**	**UL**	**FTP INV**	**FTP INV LFT**	**YIELD**	**Margin INV**	**Margin INV LFT**
Mortgage	20	2.49	0.50	0.05	0.80	0.42	3.46	4.21	1.25	-2.21	-2.96
Mortgage	18	2.25	0.50	0.05	0.80	0.42	3.22	3.97	2.746	-0.47	-1.22
SME Loans	32	2.35	0.50	0.90	3.60	0.90	4.65	7.35	3.25	-1.40	-4.10
Deposits ECB	30	2.59	0.50				3.09	3.09	2.59	-0.50	-0.50
	AMOUNT	**INTERBANK**	**OC**	**FTP FUND**	**YIELD**	**Margin FUND**					
Deposits	53	2.27	0.50	1.77	2.27	-0.50					
NMD	35	2.25	0.50	1.75	0.00	1.75					
Equity	12	2.51	0.50	2.01	0.00	2.01					
	Margin INV	**Margin INV LFT**	**Margin FUND**	**Fee**	**PGa**	**Provisions**	**PGt-1st**	**Capital**	**Capital at Risk**	**PGt-2nd**	**UL**
	-1.12	-2.27	0.59	0.30	-0.23	0.30	-1.08	12	-9%	10.92	0.45
	Hasta 1y	**1y-3y**	**3y-5y**	**5y-10y**	**10y-15y**	**15y-20y**	**20y-25y**	**>25y**			
Margin INV	-0.15			-0.45				-0.53			
Margin FUND	0.35		0.00		0.24						
PGa – Buckets	**0.20**	**0.00**	**0.00**	**-0.45**	**0.24**	**0**	**0.00**	**-0.53**			
Fees				0.30							
PGa				**-0.23**							

Source: Own elaboration.

Financial year 2025

Table 8.12: PRICING GAP Metrics and Temporary scheme (2025).

	AMOUNT	CF	OC	EL	EL (LFT)	UL	FTP INV	FTP INV LFT	YIELD	Margin INV	Margin INV LFT
Mortgage	20	2.47	0.50	0.05	0.80	0.42	3.45	4.19	1.25	-2.20	-2.94
Mortgage	18	2.28	0.50	0.05	0.80	0.42	3.26	4.00	2.784	-0.47	-1.22
SME Loans	32	2.40	0.50	0.90	3.60	0.90	4.70	7.40	3.25	-1.45	-4.15
Deposits ECB	30	2.27	0.50				2.77	2.77	2.274	-0.50	-0.50
	AMOUNT	**INTERBANK**	**OC**	**FTP FUND**	**YIELD**	**Margin FUND**					
Deposits	53	2.31	0.50	1.81	2.31	-0.50					
NMD	35	2.28	0.50	1.78	0.00	1.78					
Equity	12	2.55	0.50	2.05	0.00	2.05					
	Margin INV	**Margin INV LFT**	**Margin FUND**	**Fee**	**PGa**	**Provisions**	**PGt-1st**	**Capital**	**Capital at Risk**	**PGt-2nd**	**UL**
	-1.14	-2.29	0.61	0.30	-0.23	0.30	-1.08	12	-9%	10.92	0.45
	Hasta 1y	**1y-3y**	**3y-5y**	**5y-10y**	**10y-15y**	**15y-20y**	**20y-25y**	**>25y**			
Margin INV	-0.15			-0.46				-0.52			
Margin FUND	0.36		0.00		0.25						
PGa – Buckets	**0.21**	**0.00**	**0.00**	**-0.46**	**0.25**	**0**	**0.00**	**-0.52**			
Fees				0.30							
PGa				**-0.23**							

Source: Own elaboration.

Table 8.13: PRICING GAP Metrics.

PGt-1st	EL (LFT)	Provisions	Deficit Provisions	Deficit Capital	UL
-1.42	1.46	0.30	1.16	-0.27	0.45

Source: Own elaboration.

8.7 A reflection

The presentation in this chapter of the potential and benefits of using the Pricing Gap methodology as a tool for the SREP process may have significant implications.

In the previous chapter, this same methodology was presented and justified as an objective tool for quantifying macroprudential policies.

The use of both approaches can help authorities identify overlaps in capital buffers, since if this methodology is used first for the SREP approach and then for the macroprudential assessment, the latter's result in higher capital/provision requirements could be those identified for Pillar 2, as they are quantified using the same methodology.

9 PRICING GAP as a stress testing analysis tool

After reviewing the main aspects covered by the ECB stress tests that are relevant to the purpose of this manual, these sections will discuss how a stress test can be focused on Pricing Gap metrics and how they can complement the current tests carried out by the authorities. The results can be used both by banks themselves to guide their business models within their strategic plans and by authorities to set capital/provision levels in the SREP process.

9.1 Review of the main elements of EBA stress testing

Stress tests in banking have become a key financial supervision tool since the 2008–2009 financial crisis. In particular, the EBA coordinates biennial stress testing exercises at the European Union level, with the aim of assessing the ability of major banks to absorb losses under adverse macroeconomic scenarios and maintain adequate capital levels.

These exercises, initiated after the Great Financial Crisis, seek both to identify vulnerable banks and to restore confidence in the banking system through additional capital requirements where necessary. In 2025, a new European-wide stress test was carried out, the methodological framework for which was defined in the note "2025 EU-wide stress test – Methodological Note" published in November 2024. This academic document sets out in detail, step by step, the methodology for constructing these stress exercises following the EBA's approach for 2025.

This manual will not cover the entire methodology, but only those parts where the methodology developed by the EBA intersects with the key points of the Pricing Gap methodology and its metrics, analysing the connections between concepts to demonstrate in a simple way how the new methodology can help to complement supervisory stress test exercises. Therefore, market risk and counterparty risk, as well as operational and conduct risk, will not be addressed.

9.1.1 Design of the macroeconomic stress scenario

All stress tests are based on a set of macro-financial scenarios that drive the other modules. As in previous rounds, two scenarios are used in the 2025 exercise: baseline (expected trajectory) and adverse (severe shock with low probability and high impact). Both cover a three-year horizon (2025–2027) and are constructed from a common reference date: the end of 2024.

 | https://doi.org/10.1515/9783111328386-009

In methodological terms, the scenario is not limited to "macro" variables in the strict sense. Its function is to generate coherent trajectories of the determinants which, through satellite models and supervisory rules, ultimately affect:
- The credit quality of households and businesses.
- Market valuations of portfolios sensitive to interest rates, spreads or equities.
- The evolution of the financial margin.
- The behaviour of income/expense components not strictly linked to credit risk.

Although banks apply their own granularity and segmentation, the scenario acts as a common anchor to prevent the result from depending on idiosyncratic macro assumptions.

The adverse scenario is constructed using a risk-based narrative approach, as described by Farmer et al. (2022). This implies that behind the scenario there is a coherent story of crisis, i.e., the main latent macro-financial risks are identified (e.g., an inflation shock and interest rate hike triggering a global recession, or a pandemic scenario, etc.), and a trajectory of macroeconomic variables is constructed that reflects the materialisation of those risks.

According to Gross et al. (2022), the narrative design typically involves four steps, which are followed by the EBA and the ESRB:
1. Identification of key risks and events that will trigger stress.
2. Mapping of these risks to specific macroeconomic shocks (examples: fall in consumer confidence, increase in risk premiums, etc.).
3. Consistent projection of endogenous variables using macroeconomic models (ensuring that the relationships between GDP, unemployment, prices, interest rates, etc., remain economically consistent during stress).
4. Review of severity to ensure that the scenario is sufficiently extreme but plausible.

Key macroeconomic variables included in the scenarios are, among others:
- Economic activity: real GDP (Gross Domestic Product) growth rate, unemployment rate, consumption and investment, reflecting the depth of the recession in the adverse scenario.
- Prices and finance: inflation rate (CPI), evolution of housing prices and other real estate assets, stock market indices (stock exchange), which capture tensions in asset markets.
- Interest rates and spreads: short- and long-term interest rate levels (e.g., 3- and 6-month Euribor interbank rates and 10-year sovereign bond yields), as well as each country's sovereign credit spreads and corporate spreads. In adverse scenarios, a significant increase in sovereign risk premiums in vulnerable economies and a tightening of financial conditions are usually assumed.
- Exchange rate: exchange rates of major currencies (e.g., euro vs. dollar) in the case of global scenarios, which may affect banks with international exposure.

- Other factors: variables such as the expected default rate in the economy, confidence metrics, etc., although these are derived endogenously from the macro situation.

In addition to the general macroeconomic scenario, the EBA 2025 methodology provides for additional specific shocks linked to the scenario for certain types of risk.

The overall consistency of the scenario is essential, i.e., all variables and shocks must form a mutually plausible whole.

The time horizon is three years. In the adverse projection, it is assumed that the expectations of the authorities and the estimates of the banks' internal models fully incorporate the severity of the future path. This simplifies the analysis, as surprises are not modelled year by year, but rather a fully anticipated scenario is used, in line with common stress testing practices where a deterministic approach is used. It also means that no stochastic simulations or combinations of scenarios are used; in other words, a single deterministic adverse scenario is used for projection, unlike the usual IFRS 9 accounting, where multiple scenarios are weighted.

9.1.2 Credit risk

Credit risk is typically the main source of losses in severe recession scenarios, as economic crises lead to an increase in defaults and loan losses. The EBA 2025 methodology for credit risk focuses on estimating the deterioration in the credit quality of portfolios under the adverse scenario and its effect on both the income statement (losses from provisions and insolvencies) and capital requirements (through an increase in RWA due to higher risk). The approach is aligned with IFRS 9 accounting standards for estimating expected credit losses (ECL) but incorporates a series of conservative stress-specific assumptions.

9.1.2.1 Scope and definitions in credit risk

In the EBA test, credit risk covers all credit assets measured at amortised cost or fair value through other comprehensive income (FVOCI) on the balance sheet, including loans to customers, corporate exposures, retail exposures, mortgage loans, sovereign exposures in the banking book, non-performing exposures, etc. It does not include the credit risk of positions measured at fair value through profit or loss (treated under the market risk approach, which is not covered in this manual) or derivative counterparty exposures (treated under counterparty risk, which is also not covered in this manual). In terms of impact, credit losses are reflected in P&L through provisions or impairments, and the increase in risk is reflected in higher credit RWA, in general terms.

The stress methodology must project how exposures migrate between Stages 1, 2 and 3 under the adverse scenario, and how the corresponding expected loss provisions increase.

9.1.2.2 Projection of expected credit losses (IFRS 9 methodology under stress)

Participating banks must estimate expected credit losses (ECL) for each year of the horizon in both scenarios (base and adverse) in accordance with IFRS 9, but under common EBA criteria. The EBA provides clear guidance on the main steps in this estimation:

1. Estimation of the starting point in the base year for risk parameters: Each bank starts from its data at the end of the base year, obtaining the probabilities of default (PD) and losses given default (LGD) at 12 months for each portfolio segment, as well as the distribution of exposures in Stage 1, 2, 3. If the bank uses internal IRB models, it will have its own estimates; if not, it can use adjusted regulatory loss parameters. The EBA establishes a hierarchy of sources for these initial parameters, giving preference to internal models calibrated to 12-month PD, or failing that, to other approaches. This is the starting point for stress testing, a snapshot of credit quality at the outset.
2. Projection of the impact of the scenario on risk parameters: This involves translating the macroeconomic evolution of the scenario (especially variables such as GDP, unemployment, property prices, etc.) into changes in PDs, LGDs and stage transition rates for each portfolio year on year. Banks typically use satellite credit risk models that are sensitive to the economy. The EBA allows banks to use their own models for this, but under conservative restrictions. For example, banks must apply an increase in PD and LGD consistent with macro severity and respect any minimum parameters indicated by the supervisor. An important element is that the EBA requires projected credit losses to follow a certain conservative time pattern ("loss path"). In particular, for sovereign exposures, the EBA imposes specific loss parameters. For other portfolios, banks are expected to capture a significant deterioration in credit quality, i.e., massive migrations from Stage 1 to Stage 2 (deterioration) and from Stage 2 to Stage 3 (default) in the adverse scenario.
3. Calculation of provisions (ECL) and changes therein: Using the projected PDs, LGDs and stage distributions, banks calculate the necessary provisions each year in accordance with IFRS 9. The impact on the profit and loss account is the change in the stock of provisions between one year and the next. For example, if total provisions rise from 100 to 150 (million) in 2025 in the adverse, that difference of 50 is a charge to the 2025 P&L for credit impairment. The EBA emphasises that it is the change in the provision stock that affects the annual result. Therefore, if in the adverse scenario loans deteriorate sharply in 2025 (many move to Stage 2 or 3), there will be a large jump in provisions that year, which will hit the income statement.

Throughout this process, the EBA establishes key IFRS 9 assumptions under stress that all banks must comply with for alignment:

- Use of a single scenario for calculating ECL in each case; multiple scenarios are not weighted. In the baseline, only the baseline is used; in the adverse scenario, only the adverse scenario is used, assuming a 100% probability of that scenario during the life of the loan.
- Perfect foresight: it is assumed that the future evolution of macro variables is known with certainty for the estimation of expected losses.
- Reversion to the mean post-horizon: For Stage 1 and 2 exposures, when estimating expected losses beyond 2027 (because IFRS 9 requires lifetime ECL and some loans exceed 2027), the EBA indicates that, after the adverse horizon, risk parameters should assume a gradual reversion to normal conditions. Specifically, from 2028 onwards, it is assumed that adverse risk parameters will return linearly over six years to the levels of the 2027 baseline scenario. This avoids assuming that stress persists indefinitely beyond the horizon, which would be excessively punitive when calculating lifetime provisions. With this guideline, Stage 2 provisions (which require consideration of the entire life of the loan) do not explode without limit beyond 2027 but rather assume that conditions improve progressively after the initial shock.
- No Stage 3 "cure" during the horizon: Any exposure that enters default (Stage 3) during 2025–2027 is assumed to remain in default (not returning to Stage 2 or 1) until the end of the horizon. In other words, recoveries of non-performing loans within the three years of the scenario are not counted. This is a conservative assumption, as in reality some non-performing loans could be restructured or returned to performing status, but the EBA prohibits this in order not to artificially reduce losses.
- No release of Stage 3 provisions: Related to the above, if a loan was already in Stage 3 at the beginning (2024) with a certain provision set aside, and under the baseline scenario it improved, IFRS 9 would allow the provision to be released. The EBA does not allow any accumulated Stage 3 provisions to be released in the stress test, even in the baseline scenario. Coverage on existing non-performing loans must be maintained or increased but not reduced. This ensures that banks do not show gains from lower provisions in the baseline that then offset losses in the adverse scenario.

Following these guidelines, each bank generates its projections of volumes in Stage 1/2/3, PDs and LGDs PIT or at 12 months year-on-year and provisions.

The timing pattern of losses is crucial for the impact on capital. Losses that are highly concentrated at the beginning erode capital quickly, while more staggered losses could allow for some breathing room. The EBA reviews whether the timing pattern of losses is plausible given the scenario, avoiding implausible profiles that would trigger actions in the quality assurance exercise.

9.1.2.3 Calculation of the impact on results and capital due to credit risk

The methodology for credit risk produces high expected losses and higher RWAs under adverse conditions, both of which reduce capital ratios. The EBA expects banks to retain at least 8% CET1 (minimum requirement) even after stress but does not define an explicit threshold. However, supervisors may compare the resulting ratios against total requirements (minimums + buffers) to guide their SREP processes.

9.1.3 NII: separation of components

The EBA methodology separates projected NII into two key components: the reference rate component and the credit or liability margin component. The idea is that any interest rate applied to an asset/liability can be broken down into a base rate (e.g., an index such as Euribor, Libor, etc., or risk-free rate) plus a margin or spread specific to that instrument.

Dividing in this way allows the scenario to be applied in a granular manner. The base reference rates are given directly by the macro scenario. Meanwhile, margins may be affected by factors such as increased credit spreads (for loans) or higher differentials that a bank pays for its deposits in stress.

The EBA defines procedures for projecting both components:

- Reference rates for repricing assets/liabilities should be taken from the interest rate curves provided in the macro scenario for each relevant currency.
- Margins on assets and liabilities are projected by applying a series of rules prescribed by the EBA that reflect stress conditions. This is crucial because the EBA does not leave it entirely up to the bank's discretion how its spreads will vary, but imposes caps/floors linked to the country's sovereign spreads and certain idiosyncratic components:
  - For liabilities (e.g., interest-bearing deposits, debt issued): The EBA states that in the adverse scenario, the cost of liabilities must increase by the greater of two effects:
    - A percentage of the increase in the sovereign spread of the country where it operates (indicating that if the country is in trouble, it costs the bank more to attract funds)
    - An idiosyncratic component representing the bank's own deterioration. In other words, if a country sees its premium rise by 300 bp, the cost of new deposits or debt may be required to rise by, say, at least 50% of those 300 bp, and if the bank had its own weakness, this is added on top. This "highest of" ensures that banks in stable countries with individual problems also reflect higher financing costs, and vice versa.
  - For assets (e.g., lending rates on new loans): In an adverse scenario, the EBA assumes that they will increase, but only to a limited extent. The increase in the margin on new assets must be proportional to the increase in the sover-

eign spread. In other words, if the country premium rises, lending rates also rise somewhat because banks, facing more risk and cost, raise prices. However, the EBA does not want to assume that they can pass on the cost completely or more than completely to customers. Therefore, it defines a percentage of transfer. The baseline also requires them to reflect a proportion of changes in the sovereign spread in their deposit rates, symmetrically. If conditions improve (spreads fall), they cannot assume that they will reduce their costs too much; there is a floor.
  - In addition, it sets a cap on adverse NII at the aggregate level: the EBA explicitly mandates that in the adverse scenario, the bank's total NII cannot exceed the NII for the base year.
- Treatment of volumes: Remember, the balance sheet is static, so in NII projections, when an asset or liability matures, it is replaced by a similar one. This means that the volumes in each category remain the same, only the rates are adjusted. However, there is a nuance: the EBA allows for a certain repricing gap in terms of maturities. For example, suppose a bank has many demand deposits (which are repriced on an almost daily basis) versus 5-year fixed-rate loans. In a scenario of rising rates, this bank may see the cost of deposits rise rapidly, but not the income from loans until they mature. The EBA therefore requires banks to implement their own repricing modelling, indicating what fraction of assets/liabilities is repriced each year. Variable-rate instruments reprice immediately with the reference rate; fixed-rate instruments only when they mature and are replaced. Thus, they must reflect the time lag in NII.

9.1.4 Integration of other elements

9.1.4.1 Net fee and commission income

The term NFCI (Net Fee and Commission Income) refers to net income from fees charged minus fees paid, together with other service income. These include items such as asset management fees, investment banking (advisory services), payments, cards, etc. Their behaviour under stress may depend on economic activity (less business = fewer fees), but there is no easy macro model.

The EBA addresses NFCI by applying predetermined maximum/minimum growth rates (cap and floor). In other words, it provides growth parameters for NFCI for baseline and adverse scenarios that banks must use. In the baseline scenario, a non-negative minimum growth (floor) is usually imposed if the historical trend is positive or basically does not allow for excessive increases to be projected. In adverse scenarios, both a maximum growth (cap) and a negative minimum (floor) are set, ensuring that commissions do not plummet excessively or grow.

9.1.4.2 Other operating income and extraordinary results

These items include:

- Dividends received from shareholdings (for example, if the bank has minority shareholdings in other companies).
- Share in profits of associates or joint ventures outside the consolidated perimeter (this sometimes applies to groups that have JVs in insurance or other areas).
- Other miscellaneous operating income (rentals, etc.).
- Results from financial transactions not included in trading – although most are captured in trading, there may be, for example, sales of banking portfolio assets (which would generate extraordinary gains/losses).

The EBA's assessments of limitations in stress tests will not be taken into account as they do not apply to the Pricing Gap metrics approach.

9.1.4.3 Operating cost

In stress tests, banks sometimes assume that they will cut costs (e.g., lower personnel costs, marketing costs, etc.) in an adverse scenario to offset lower revenues. The EBA, however, limits the reduction in operating costs allowed:

- It stipulates that certain expenses cannot fall below the base year level. Specifically: "Other remaining administrative expenses", "other remaining operating expenses", "depreciation" and "other provisions" cannot fall below the base year value, except for small adjustments for approved one-offs. In other words, recurring expenses must at least be maintained. A bank cannot project significant structural savings unless they were already in place before the base year (even then, justification is required).
- If there are adjustments for non-recurring items (one-offs) from the base year to be removed for projection purposes, this is only permitted up to a threshold of 5 basis points of RWA from the base year.
- In general terms, mandatory payments to resolution funds and deposit guarantee schemes (DGS) cannot be projected downwards either: they cannot be below the base year value.
- In the baseline, expenses are supposedly allowed to grow with moderate inflation, but the restriction is mainly that they cannot fall. In adverse conditions, it is assumed that expenses cannot fall either (although in reality, a bank in crisis might cut variable expenses; the EBA prefers not to count on this "self-help").

9.1.5 Limitations of the EBA's methodological approach

Static balance sheet

The main limitation is the assumption of a static balance sheet. The EBA does not allow banks to change the size or composition of their balance sheets during stress. This improves comparability but reduces realism, because in a crisis banks normally react (by deleveraging, selling assets, adjusting financing or restricting credit). The static approach, therefore, may overestimate losses by preventing management defences and, at the same time, underestimate second-round effects, as the macro scenario remains exogenous and does not incorporate feedback.

As Haldane (2009) points out, a more comprehensive stress test should be dynamic and iterative:

1. First impact analysis.
2. Bank reaction.
3. New macro environment.
4. New losses.

Along these lines, there are frameworks that introduce feedback between solvency, financing costs and credit supply or contagion channels.

Financial contagion

The stress test designed by the EBA does not accurately capture a systemic event. It does not simulate a banking domino effect.

Financial contagion through different channels is key. Direct contagion through contractual exposures, to a lesser extent due to its lower impact, or indirect contagion through fire sales and massive deposit withdrawals, which were key factors in the 2008 crisis. Identifying and incorporating these effects into the analysis is key to assessing the resilience of financial systems.

Liquidity risk

Supervisory stress tests have focused almost exclusively on the adequacy or inadequacy of banks' capital, implicitly assuming that liquidity is managed by other means. However, the 2008 crisis showed that liquidity problems can precipitate crises even in banks that are solvent on paper.

The EBA 2025 exercise does not include an explicit liquidity stress test component in parallel with the solvency test. This is a limitation, as an adverse macro scenario could lead, for example, to deposit outflows, the closure of wholesale funding markets, etc., which would put pressure on banks' liquidity. The EBA probably assumes that banks comply with LCR/NSFR and that, if this were to occur, central banks would provide liquidity as a hypothesis.

There is a disconnect: a bank could comfortably pass a capital stress test, but in reality, have a fragile liquidity profile that makes it prone to a bank run, as seen in cases of banks with good capitalisation but without market confidence. Some analysts have advocated combining solvency and liquidity stress tests or at least assessing them simultaneously. Clark et al. (2022) mention that the link between capital and liquidity needs under stress needs to be explored.

Use of internal models

The bottom-up approach relies on banks' internal models (for PD, LGD, NII, etc.), with limitations. Although there is review, there is always a risk that certain banks' models will underestimate losses (either intentionally or due to optimistic bias). A supervisory challenge is to balance heterogeneity (each bank has different portfolios and tailor-made models) with consistency. The EBA imposes dozens of restrictions to limit freedoms, but even so, comparing results bank by bank is difficult because methodologies differ.

Severity of scenarios

Another limitation is the possible lack of diversity in scenarios. EBA stress tests tend to focus on a fairly standard adverse macroeconomic scenario (deep recession, property market crash). However, scenarios of a different nature could be considered.

On the other hand, some specific risks, such as systemic cyberattacks and extreme geopolitical events, are not usually covered. The EBA 2025 in particular does not include climate testing (this has been done separately). Integrating climate factors into stress testing is debatable because they operate in the long term, but the impacts of events such as DANA in Spain could be added.

9.2 PRICING GAP. Integration of stress test concepts

9.2.1 A reflection

The stress test exercises coordinated by the EBA constitute, in general terms, a solid framework for assessing the resilience of the European banking system. Their main strength lies in the breadth of the risk perimeter considered, the reporting discipline and the effort to standardise assumptions to promote comparability between institutions. However, this very pursuit of comparability leads to significant methodological constraints, some of which are difficult to avoid (e.g., the static balance sheet), while others could be reviewed through conceptual changes, especially in the treatment of certain accounting dynamics under IFRS 9 and in the modelling of the financial margin.

1. **IFRS 9, impaired assets and the problem of definitions**
A first source of methodological friction lies in the very framework of IFRS 9 applied in the stress test, particularly for impaired assets. The operational definitions (staging, significant impairment, default, cure) and their translation into stress projections do not always accurately capture the economic reality of impairment, but rather reproduce, in part, limitations inherent in provision accounting. In this sense, the exercise may end up accurately measuring "the accounting" without necessarily reflecting the economic profile of the risk with the same accuracy. As already highlighted in this manual, the use of 12-month PDs is very limiting for Stage 1, and combined with the highly competitive environment in the banking sector, causes pricing problems, such that when credit risk materialises, the increase in provisions in stress environments works against capital. In this regard, if PDs were LFT for all stages, many of the problems already mentioned would be avoided and stress tests would be improved, since for credit risk only EL LFT would be used and the approach would be to analyse the growth of non-performing loans above the economic cycle averages and see if this has an impact on capital. Meanwhile, it should be treated with a dynamic provision fund, as proposed in various places in this book.

In addition, the temporal pattern of losses may be "distorted" by the provisioning approach. In some cases, the impact appears to be very concentrated at the beginning and then stabilises by construction, when in practice there could be more persistent trajectories, with second waves of deterioration or gradual materialisation of risk (e.g., via refinancing or effects on collateral). This situation would have no impact if banks worked not with the current IFRS 9 model, but with the proposal made in this manual.

Added to this is the mean reversion hypothesis used to estimate expected losses beyond the explicit horizon. Although this convention prevents stress from being artificially prolonged over time and thus prevents accounting regulations on provisions from generating greater future needs after the end of the projection period.

2. **Margin projection: fixed rate rigidity and competitive realism**
Several debatable issues arise in the financial margin section. The projection of fixed-rate loans maintaining their instalments constant until maturity is technically consistent with the contract, but it may hide the underlying problem of an environment of sharp rate rises, as this financial risk would not be correctly remunerated. The tension is not so much evident in fixed assets (which "do not move") as in liabilities, especially deposits, where there may be an increase in remuneration and a greater shift towards more expensive products involving higher beta remuneration. In other words, economic risk may emerge on the financing side before fixed assets are "repriced", and an overly mechanical projection may underestimate this fragility. All of the above can be perfectly captured using the Pricing Gap methodology, revealing problems that are not correctly reflected in the accounts.

Furthermore, although the exercise incorporates the idea that in times of stress the cost of liabilities rises more than the return on assets, comparability suffers when repricing depends largely on each institution's internal estimates. This point is particularly sensitive for banks with balance sheets highly exposed to fixed-rate portfolios originating in the ultra-low-interest rate period: small differences in internal assumptions (deposit betas, repricing pace, elasticities) can substantially change the projected margin generation capacity. Paradoxically, the exercise is very restrictive in some respects to ensure comparability but leaves room for discretion precisely in parameters that are decisive.

Another relevant methodological element is the treatment of renewals or maturity substitutions: if prices are set according to projected curve levels, but without adequately incorporating the sectoral competitive environment, the exercise may implicitly assume a capacity to pass on prices to the customer that is not always realistic. Competition, especially in deposits, is not a "detail"; it is one of the mechanisms that most influences the transmission of rates and margin erosion.

3. **Financing cost: limits of approximating it by sovereign premium**
Linking certain country costs to sovereign premiums makes sense to a certain extent (country risk, financial environment), but it is incomplete if the aim is to interpret the reality of bank financing. In practice, the cost of funding depends on a combination of factors: ratios such as LtD, interbank behaviour, monetary policy orientation, perception of idiosyncratic risk (mainly reputational events), deposit structure (NMD) and, above all, the dynamics of substitution between sources of funding in times of stress. If the exercise sets too narrow a main channel, there is a risk of explaining the cost of financing by a variable that is not always the dominant one, especially in episodes where confidence in a particular institution deteriorates more than the country's sovereign risk.

4. **Excessive restrictions and tension between severity and realism**
In stress testing, severity is necessary; the question is whether it should be severe and realistic. Some restrictions—for example, not recognising benefits derived from a steepening of the curve even under a constant balance sheet—may be considered excessively strong. If the balance sheet cannot be adjusted through management (already a very demanding restriction), also preventing certain economic mechanisms from operating in the result can produce a scenario that "punishes" by construction, rather than by economic transmission of the shock. This does not invalidate the exercise, but it does affect its interpretation: it ceases to be an economically coherent stress test and becomes more like a test of accounting conservatism.

5. **Towards a richer approach: supervisory dialogue, idiosyncrasy and second round**
If the objective is to compare entities, the limitation of static balance sheets is difficult to avoid. However, a reasonable approach would be to separate them into two layers:

- A comparable stress test (like the current one).
- A complementary, more "supervisory" exercise linked to P2G, where assumptions are adjusted to idiosyncratic issues and elements that are currently left out are explored (plausible management actions, sensitivity to competition, and, above all, second-round effects). This approach would allow for more interpretable and useful results for specific prudential decisions, without sacrificing the transparency and comparability of the public exercise. The feasible way to integrate this vision into management would be through GAP methodologies.

6. **Solvency-liquidity integration: a useful proxy from the first liquidity defence mechanism**
Finally, it is pertinent to consider a combined solvency and liquidity stress from the first defence mechanism: the bank's ability to remunerate deposits under stress based on its balance sheet structure and interest rate risk management. A plausible proxy would be to assess whether the bank adequately "covers" its duration to market curves and whether, in an adverse scenario, it could sustain a more aggressive remuneration of deposits (even with high betas), recognising that assuming a beta equal to 1 for the entire deposit base is unrealistic and that the stability of NMDs is a fundamental buffer for when the market demands to pay betas well above 1 for term deposits. This type of analysis would help to explore more explicitly the link between capital and liquidity needs under stress, a point that the Pricing Gap methodology is able to address effectively and which could improve the EBA's current stress tests.

7. **The usefulness of the pricing gap: more than just an accounting result**
Given these limitations, it is very valuable to view the stress test from a Pricing Gap perspective, not as an exercise that produces only an accounting result (better or worse), but as a diagnosis that allows the origin of the problem in the banking business model to be identified. This perspective shifts the focus from the "final result" to the mechanisms that generate it (repricing, deposit betas, maturity structure, sensitivity to curves and spreads), associated with different macroeconomic scenarios, allowing for an assessment of the viability and, above all, the sustainability of the margin, indicating the fundamentals that support profitability and the vulnerabilities that could erode it in the long term.

As can be seen in the table (Figure 9.1), each macro scenario would be identified with the impacts[49] that they would have on each of the components of the Pricing Gap metrics, which would then allow for the analysis of both the sustainability and viability

49 In the same way as the methodology established in the EBA and ESRB. European Systemic Risk Board & European Central Bank. (2025). Macro-financial scenario for the 2025 EU-wide banking sector stress test (updated 26 February 2025).

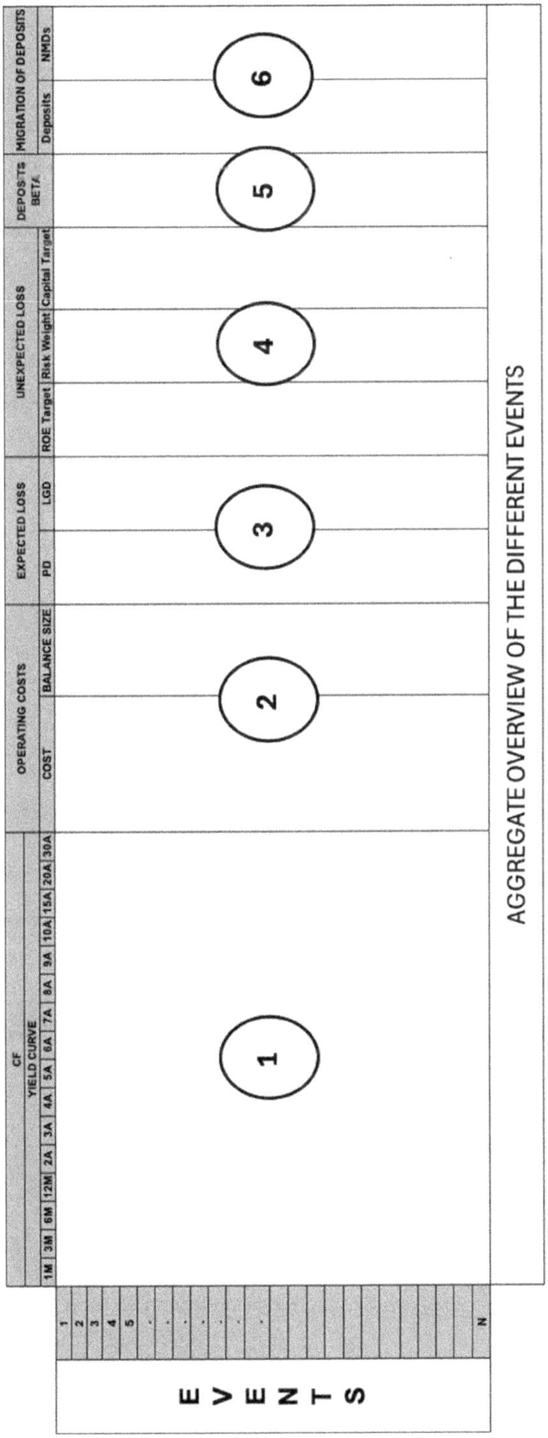

Figure 9.1: Parameters for Pricing Gap.
Source: Own elaboration.

of the banking business in stress environments. The different scenarios can have an impact on:

1. Yield Curve: Through satellite models, the scenarios have an impact on the yield curve. Subsequently, all impacts may converge towards a deterministic future curve given by the authorities, which will obviously be different from that projected by the implied yield curve.
2. Operating Costs: Macro scenarios may involve, for example, reactions in the banking system to deleveraging processes, which under a constant cost scheme may affect the sustainability of the business.
3. Expected Loss: Similarly, different macro situations will lead to increases in PD and LGD. It should be remembered that the Pricing Gap methodology works with average cycle PDs. For PGa, they are adjusted to the investment repayment schedule to ensure that the financial institutions' profitability model is sustainable over time and generates enough to cover their credit risk. For PGt, PD LFT is also taken into account and is triggered in full in the financial year. Subsequently, checks are made to see whether the stressed PDs in the system are above or below the economic cycle average. If they are above the economic cycle, the worst-case scenario is taken; if they are below, the model works on a prudent basis and the average PD LFTs for the economic cycle are taken as valid.
4. Unexpected Loss: In principle, no macro scenario should impact these items, as these parameters consider the margin of protection against unexpected events. However, this information is used as a profitability buffer with the capacity to absorb provisioning needs in stress scenarios until profit is reduced to zero.
5. Deposits Beta: Macro scenarios that have an impact on financing conditions will be captured through this parameter. This parameter, together with the next one, is key to assessing the sustainability of banking businesses.
6. Migration of Deposits: As with the previous parameter, deposit migration is key to assessing the cost of financing, as well as being an essential element for the sustainability of the banking business. This parameter can be used to capture events affecting the reputation of banks, where institutions have to make an additional effort in terms of remuneration and migration of NMD deposits to term deposits in order to stabilise liquidity.

The authorities and supranational bodies involved in scenario design obviously cannot be certain that the results of the modelling exercise will occur for each stress exercise. One of the issues of interest is to identify where the thresholds of the parameters involved in assessing the sustainability and viability of the banking business lie. In other words, to know how to quantify the level at which a parameter has an impact in one direction or another.

The Pricing Gap methodology allows reverse stress tests to be carried out, which can answer these types of questions that are of real interest to these authorities. Questions such as the following:

1. What is the maximum LGD that can be accepted in a stress test for a given capital at risk?
2. What is the maximum beta for deposits that can be accepted for a given institution, allowing it to have a break-even profitability measured through the PGa?
3. For a constant balance sheet, what are the maximum swap rates that can be achieved to reach the break-even point measured through the PGa?

Finally, and increasingly important, geopolitical risks, which can be identified, can be treated in the same way as different macro scenarios. After completing the entire modelling process, sensitivity analyses could be performed to address the impacts on the stability of the financial sector of different geopolitical risks that are of great concern to the authorities.

9.2.2 Case study

The hypothetical stress test exercise that could be carried out using the Pricing Gap methodology would begin with the presentation of the balance sheet (Figure 9.2) and balance sheet pricing structure of Bank X, for which the same balance sheet as the financial institution in the case study in the previous chapter (SREP) will be used.

The data tape (Table 9.1) with additional information on the balance sheet structure, risk profile of investment operations, the duration structure of assets and liabilities, risk weight, and other parameters necessary to calculate the PGa and PGt metrics.

The yield curve together with market implicites is shown in Table 9.2.

The valuation of the business model, both from the point of view of sustainability and viability through the Pricing Gap metrics, is shown in Table 9.3.[53]

The macro scenario (random and for the sole purpose of presenting a practical case) and its impacts on the different components are defined below:

- Real GDP: Significant cumulative decline over the next three years
  - Impact on ECL LFT, as the average risk is estimated to rise above the economic cycle average.
  - Impact on provisions.
  - Impact on fees due to lower activity.
  - Initially, there will be no deleveraging on the balance sheet and therefore no impact on operating costs.
- HICP (Harmonised Inflation): Strong and sustained increase in inflation
  - Impact on the swap curve, with increases in short-term segments due to monetary policy decisions causing a curve inversion.
  - Impact on operating costs due to their indexation.
  - Impact on PDs due to lower payment capacity.
- Residential housing: Bubble burst. Generalised fall in house prices

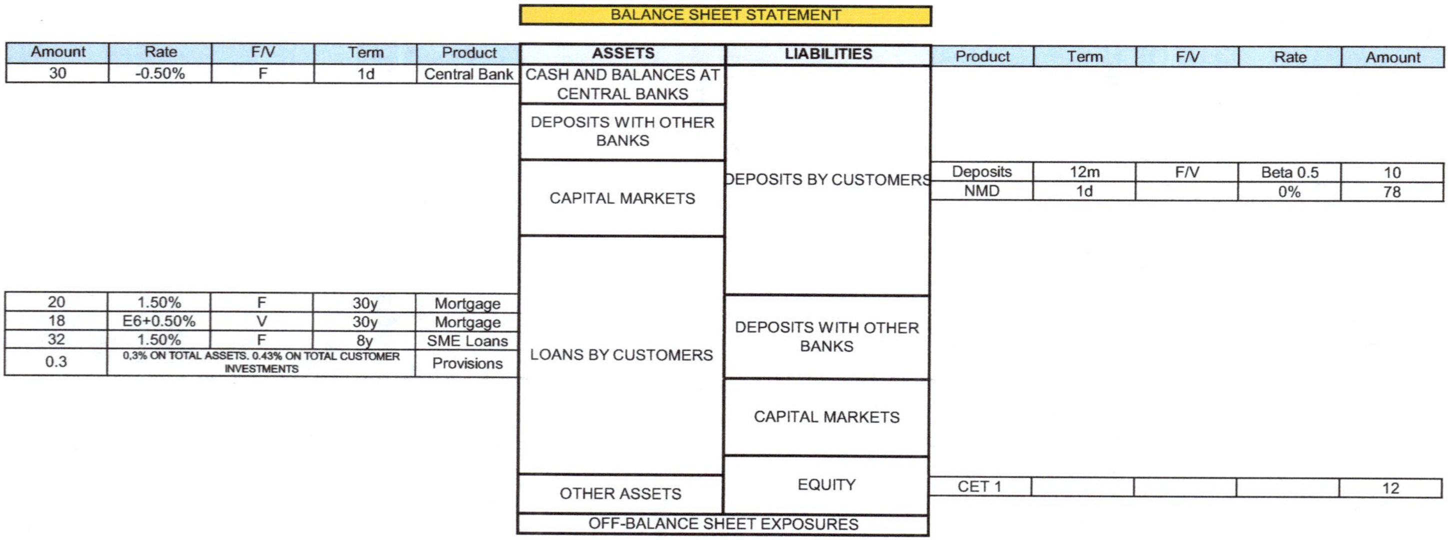

Figure 9.2: Balance Sheet Statement.
Source: Own elaboration.

Table 9.1: Balance Sheet Data Tape.

BALANCE SHEET DATA TAPE

Product	Amount	Rate	Fee	F/V	Term	Duration	PD LFT	LGD	OC	Provisions	RW	ROE	CAPITAL
Mortgage	20	1.50%		F	30y	15	2%	40%	0.5%	0.2	35%		
Mortgage	18	E6+0.50%		V	30y	0.5	2%	40%	0.5%	0.2	35%		
SME Loans	32	1.50%		F	8y	4	6%	60%	0.50%	0.7	75%	10%	12%
Deposits ECB	30	€STER			1d	0.0			0.50%	0	0%		
			0.30%										
Deposits	10	Beta 0.5		F/V	12m	1							
NMD	78	0%			1d	4.0							
Equity	12	0%				10							

Source: Own elaboration.

Table 9.2: Yield Curve and Forward Rate.

	SPOT RATE	FORWARD RATE		
		1Y	2Y	3Y
€STER	-0.091	1.778	2.59	2.274
EURIBOR 6M	1.203	2.373	2.246	2.284
EURIBOR 12M	1.778	2.59	2.274	2.309
SWAP 4Y	2.234	2.389	2.35	2.402
SWAP 10Y	2.416	2.504	2.505	2.545
SWAP15Y	2.487	2.52	2.485	2.472

Source: Own elaboration (in %).

  - Impact on LGDs, increasing in line with the average estimate for the economic cycle.
  - Impact on provisions.
- Credit spread: Significant increase in wholesale financing spreads
  - Impact on the valuation of ALCO portfolio bonds.
  - Transfer to retail financing. Generalised and gradual increase in betas and transfers from NMDs to term deposits.

These scenarios may be sufficient. Obviously, others can be used, such as events in the commercial real estate sector, exchange rates, equities, geopolitical events, etc.

All macro events must be translated, using satellite models, into the factors that impact the valuation of the Pricing Gap methodology, i.e., yield curve, operating cost, expected loss, unexpected loss and behaviour of the financing structure.

For the baseline scenario, the translation of the different events would result in the following changes in the banking environment:

- Yield Curve: As a result of the different events, the new projected curve is shown in Table 9.4.

This curve will affect repricing, and no new spreads will be applied to variable transactions, while fixed rates will be renewed at the same rate as they appear on the balance sheet.

- Expected Loss: The new economic deterioration scenario shows significant growth in credit risk above the cycle average, see Table 9.5:

As can be seen, the stress test implies a significant increase in credit risk, from 1.46 in the average BaU scenario for the cycle to 3.75 ECL in 2025. These parameters will affect the PGt metrics, which provide information on the viability of the banking business. For the PGa metric, the average cycle parameters are always used, as pricing to assess the sustainability of the banking business cannot be expected to be under stress conditions.

Table 9.3: Pricing Gap Metrics and Temporary Scheme.

	AMOUNT	CF	OC	EL	EL (LFT)	UL	FTP INV	FTP INV LFT	YIELD	Margin INV	Margin INV LFT
Mortgage	20	2.49	0.50	0.05	0.80	0.42	3.46	4.21	1.25	-2.21	-2.96
Mortgage	18	1.20	0.50	0.05	0.80	0.42	2.18	2.92	1.703	-0.47	-1.22
SME Loans	32	2.23	0.50	0.90	3.60	0.90	4.53	7.23	3.25	-1.28	-3.98
Deposits ECB	30	-0.09	0.50				0.41	0.41	-0.091	-0.50	-0.50
	AMOUNT	**INTERBANK**	**OC**	**FTP FUND**	**YIELD**	**Margin FUND**					
Deposits	10	1.78	0.50	1.28	0.89	0.39					
NMD	78	2.23	0.50	1.73	0.00	1.73					
Equity	12	2.42	0.50	1.92	0.00	1.92					
	Margin INV	**Margin INV LFT**	**Margin FUND**	**Fee**	**PGa**	**Provisions**	**PGt-1st**	**Capital**	**Capital at Risk**	**PGt-2nd**	**UL**
	-1.09	-2.24	1.63	0.30	0.84	0.30	-0.01	12	0%	11.99	0.45
	Until 1y	**1y-3y**	**3y-5y**	**5y-10y**	**10y-15y**	**15y-20y**	**20y-25y**	**>25y**			
Margin INV	-0.15			-0.41				-0.53			
Margin FUND	0.04		1.36		0.23						
PGa – Buckets	**-0.11**	**0.00**	**1.36**	**-0.41**	**0.23**	**0**	**0.00**	**-0.53**			
Fees				0.30							
PGa				**0.84**							

Source: Own work.

Table 9.4: Forward Rate Scenario.

	SPOT RATE	FORWARD RATE		
		2023	**2024**	**2025**
€STER	-0.091	**2.5**	**3**	**3.25**
EURIBOR 6M	1.203	**2.6**	**3.1**	**3.3**
EURIBOR 12M	1.778	**2.75**	**3.2**	**3.3**
SWAP 4Y	2.234	**2.7**	**2.8**	**2.6**
SWAP 10Y	2.416	**2.6**	**2.6**	**2.5**
SWAP15Y	2.487	**2.5**	**2.5**	**2.4**

Source: Own elaboration (in %).

Table 9.5: Expected Loss Scenario.

	2023		2024		2025	
	PD LFT	**LGD**	**PD LFT**	**LGD**	**PD LFT**	**LGD**
Mortgage	3.0%	45%	4.5%	50%	6.0%	55%
Mortgage	3.0%	45%	4.5%	50%	6.0%	55%
SME Loans	8.0%	65%	9.5%	65%	12.0%	65%
ECL Stress	2.18		2.83		3.75	
ECL LFT			1.46			

Source: Own elaboration.

- Operating Costs: Inflation and its derivation towards indexed costs causes an increase in costs and has the following impacts, see Table 9.6:

Table 9.6: Operating Costs Scenario.

	OPERATING COSTS		
	2023	**2024**	**2025**
Operating Costs	**0.55**	**0.55**	**0.55**

Source: Own elaboration (in %).

- Funding Conditions: The result of the different events translates into a more volatile environment in both the wholesale and retail funding markets. In the case study, the main impact is the financing scheme through term deposits and NMDs, how they migrate between them, what beta term deposits have and, in a volatile environment, assuming that the value contribution of NMDs is measured against short-term rates (Euribor 6M), see Table 9.7:

Table 9.7: Funding Conditions Scenario.

	2023		2024		2025	
	BETA	**MIX**	**PD LFT**	**MIX**	**PD LFT**	**MIX**
NMDs	0	65%	0	50%	0	40%
Deposits	0.7	35%	0.8	50%	0.9	60%
Volatility Deposits	It is assumed that all deposits are subject to the risk of leakage and their value is compared against the 6-month Euribor.					

Source: Own elaboration.

Stress test results (year-on-year)

Table 9.8 to 9.10, shows the results year by year. It shows the different balance sheet items with the components needed to obtain the Pricing Gap metrics (PGa, PGt-1st and PGt-2nd), as well as the levels of capital at risk, under the stress test scenarios presented.

Year 2023

Table 9.8: Pricing Gap Metrics and Temporary Scheme (2023).

	AMOUNT	CF	OC	EL	EL (LFT)	UL	FTP INV	FTP INV LFT	YIELD	Margin INV	Margin INV LFT
Mortgage	20	2.50	0.55	0.05	0.80	0.42	3.52	4.82	1.25	-2.27	-3.57
Mortgage	18	2.60	0.55	0.05	0.80	0.42	3.62	4.92	3.1	-0.52	-1.82
SME Loans	32	2.70	0.55	0.90	3.60	0.90	5.05	9.35	3.25	-1.80	-6.10
Deposits ECB	30	2.50	0.55				3.05	3.05	2.5	-0.55	-0.55
	AMOUNT	**INTERBANK**	**OC**	**FTP FUND**	**YIELD**	**Margin FUND**					
Deposits	31	2.75	0.55	2.20	1.93	0.28					
NMD	57	2.60	0.55	2.05	0.00	2.05					
Equity	12	2.60	0.55	2.05	0.00	2.05					
	Margin INV	**Margin INV LFT**	**Margin FUND**	**Fee**	**PGa**	**Provisions**	**PGt-1st**	**Capital**	**Capital at Risk**	**PGt-2nd**	**UL**
	-1.29	-3.16	1.50	0.30	0.51	0.30	-1.06	12	-9%	10.94	0.45
	Until 1y	**1y-3y**	**3y-5y**	**5y-10y**	**10y-15y**	**15y-20y**	**20y-25y**	**>25y**			
Margin INV	-0.17			-0.58				-0.55			
Margin FUND	1.26		0.00		0.25						
PGa – Buckets	**1.09**	**0.00**	**0.00**	**-0.58**	**0.25**	**0**	**0.00**	**-0.55**			
Fees				0.30							
PGa				**0.51**							

Source: Own elaboration.

Year 2024

Table 9.9: Pricing Gap Metrics and Temporary Scheme (2024).

	AMOUNT	CF	OC	EL	EL (LFT)	UL	FTP INV	FTP INV LFT	YIELD	Margin INV	Margin INV LFT
Mortgage	20	2.50	0.55	0.05	0.80	0.42	3.52	5.72	1.25	-2.27	-4.47
Mortgage	18	3.10	0.55	0.05	0.80	0.42	4.12	6.32	3.6	-0.52	-2.72
SME Loans	32	2.80	0.55	0.90	3.60	0.90	5.15	10.43	3.25	-1.90	-7.18
Deposits ECB	30	3.00	0.55				3.55	3.55	3	-0.55	-0.55
	AMOUNT	**INTERBANK**	**OC**	**FTP FUND**	**YIELD**	**Margin FUND**					
Deposits	44	3.20	0.55	2.65	2.56	0.09					
NMD	44	3.10	0.55	2.55	0.00	2.55					
Equity	12	2.60	0.55	2.05	0.00	2.05					
	Margin INV	**Margin INV LFT**	**Margin FUND**	**Fee**	**PGa**	**Provisions**	**PGt-1st**	**Capital**	**Capital at Risk**	**PGt-2nd**	**UL**
	-1.32	-3.84	1.41	0.30	0.39	0.30	-1.84	12	-15%	10.16	0.45
	Until 1y	**1y-3y**	**3y-5y**	**5y-10y**	**10y-15y**	**15y-20y**	**20y-25y**	**>25y**			
Margin INV	-0.17			-0.61				-0.55			
Margin FUND	1.16		0.00		0.25						
PGa – Buckets	**1.00**	**0.00**	**0.00**	**-0.61**	**0.25**	**0**	**0.00**	**-0.55**			
Fees				0.30							
PGa				**0.39**							

Source: Own elaboration.

Year 2025

Table 9.10: Pricing Gap Metrics and Temporary Scheme (2025).

	AMOUNT	CF	OC	EL	EL (LFT)	UL	FTP INV	FTP INV LFT	YIELD	Margin INV	Margin INV LFT
Mortgage	20	2.40	0.55	0.05	0.80	0.42	3.42	6.67	1.25	-2.17	-5.42
Mortgage	18	3.30	0.55	0.05	0.80	0.42	4.32	7.57	3.8	-0.52	-3.77
SME Loans	32	2.60	0.55	0.90	3.60	0.90	4.95	11.85	3.25	-1.70	-8.60
Deposits ECB	30	3.25	0.55				3.80	3.80	3.25	-0.55	-0.55
	AMOUNT	**INTERBANK**	**OC**	**FTP FUND**	**YIELD**	**Margin FUND**					
Deposits	53	3.30	0.55	2.75	2.97	-0.22					
NMD	35	3.30	0.55	2.75	0.00	2.75					
Equity	12	2.50	0.55	1.95	0.00	1.95					
	Margin INV	**Margin INV LFT**	**Margin FUND**	**Fee**	**PGa**	**Provisions**	**PGt-1st**	**Capital**	**Capital at Risk**	**PGt-2nd**	**UL**
	-1.24	-4.68	1.09	0.30	0.15	0.30	-2.99	12	-25%	9.01	0.45
	Until 1y	**1y-3y**	**3y-5y**	**5y-10y**	**10y-15y**	**15y-20y**	**20y-25y**	**>25y**			
Margin INV	-0.17			-0.54				-0.53			
Margin FUND	0.85		0.00		0.23						
PGa – Buckets	**0.69**	**0.00**	**0.00**	**-0.54**	**0.23**	**0**	**0.00**	**-0.53**			
Fees				0.30							
PGa				**0.15**							

Source: Own elaboration.

These results should not be interpreted in the same way as accounting figures. The capital at risk[50] of -25% in the 2025 financial year (Table 9.10) is the highest point of impact in the stress scenario. How is the breakdown carried out?

1. The main conclusion that can be drawn from the simulation exercise, about the viability of the banking business, is that the capital deficit is determined by the PGt-1st metric and is equal to -2.99 at the end of the stress test period, in 2025. Setting the final capital level, defined by the PGt-2nd of 9.01, therefore, makes it unnecessary to allocate capital by P2G. However, the level of capital would pose problems for the proper performance of the business model, as it does not have sufficient capacity to continue growing organically.

This conclusion is even more meaningful if the metric is analysed carefully. It should be remembered that if it recognises the full ECL defined in the stress test, but still with a capital level of 9.01, it would contemplate a complete transfer of deposits and a beta equal to 1, which is not defined in the scenario, but as mentioned above, the metric recognises this through a more negative margin on investment.

2. This deficit is determined by three parameters:
   a. Margin INV LFT, which is equal to -4.68
   b. Margin FUND equal to 1.09
   c. Fees equal to 0.30
   d. Provisions equal to 0.30

As mentioned above, the negative value of Margin INV LFT marks the profitability deficit in the sudden materialisation of the credit event projected for 2025 and also the materialisation of the interest rate risk that could materialise if all deposits were paid with beta 1 and there were no NMDs, something to take into account in periods after the time horizon of the stress test exercise and this marks its evolution in each of the years shown in Tables 9.8, 9.9 and 9.10.

3. Provisions are 0.30. The ECL LFT is 1.46. The recommendation is that financial institutions should have that expected loss covered by a dynamic provision.
4. The ECL stress is 3.75. If the prudence of establishing this provision policy were applied, 2.29 would remain uncovered.
5. The unexpected loss is 0.45 per annum, which over three years would amount to an absorption capacity without touching capital of 1.35.
6. The 2.29 remaining to be covered, minus the 1.35 absorption capacity for the unexpected loss, would ultimately result in an uncovered risk and a capital requirement of 0.94 to remain above 12.

50 It is equal to PGt-1st/Capital.

The vision of how the sustainability of the banking business would look in the process of this simulation exercise would be achieved through the evolution of the PGa metric:

- With a PGa of 0.51 in 2023 falling to 0.15 in 2025, it can be concluded that the business model is sustainable.
- The key to the decline is the transfer of deposits identified in the stress test scenarios, which is represented by a decrease in the margin on funding. In 2023, it was 1.5, falling to 1.09 in 2025, even with the rise in short-term rates, but the transfer has had a greater impact.
- When analysing the tables of PGa components by time buckets in the figures 9.8 to 9.10, it can be seen that their evolution is due to the lower subsidy provided by liabilities. This draws attention to the qualitative aspect of the entity's management in terms of its funding strategy.
- The margin on investment has not had much impact on the movements. The main factor that may affect it is long-term fixed-rate mortgages. These depend on the greater or lesser risk of long-term rates, which in the defined scenario remain virtually unchanged.
- Efficiency has an impact of less than 0.05 on the BaU scenario.
- Finally, the expected loss for PGa has no impact because it continues to be valued using the LFT economic cycle approach adjusted to the amortisation schedule for operations. It makes no sense to value an institution's balance sheet prices in order to draw conclusions on the sustainability of the banking business using stressed credit risk parameters.

From the stress test, using the PGa metric, it can be concluded that the inversion of the yield curve has added value to the entity's liquidity and kept PGa positive, although there is still a significant risk of additional transfers and higher beta, which implies a lower capacity for subsidisation through the Margin on Funding, to the point of jeopardising the sustainability of the business.

It should be noted that this same analysis exercise could obviously be carried out year after year to see how the impacts would gradually unfold, but this has been avoided for the sake of simplification.

The authorities may be interested in carrying out a reverse stress test for the financial institution's balance sheet structure in a BaU environment, once the time horizon of the stress test has ended, on what the maximum level of swap rates would be in 15 years (already assuming a normalisation process of the interest rate curve), which would entail a chain of higher 6-month Euribor rates for certain deposit transfer levels, since after a period of stress, banks tend to suffer both financially and in terms of reputation, and one of their greatest weaknesses is maintaining adequate levels of profitability to ensure the sustainability of the banking business. Through this exercise, the supervisor could monitor this scenario on an institution-by-institution basis to control the stability of the financial system.

Finally, it should be noted that there are many advantages, and it would strengthen the current vision of the EBA's stress test exercises to complement them with the contribution of Pricing Gap metrics. Furthermore, as it is carried out with a bottom-up approach, it is possible to work with a granular view, providing a great deal of flexibility in the analyses to be developed.

10 PRICING GAP, a tool for design of a strategic plan in banking based on profitability

The aim of this chapter is to provide a brief introduction to the fundamentals of strategic planning for a financial institution. Secondly, it analyses how the concepts of sustainability and viability could be integrated into strategic plans through metrics associated with the Pricing Gap methodology. Finally, it reviews the main characteristics of the different business models and where the keys to management lie from an ALM perspective.

10.1 Strategic planning process in a banking institution

Strategic planning is the pillar that guides all high-level decisions in a banking organisation. It consists of a systematic process to define the future direction of the bank (its vision and strategic objectives) and detail the path to achieve that direction, optimising the use of resources and managing the associated risks. In the banking sector, this process takes on special relevance due to the complex and delicate nature of the financial business. Banks are highly leveraged, tightly regulated institutions whose viability depends largely on public confidence and perceived soundness (Choudhry, 2018). A strategic error can compromise not only profitability, but the survival of the institution. Hence, Chorafas (1999) stated that “failing to plan is planning to fail”, emphasising that a robust planning methodology should characterise every banking strategy.

The objectives of strategic banking planning include:

1. Ensuring profitable and sustainable growth.
2. Proactively adapting to changes in the environment (economic, technological, regulatory, competitive).
3. Aligning the organisation (resources, structure, culture) with long-term goals.
4. Managing the balance between risk and return according to the risk tolerance defined by the Board of Directors.
5. Meeting the expectations of key *stakeholders* (shareholders, customers, regulators, employees and society).

In essence, an effective strategic plan answers the following questions:

- What kind of bank do we want to become?
- Which markets and customers will we serve?
- What value proposition will we compete with?
- What financial and operational capacity do we need?
- How will we manage the inherent risks?

 | https://doi.org/10.1515/9783111328386-010

Clearly defining these questions allows management to focus their efforts and avoid "strategic drift", in which the bank tries to define a strategy without a clear direction, leading to disorderly growth, excessive exposure to ununderstood risks, and eventual destruction of value. These issues were seen prior to the 2008 crisis in institutions that aggressively pursued market share and profitability without considering the robustness of their balance sheets (Choudhry, 2018). Hence, all this underscores the importance and necessity of incorporating the vision of sustainability and viability into the banking business model.

10.1.1 Stages of the strategic planning process

Although each bank may have its own particular approach, many strategic planning processes in banking follow a general cycle comprising several interrelated stages. These stages can be summarised as follows:

1. Strategic diagnosis (analysis of the current situation).
2. Formulation of the strategic vision and objectives (defining *where we want to be* in the future).
3. Development of strategy and plans (outlining *how* we will achieve these objectives through initiatives and action plans).
4. Execution, monitoring and feedback (implementing the plan, measuring results and making adjustments as necessary). Each of these phases and their best practices are detailed below, with a focus on the banking context.

10.1.1.1 Strategic diagnosis: Starting point

Every strategic plan starts with a deep understanding of the bank's current position and the environment in which it operates (Choudhry, 2018). In this analytical phase, both internal and external information is gathered, covering aspects such as:

- Assessment of stakeholder expectations.
  - Shareholders
    - Profitability, dividend and growth targets, etc.
  - Regulators
    - Solvency, liquidity, IRRBB, etc.
  - Customers
    - Quality of service, products, channels
- Analysis of the macroeconomic and market environment, creating alternative scenarios with stress tests to assess the robustness of the strategy.
  - Projection of macroeconomic trends.
    - GDP, inflation, yield curve, exchange rates.
  - Projection of trends in the financial sector.
  - Analysis of markets and segments where the entity operates.

    - Analysis of credit demand.
    - Demographic changes in the customer base.
    - Other factors.
- Analysis of the competitive environment.
  - Understanding competitive dynamics,
    - Identifying direct and indirect competitors,
    - Assess their strengths and how they are changing the rules of the game.
  - The organisation's response to competitors' moves.
  - Analysis of customer value. How is their behaviour evolving? (Omarini, 2015)
    - Channel migration.
    - Product demand.
    - Satisfaction levels.
    - Risk of churn.
- Internal diagnosis and key competencies.
  - Honest identification of strengths and weaknesses.
  - Analysis of essential and non-essential competencies (Choudhry, 2018). Leverage to grow in those areas with the highest probability of success and those where a cautious approach is required.
- Analysis of the organisation's processes, systems and culture. The vast majority of strategies fail due to a lack of internal capabilities.
- Resource capacity and structure.
  - Quantification of available resource capacity (financial, human, technological) and adequacy of the current organisational structure.
  - Assessment of liquidity, capital and financial risk position.
  - Identification of new skills required in the workforce, as well as organisational size and structure (Choudhry, 2018).

At the end of this phase, the bank should have a clear understanding of its starting point, the external trends and forces that will shape the future, its relative competitive position and its available or deficient internal capabilities. This is the information base on which the strategy will be built.

10.1.1.2 Formulation of the vision and strategic objectives. Where do we want to be?

With the result of the previous point, entities proceed to define the strategic vision and the major long-term objectives.

The vision is a concise statement of the desired future state of the bank, capturing its fundamental aspiration. It should answer the following question:

- What do we want to become within the planned timeframe?

An effective vision provides a "call to action" that inspires and aligns all staff (Choudhry, 2018). Furthermore, it is important that it is aligned with the expectations of all relevant stakeholders (Choudhry, 2018). Balance in the vision is key.

Based on the vision, specific strategic objectives are established to enable the vision to be realised. These objectives are usually formulated in different dimensions:

- Financial objectives (for example)
  - Return on capital > X%
  - Annual credit growth of Y%
  - Diversification of income to reduce dependence on a certain line to Z%
  - Maintain a default ratio below N%
- Commercial objectives
  - Achieve a certain number of new customers in specific segments
  - Increase customer satisfaction or loyalty as measured by NPS (Net Promoter Score) or satisfaction index
  - Achieve X% market share for a certain product
- Operational objectives
  - Automate X% of transactions
  - Reduce the efficiency ratio (cost/income %) to a target level
- Solvency and risk objectives
  - Maintain CET1 > certain threshold
  - Achieve AA credit rating, etc.
- Other factors

Objectives must be specific, measurable, achievable, relevant and time-bound so that they guide implementation and can be properly monitored.

It is also essential that the vision and strategic objectives defined are realistic and consistent with the diagnosis made.

To ensure the viability of the objectives, it is advisable to preliminarily validate that they comply with critical restrictions on available capital and liquidity, and risk appetite defined through a framework approved by the Board of Directors. In fact, many banks now integrate long-term financial planning tools at this stage: models that project financial statements under assumptions of plan implementation, verifying whether key metrics (regulatory capital, LCR, etc.) remain within acceptable limits in each year of the plan (Choudhry, 2018). If the numbers do not add up, the objectives must be adjusted. This iteration ensures that the desired strategy is also the one the bank can safely execute.

10.1.1.3 Initiatives, levers and plans. How do we get there?

Once the bank has defined where it wants to go, there is the need to focus on how to get there. This phase corresponds to the formulation of the strategy in the strict sense. It consists of identifying and designing the strategic initiatives, projects and policies through which the bank will achieve its objectives. Here, the vision is transformed into concrete actions that can be assigned to responsible parties and scheduled.

A useful conceptual tool is to conceive of a strategic gap: the distance between the current situation (diagnosis) and the desired situation (objectives). Each strategic initiative should contribute to closing part of that gap.

Strategic initiatives are usually classified by area or axis, for example:
- Business development.
- Operational efficiency.
- Digital transformation.
- Risk, liquidity and capital management.
- Talent and culture.

Each initiative must be detailed in the following terms:
- What will be done
- Who will be responsible
- What resources are needed
- What results are expected

A key component of this development is identifying the management levers, or key success factors, that the bank must activate to drive change. These levers are the areas of focus for achieving significant improvements in performance indicators.

During this stage, it is also crucial to set intermediate goals or milestones for each initiative. Since the implementation of the strategy usually spans several years, setting annual or semi-annual milestones allows for progress to be monitored.

Likewise, key performance indicators (KPIs) should be assigned to each initiative or objective, which links to the next section on monitoring. For now, in the design phase, it is sufficient to define what will be measured to determine whether the initiative was successful.

During the development of the plan, there are two key issues that require close attention. The first is the execution risks of each initiative and the new risks that may arise from the implementation of the new strategic plan, which must be identified, measured, quantified, monitored, and controlled. The second issue is regulatory constraints that may affect the plan, which must be addressed in the development of the strategic plan.

A common mistake that Choudhry (2018) and others point out is to establish too many unrelated initiatives or to pursue too many fronts at once. It is preferable to identify and prioritise those strategic moves with the greatest expected impact or those that are most urgent and concentrate resources on them. Less critical initiatives can be scheduled for later phases or even discarded if they do not add sufficient value. This prioritisation should be reflected in the allocation of capital and budget and in the development of the strategic plan. Economic capital and investment expenditure should be channelled towards prioritised initiatives.

The final outcome of this stage usually takes the form of a documented strategic plan, which includes the vision, objectives, detailed strategic initiatives, milestones, KPIs, and resource allocations. Given the level of detail, this document is often summarised in matrices or strategic maps to facilitate communication.

10.1.1.4 Strategy execution and monitoring systems

Strategic planning does not end with the development of the strategic plan; in fact, it could be said that this is when the real challenge begins: making things happen as planned. The best strategy on paper will fail without disciplined execution and timely adjustments. Therefore, successful banks devote considerable attention to the governance, monitoring, and feedback on the strategic plan.

In terms of execution, it is advisable to establish clear governance structures for the implementation of the plan. This oversight should be led by a senior executive or area that centralises the coordination of initiatives. Likewise, those responsible for each strategic initiative are assigned, usually senior executives responsible for that part of the plan, and the chain of accountability is defined. The Board of Directors should receive regular reports (quarterly, for example) on the progress of the strategic plan, comparing the results obtained with the established milestones (Choudhry, 2018, p. 517), without the need for any reconfiguration work in response to each tactical variation or negative results in short-term execution.

Monitoring through KPIs, as already mentioned, each objective and initiative is accompanied by indicators. In the execution stage, a KPI monitoring system (e.g., strategic scorecards) is deployed to measure progress. These indicators must be integrated into the bank's regular management cycle. A balanced scorecard is used to translate the strategy into a series of objectives and indicators from various perspectives (financial, risk, business, processes, customers, segments, channels, etc.) with specific annual targets, which are then analysed by a monitoring committee.

Control and adjustment mechanisms must also be implemented. The strategy should not be viewed as static, as the environment changes and deviations in execution may arise. A good strategic system includes continuous feedback. If certain indicators show a lag, senior management must investigate the causes. Based on the conclusions, corrective actions can be taken. Tactical flexibility is important without losing sight of the ultimate vision and not changing course for trivial reasons (Choudhry, 2018). Financial institutions should place special emphasis on conducting annual ICAAP updates with stress scenarios to assess the financial risks associated with the strategic plan.

When executing a plan, it is vitally important to keep employees informed and engaged. Internal communication plays a vital role. All levels of staff must understand the strategy, the rationale behind the initiatives and how their work contributes to the goals. This increases the sense of purpose and minimises resistance. Many organisations implement change management programmes to accompany strategic transformations, especially when they involve significant cultural or process changes.

10.2 Incorporating sustainability and viability into strategic banking planning

As outlined in previous chapters, competition in the banking sector creates friction affecting profitability, stability, and risk-taking behaviour. This competition often results in a pricing gap at the point of origination, which can be further exacerbated by balance sheet management decisions in response to interest rate fluctuations. Consequently, assets and liabilities are frequently held at prices that do not sufficiently compensate for the financial risks to which they are exposed.

The pricing-versus-risk issues on the balance sheet, when viewed through accounting information, constrain the ability to draw definitive conclusions, as discussed in earlier chapters.

Under IFRS 9, the treatment of provisions for Stage 1 transactions—based on a 12-month forward-looking, point-in-time (PIT) view—prevents the accumulation of provisions that could be built up over time and drawn upon during periods of economic downturn. As a result, banks cannot rely on these provisions in times of stress but on existing capital buffers, which are unlikely to be deployed due to the reputational stigma they would face in the capital markets.

The previous point emphasised a critical aspect of developing a strategic plan. Best practice in the sector focuses on business model design—defining which customers the bank should target and how to strengthen its market presence and positioning. This includes organising channels to meet customer needs, designing an appropriate product portfolio, and implementing efficient processes to execute the business model. With the advent of artificial intelligence, the focus is increasingly on leveraging the relationships between financial institutions and their customers, gaining insights from payment patterns, digital banking usage, and other behavioural data.

A bank, to use a simile, could be likened to a walnut, see Figure 10.1. The outer layer, i.e., the outside, is where the institution's business model is defined and developed, i.e., the relationship with customers, through different markets, with specific segmentations, through digital channels or advice, products, processes, etc.

The inside of the nut is the true heart of a bank. This is where lending and funding policies are decided. The price at which transactions should be entered is analysed in order to balance profitability in relation to the financial risks involved. These risks are managed over time, i.e., the sustainability and viability of the business model characterised in the layer outside the nut is directed and planned. The current problem is that the ALM management model often has the mission of improving the accounting view of a bank's results, which is not the optimal way to make decisions.

A bank does not go bankrupt because of better or worse use of the outer layer, i.e., in the design of the business model. This issue has an impact on its greater or lesser positioning in the market. There is no better or worse strategy than another; it all depends on how it is executed, and it is in execution problems or strategies that are too focused on increasing market share that problems originate within bank balance

Figure 10.1: Graphic Illustration of a Bank.
Source: Own elaboration through Chat GPT.

sheets. Intense competition within banking systems amplifies these challenges, leading to the recognition of financial risks on balance sheets without adequate remuneration.

Therefore, a bank can face the risk of bankruptcy if it does not operate properly—that is, if it fails to manage the "core" decisions, ensuring that the financial risks it assumes are adequately compensated. As highlighted earlier, this arises in highly competitive financial systems when growth strategies focus on market share acquisition without first developing robust commercial capabilities.

Strategic plans generally do not address this issue correctly due to the "accounting" approach of the financial analyses carried out. Strategic diagnosis often focuses primarily on balance sheet indicators, P&L, and financial risks, which are then used during the formulation of the strategic vision and objectives. Many institutions, during implementation planning, place excessive emphasis on keeping these metrics within the thresholds approved by the Board of Directors.

One approach to improving the development of strategic plans is to place greater emphasis on ALM, using the Pricing Gap methodology to evaluate the institution both at the start of the plan and as it evolves. This assessment helps guide the necessary management decisions while simultaneously developing a business model tailored to the customers aligned with the bank's strategic vision. The approach serves a dual purpose: first, to ensure that the business model is sustainable over time, and second, to maintain the institution's viability during periods of uncertainty, preventing potential financial stability issues.

The Pricing Gap methodology has already been presented in previous chapters. Graphically, we can summarise it in Figure 10.2.

As can be seen, the figure represents the formulations already presented in previous chapters.

Once the various components of FTP investment operations are calculated, they are compared with market prices to determine the investment margin, with a view to the business's sustainability, in order to obtain the PGa. In this process, the expected loss is considered from an economic cycle or lifetime perspective but is adjusted according to the amortisation schedule of the operations.

For the margin on investment (LFT) related to the viability of the banking business, the expected loss is also viewed from an economic cycle perspective but is not adjusted for the amortisation schedule; instead, it is assumed to occur suddenly, as if an economic crisis were to strike immediately.

The funding margin is calculated as the difference between FTP funding operations and the market price. This approach is preferred because applying liquidity premiums can introduce noise. In medium- and long-term operations, assuming constant premiums—even if they increase over time—can lead to pricing errors, especially for banks with significant retail funding, where remuneration and betas are highly volatile.

Separating investment and funding calculations also allows for better identification of pricing errors, clarifies how issues are financed, absorbed, or subsidised, and enables a focused approach to the financing strategy within a strategic plan, particularly as investment-side problems accumulate.

Once the PGa, PGt-1st and PGt-2nd are obtained, the provisioning and capital policies are analysed outside the environment required by prudential regulation. Delving deeper into these policies helps to improve understanding of the absorption capacity required for the business model in place.

Additionally, the methodology can be used to analyse credit policy through market prices, providing a valuable indicator: the internal default indicator. In other words, by covering the funding component based on market prices and accounting for overheads, it is possible to estimate the maximum level of delinquency that can be assumed at the traded prices, with or without considering the entity's profits or the capital component. This gives risk departments insight into the appropriate level of leniency when originating transactions.

Any delinquency above this threshold that can be absorbed without compromising the sustainability of the banking business depends on the non-realisation of balance sheet risks—specifically, the institution's ability to maintain funding with a beta below 1 and to minimise transfers from non-maturity deposits (NMDs) to term deposits.

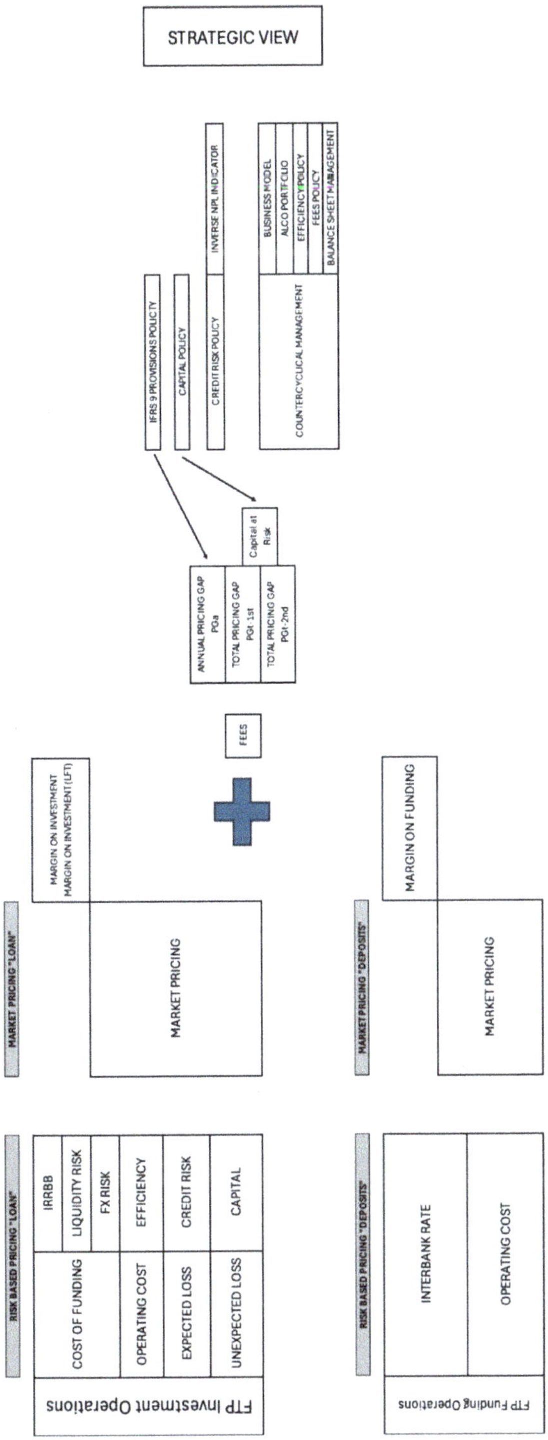

Figure 10.2: Pricing Gap Methodology.
Source: Own elaboration.

Finally, what the graph shows is that, once all the analysis information has been obtained through the Pricing Gap methodology, which originates in the ALM world, it is the countercyclical management capacity available to financial institutions. Countercyclical capacity is defined as, once vulnerabilities in the sustainability and viability of the banking business have been identified, what different instruments or policies can be implemented to minimise these risks. These focus on changes in the business model and how the business model is being executed and whether it is worth sustaining over time, for example, in new positioning decisions in the ALCO portfolio, in decisions regarding the efficiency policy in the distribution model of the business model, as well as the processes used for them. Fee policy decisions can help minimise pricing errors by enabling more effective cross-selling to existing customers.

Now the necessary steps are presented for a possible integration of the Pricing Gap methodology into a strategic plan, as well as into the daily management of a financial institution.[51]

10.2.1 Case study

1. Presentation of the starting point.
We start with the initial balance sheet of the institution, which is represented in Figure 10.3.

In addition, a data set of basic information on the risk structure of operations must be available (Table 10.1).

From an accounting point of view, this entity presents very good results, which are represented in Table 10.2.

In principle, based on this information, an entity can consider that it has an optimal starting point. The accounting figures comply with all prudential regulations. Its starting income statement is positive, it has profit generation capacity, it is profitable from an accounting perspective, and therefore, in its new strategic plan, based on a very simple analysis as this is an illustrative example, it could consider continuing to focus on the mortgage and SME business model in which it is positioned, with retail financing that has been performing steadily. The market is focusing on attracting fixed-rate mortgage customers, so it has to work in that scenario.

2. Integration of the Pricing Gap vision into the starting point analysis.
The entity proceeds to integrate the entire Pricing Gap methodology shown in Table 10.3.

51 The example of a typical entity from the previous chapter will be used.

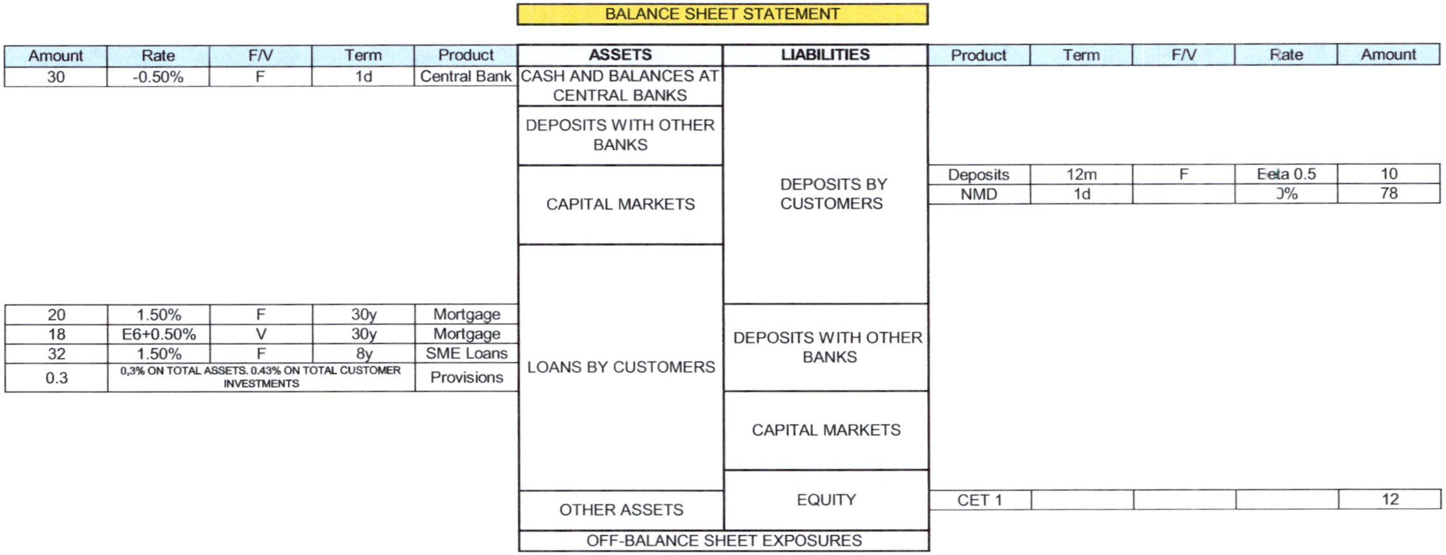

Figure 10.3: Opening Balance Sheet.
Source: Own elaboration.

Table 10.1: Balance Sheet Data Tape.

BALANCE SHEET DATA TAPE													
Product	**Amount**	**Rate**	**Fee**	**F/V**	**Term**	**Duration**	**PD LFT**	**LGD**	**OC**	**Provisions**	**RW**	**ROE**	**CAPITAL**
Mortgage	20	1.50%		F	30y	15	2%	40%	0.5%	0.2	35%		
Mortgage	18	E6+0.50%		V	30y	0.5	2%	40%	0.5%	0.2	35%	10%	12%
SME Loans	32	1.50%		F	8y	4	6%	60%	0.50%	0.7	75%		
Deposits ECB	30	€STER			1d	0.0			0.50%	0	0%		
			0.30%										
Deposits	10	Beta 0.5		F/V	12m	1							
NMD	78	0%			1d	4.0							
Equity	12	0%				10							

Source: Own elaboration.

Table 10.2: P&L for Year 2022.

	P&L
	22
YIELD INVESTMENT	1.57
YIELD FUNDING	0.10
NII	**1.47**
FEE	0.30
TOTAL OPERATING INCOME	**1.77**
OC	0.50
PRE-PROVISION PROFIT	**1.27**
PROVISION FOR CREDIT LOSS	0.00
PROFIT BEFORE TAX	**1.27**

Source: Own elaboration.

With this information, the approach to the strategic plan differs, and this is where the value contribution can be found.

- First, it should be noted that the business model is sustainable. It has a PGa of 0.84. However, it is important to analyse the different components that make up this metric, which help to improve the management of the business model:
  - The margin on investment for operations is very negative, and even more so for fixed-rate operations, which were constructed during a period when the interest rate curve was negative. This occurs because these operations have a very high cost of funding compared to the rates set in the balance sheet, mainly. This makes it a risk to assess its materialisation, which would be through higher remuneration of deposits with a beta equal to 1 and strong transfers of NMDs to term deposits. In such a situation, these operations would not be able to cover the remuneration of the portion of deposits that would finance them.
  - The same applies to SME operations. However, as these operations have a UL of 0.9 and a margin on investment of −1.28, this implies that, assuming no distributions to shareholders (UL = 0), they exhibit a profitability shortfall of at least 0.38 to break even, excluding profits or coverage for unexpected losses. This insight is valuable, as it can serve as a benchmark for planning additional profitability measures to be introduced for this segment, for example through fees.
  - As in previous point, variable-rate mortgage operations, with a UL of 0.42 and a margin on investment of -0.47, also show a profitability shortfall. This implies that these operations should be through additional income sources, for example via fees. By contrast, fixed-rated mortgage transactions, with a margin on investment of -2.21, cannot be balanced through cross-selling. This information is highly valuable, as the entity should take it into account when defining its strategy. In particular, it should analyse market conditions - if a sustained decline in long-term interest rates is expected, hedging against

Table 10.3: Pricing Gap Methodology for the Year 2022.

	AMOUNT	CF	OC	EL	EL (LFT)	UL	FTP INV	FTP INV LFT	YIELD	Margin INV	Margin INV LFT
Mortgage	20	2.49	0.50	0.05	0.80	0.42	3.46	4.21	1.25	−2.21	−2.96
Mortgage	18	1.20	0.50	0.05	0.80	0.42	2.18	2.92	1.703	−0.47	−1.22
SME Loans	32	2.23	0.50	0.90	3.60	0.90	4.53	7.23	3.25	−1.28	−3.98
Deposits ECB	30	−0.09	0.50				0.41	0.41	−0.091	−0.50	−0.50
	AMOUNT	**INTERBANK**	**OC**	**FTP FUND**	**YIELD**	**Margin FUND**					
Deposits	10	1.78	0.50	1.28	0.89	0.39					
NMD	78	2.23	0.50	1.73	0.00	1.73					
Equity	12	2.42	0.50	1.92	0.00	1.92					
	Margin INV	**Margin INV LFT**	**Margin FUND**	**Fee**	**PGa**	**Provisions**	**PGt-1st**	**Capital**	**Capital at Risk**	**PGt-2nd**	**UL**
	−1.09	−2.24	1.63	0.30	0.84	0.30	−0.01	12	0%	11.99	0.45
	Hasta 1y	**1y-3y**	**3y-5y**	**5y-10y**	**10y-15y**	**15y-20y**	**20y-25y**	**>25y**			
Margin INV	−0.15			−0.41				−0.53			
Margin FUND	0.04		1.36		0.23						
PGa – Buckets	**-0.11**	**0.00**	**1.36**	**-0.41**	**0.23**	**0**	**0.00**	**-0.53**			
Fees				0.30							
PGa				**0.84**							

Source: Own elaboration.

such a decline could be an option - and assess the overall viability of operating this market. Although fixed-rate mortgages may offer accounting benefits, these reflect a short-term perspective that should be avoided when designing a long-term strategic plan.

- Current commissions amount to 0.30 (it is assumed that all segments contribute the same amount in commissions) and do compensate for the SME and variable-rate mortgage segments, but fixed-rate mortgages are far from being able to balance themselves out.
- The margin on funding is what subsidises the incorrectly remunerated risks of investments. This can be assessed in the PGa table by buckets in Table 10.3. The value is 1.63, and a large part of that value is in the 3y-5y range, since in a BaU environment, the value given to NMDs is 4 years. However, if the entity's funding were 100% in term deposits and with a beta equal to 1, the margin on funding would be reduced to 0 and there would be no subsidy as in the example. The origin of this value comes from having 11% term deposits with a beta equal to 0.5 and 78% of total funding in NMDs, which are considered very stable and contribute a lot of value, as it is assumed (based on NMD modelling) that they have a modified duration of 4 years. All this information is key to managing the strategic plan, because if the entity has to defend its position in the mortgage market, which is committed to fixed rates, the key to the sustainability of the business model lies in the structure of liabilities, how customer loyalty is worked on and how value is provided to them so that they place their trust in the entity and that strategy can be returned in added value.
- The conclusions initially obtained at the aggregate level can be broken down by segments, markets, geographies, and other dimensions, given the bottom-up nature of the PGa analysis. This significantly enhances the added value of the methodology, particularly for universal banks, whose structures and operations are inherently more complex.
- From a viability standpoint, PGt-1st is equal to -0.01, with capital at risk of 0 and PGt-2nd of 11.98, so it can be concluded that the entity is viable. However, additional information can be extracted.
  - Provisions comply with regulations and currently stand at 0.3. The average expected loss for the cycle is 1.46, so the institution should take this situation into account when planning its profit policy to allow it to accumulate sufficient provisions for use in the event of changes in the economic cycle.
  - The inverse delinquency indicator can be obtained from the market prices of the investments. This indicator is obtained by subtracting the funding curve estimated by the institution and the operating costs from these market prices. The UL could also be subtracted or not, to obtain the indicator information with or without profits (to be distributed to shareholders). All components are cleared and the implicit ECL embedded in market prices is obtained. By subtracting the LGD, the resulting figure

represents the implicit PD assumed by market prices for the operations under analysis. This information is also highly relevant as a management KPI when assessing whether to enter specific markets or segments.

3. Projections of the Pricing Gap methodology metrics.
As in the classic construction of a strategic plan, where projections are made for the balance sheet, income statement and financial risk, liquidity and capital indicators, projections should be made using the Pricing Gap methodology in the same way as in the case presented in the SREP methodology and stress test. The implicit interest rate curves should also be projected. Credit risk scenarios, term deposit betas, different transfer scenarios, etc., should be estimated too.

With the information projected in the same way as presented in Chapter 8 (both in the BaU scenario and in stress test mode), the results would be analysed again to try to conclude whether or not the entity's picture has improved. This assessment determines whether the business model planned under the estimated competitive environment and the assumptions of the strategic plan is adequate, or whether it is necessary to return to the starting point and reconfigure the strategy in the event that projected scenarios reveal balance sheet risks that could jeopardise the sustainability or viability of the business.

At this stage, it is important to initiate the analysis of countercyclical capacity. Countercyclical capacity means that, based on the information analysed, entities decide to change the markets, segments, customers and products they want to target, or at least consider a different way of targeting or approaching them. This is because, although the short-term profit may be positive in accounting terms, in the long term the financial risks (it should be remembered that this is the raw material of banks) could, if they materialise, lead to serious problems for the sustainability or viability of the banking business. To this end, the following dimensions are analysed:

a. ALCO Portfolio: With the existing liquidity and the commercial gap resulting from the planned period, institutions can change their investment policies in the ALCO portfolio to compensate for potential sub-optimal results of the business model, represented by the Pricing Gap metrics, either by taking on more duration or greater credit risk, as long as prudential regulation allows it.
b. Efficiency Policy: Either due to actual excess capacity (excess branches or employees) deduced from productivity indicators, or because the levels of profitability in the market where the competition is so strong that decisions have to be made to balance profitability through efficiency decisions. Many, but not all, bank mergers are motivated by this issue. On the other hand, while maintaining costs and structure, institutions may be interested in calculating the target operating cost level, the turnover required to achieve it, and whether the growth in the planned strategic plan would allow them to achieve it.
c. Fees Policy: Using the information obtained from the entire Pricing Gap analysis and metrics process, and specifically an in-depth analysis of the.PGa, its compo-

nents, etc., a comprehensive cross-selling strategy can be developed with customers across different segments, markets and geographies to determine what the marketing policy for products linked to investment and financing operations should be and to find the break-even points. At this point, it is vital to establish KPIs on the customer fee policy by segment to be achieved. Here, universal banking has greater capacity to develop a more diversified business model with a greater weighting on investment banking, whose performance is focused on fees for its advisory operations.

d. Balance Sheet Management: Financial institutions, through different balance sheet management strategies (mainly financial and derivative strategies), can boost balance profitability levels by taking advantage of movements in the curve. For this part, which is not covered by this manual, there are essential references such as Choudhry (2007, 2018, 2023).

4. Monitoring of Pricing Gap and Governance indicators.
The biggest problems that entities tend to encounter with strategic plans are execution risks. This is where most problems arise.

A robust scorecard must be established, as discussed in point 2 of this chapter. All information derived from the Pricing Gap methodology (Figure 10.2 and Table 10.3) used during the plan construction phase should be incorporated to monitor its evolution and assess how the two most important concepts within a financial institution—namely, the sustainability and viability of the business—are developing. These concepts should be supported by their respective factors and indicators to facilitate their proper assessment.

The information provided by the Pricing Gap methodology will support decision-making across the business model, ALCO policies, efficiency initiatives, fee-setting policies, and balance sheet management, enabling the evolution of the business to be aligned with the desired target levels—not from a purely accounting perspective, but in accordance with the principles of the Pricing Gap framework.

10.3 Banking business models: Approaches, key elements and new competitors

The banking industry encompasses a variety of business models that define how each institution creates and captures value in the market. A banking business model can be understood as the particular configuration of products and services offered, customer segments served, distribution channels used, revenue generation mechanisms and sources of competitive advantage that characterise a bank (Omarini, 2015). While the basic function of banking is to buy and sell money and provide a range of services for which a series of fees are charged, the way in which banks perform that function is the business model.

Here is a brief overview of the main business models:

a. Traditional retail banking.
b. Universal banking.
c. New ways of banking. Fintech and Bigtech.

After briefly presenting the characteristics of each model in terms of target markets, customer base, channels, management levers, revenue mechanisms and competitive advantages in a summary table (Table 10.4), we will briefly reflect on the Pricing Gap methodology for the different types of business models in order to compare them.

Table 10.4: Bank Business Model.

	Traditional Consumer Banking	Universal Banking	Fintech/Bigtech Banking
Customer segment	Individuals, families, local SMEs.	All segments: retail, SMEs, corporate, institutional.	Varies depending on the fintech: many focus on niches (digital youth, underserved SMEs, etc.). Bigtech targets its massive base of tech users.
Geographic reach	Generally national or regional.	Multinational or global (geographical diversification).	Mainly digital/global (fintechs can operate globally via the internet, bigtech has global platform reach).
Products/ Services	Accounts, payments, consumer credit/mortgages, cards, basic investment/ insurance.	Broad portfolio: retail products + corporate banking (corporate credit, foreign trade) + investment banking (M&A, capital markets) + asset management, etc.	Specific offerings depending on the start-up: mobile payments, P2P lending, crowdfunding, neobanks (digital accounts), *robo-advisors*, crypto, etc. Bigtech offers payments (e.g. Apple Pay), consumer credit, person-to-person payment services, etc., integrated into its ecosystem.

Table 10.4 (continued)

	Traditional Consumer Banking	Universal Banking	Fintech/Bigtech Banking
Distribution channels	Physical branches, ATMs, online and mobile banking, call centres (in transition to digital-physical omnichannel).	Multiple: extensive physical network in major retail markets, plus digital channels; sales forces for corporate clients; presence in global financial markets (traders, investment bankers).	Predominantly digital: mobile apps, web platforms, online marketplaces. Little or no physical infrastructure of their own (they take advantage of existing partner channels or are 100% online). Bigtech integrates financial services into their existing apps/ platforms (e.g. WhatsApp, e-commerce).
Main sources of income	Interest margin (loans vs. deposits) + banking service fees.	Diversified: retail interest margin + commissions + investment banking fees (underwriting, advisory) + proprietary trading and investment + wealth management (fees).	Model varies: some fintech companies earn from commissions (e.g. per transaction), loan spreads (crowdlending), subscriptions (freemium neobanks), software sales (BaaS). Bigtech companies tend to monetise indirectly (e.g. financial services increase core sales, obtain data, build user loyalty).
Cost structure	High fixed operating costs (branch network, large staff). Cost/income ratio typically 50-65%. Focus on efficiency through digitalisation.	Complex structure: retail network costs + wholesale banking costs (high salaries in investment banking, technology). Significant economies of scale, but also high global compliance costs. Cost/income ratio varies by division (consolidated may be 60% retail, 40% wholesale banking).	Lower operating costs due to lack of traditional physical infrastructure; scalable technology base. However, they require high initial investment in technology. They can operate with very low cost/income ratios (<40%) if they scale successfully. Bigtech has minimal marginal costs in financial services (leveraging existing infrastructure).

Table 10.4 (continued)

	Traditional Consumer Banking	Universal Banking	Fintech/Bigtech Banking
Competitive advantages	Trust and established brand; local proximity; broad deposit base (cheap funding); mass customer diversification; personal relationship with customers (historically).	Synergies between businesses (cross-sell); revenue diversification that can stabilise profits; ability to comprehensively meet the complex needs of large customers; large capital base and internal liquidity; global reach.	Agile innovation; superior focus on digital user experience; low costs and attractive prices; intensive use of data for personalisation; for big tech: already built ecosystem, big data, deep customer knowledge and enormous financial resources.
Challenges	Digitise to avoid losing young customers; high price competition (commoditisation of products); maintain profitability with low rates; comply with strict consumer protection regulations.	Management complexity; risk of contamination between divisions; greater regulatory scrutiny ("too big to fail"); risk of not being a leader in anything due to diversification; fragmented internal culture; fintechs attacking profitable niches; continuous need for recapitalisation d s due to growing demands.	Gaining trust (as they are not traditional banks, they must convince users to migrate); facing regulations as they grow (many fintechs initially operate with less regulation); scaling their customer base against the distribution power of banks; for big tech, avoiding regulatory or antitrust reaction that limits their foray into finance.

Source: Own elaboration based on Choudhry, 2018; Omarini, 2015; King, 2018.

10.3.1 Traditional retail banks/Commercial banks

From the point of view of the Pricing Gap methodology, traditional retail banks, in their normal business process (buying/selling money and providing services in exchange for commissions), face highly competitive environments. This is because, in general terms, their target customers, private individuals and SMEs, are characterised by a demand for commodity products, where the differentiating factor is usually price, meaning that margins or investment are often under considerable pressure. SMEs, which are also based more on products that rely on financial advice, have less weight. Depending on the competitive environment, the management of the different cycles of the interest rate curve, the risks they have taken at a fixed rate in the long term, etc., these financial institutions will have a more negative value than others.

This negative margin on investment is partially offset by cross-selling strategies aimed at achieving higher fee levels to balance pricing errors for the reasons already mentioned.

Efficiency in this type of institution is always a challenge. On the one hand, they have to maintain a sufficiently balanced number of branches to continue to maintain the proximity on which their business and distribution model is based. On the other hand, they cannot lose sight of innovation in terms of digitalisation, which allows them to compete reasonably with other much stronger players in this area. Therefore, pricing is usually a fairly rigid factor, and in many cases, it is mergers and acquisitions that tend to improve this area.

In terms of expected losses, these types of more domestic institutions should, in theory, have a credit risk that is very much in line with the economic cycle and, depending on whether they have pursued aggressive strategies in the past to grow their market share, they should not have any viability problems in this regard. In addition, the prudential regulation implemented after the great financial crisis prevents institutions from maintaining growth levels similar to those of the last crisis.

This issue must be linked to a proper provisioning policy, which, as already stated, should maintain a dynamic provisioning policy of at least the economic cycle average of expected losses.

Their distribution channels are predominantly branches, although they also rely on digital channels. This proximity to customers allows them to maintain a very positive margin on funding, which is also fairly stable. Even in times of maximum volatility, when term deposits are paid at betas well above 1, they are offset by the more stable and lower-cost structure of NMDs. This prudent management, proximity to customers, and provision of value and trust is what protects these types of institutions and businesses in times of uncertainty. Exacerbated growth policies with greater dependence on markets where financing is paid above the curve with a concentration of maturities can expose them to a less positive margin on funding, which, when more negative economic cycles occur, does not find sufficient compensation in this part of management to protect the balance sheet and the need for greater provisions, when combined with environments of higher credit risk, represented by the PGt.

If capital policy is not robust, it can affect the entity's organic growth, as a significant dividend policy and maximisation of short-term profits to grow without impacting the solvency ratio, without maintaining consistency with the provisioning policy, is something to be taken into account when assessing the bank's future viability.

As countercyclical policies, these entities, due to their smaller size but higher levels of structural liquidity, can rely on ALCO portfolio management originating from the positive commercial gaps obtained from this greater inflow of customer liabilities. A thorough understanding of the origin of the customer segments and products that generate imbalances is key to successfully navigating changes in business models in strategic plans, deciding which businesses to accelerate, which types of customers to target with cross-selling policies to offset price deficiencies, etc. Finally, when analysing the overall situation, make balance sheet management decisions to the extent that there are curve movements that improve negative margin on investment levels, make balance sheet hedging decisions (always under the umbrella of IRRBB regulatory compliance, etc.) to improve the entity's risk profile, even if these decisions do not optimise the accounting result.

10.3.2 Universal banks

As for universal banking, the conclusions are similar to those for commercial banking, with certain nuances. Its business, having a broader customer target that includes large corporations and institutions, with a wide geographical spread, and with a set of activities that are more advisory-based, in theory, they have much more robust fees than commercial banking due to the dynamism of their investment banking and a margin on investment that is, in theory, less stressed than domestic commercial banking, depending on the growth policies they have pursued in each of the countries in which they operate. Therefore, they have a more balanced margin generation profile.

Their deposit base is generally less stable due to their business model in terms of branch distribution and less proximity to the territory, as they are committed to a hybrid model between digital and branch channels in their quest not to lose market share to neobanks/bigtech/fintech.

The challenges faced by these types of entities are enormous. Their size makes management much more complex, with geographical diversity, different regulations and constant competition, meaning that the development of this type of methodology generates a lot of value in management. Far beyond accounting information, the PGa methodology allows the management team to ask an infinite number of questions and assess in real time the two key variables of business management: sustainability and viability. For example, the same question regarding a global problem in the commercial real estate sector can obtain immediate answers through the model, such as what profitability model should be implemented to balance the PGa, what provision policy should be anticipated to absorb possible uncertainties, and all by country, different divisions, etc.

Universal and commercial banks, with the new prudential regulation of capital, solvency, macroprudential requirements, MREL and TLAC, have slowed down their organic growth in credit investment, so given the debt ratios of households and companies and the growth of balance sheets since the great crisis, it is difficult to imagine a repeat of what happened in the past. The difficulties they face are primarily related to the correct pricing of new originations and existing balance sheet exposures, specifically ensuring that balance sheet duration is properly priced after a prolonged period of negative interest rates, during which monetary policy and central bank balance sheet management did not facilitate effective price formation. Institutions with the most robust and stable funding structures would be best prepared, as the risk would materialise during periods of uncertainty—such as an event affecting reputation—that could trigger a structural change in deposit betas, or a shift of such magnitude that non-maturity deposits (NMDs) are insufficient to offset the beta of term deposits.

Therefore, those institutions with a positive PGa and little dependence on margin on funding that are financing a lot of margin on investment in the long term and at a fixed rate will be much more resilient in times of uncertainty (an example of this would be Silicon Valley Bank). From an ALM perspective, all of the above explains why many financial institutions adopt a customer-centric approach in their strategic plans.

10.3.3 Fintech/Bigtech banking

To summarise, the neobank/bigtech/fintech world (hereinafter neobanks) does not represent a single banking business model, but rather multiple emerging models that compete with parts of the traditional banking business. Their presence forces us to rethink existing models: consumer banking is becoming more technological and customer-centric, and universal banking must focus on areas of added value (expert advice, complex operations) while automating and streamlining its basic processes.

Neobanks originate their business by breaking down customer payments into consumer transactions. Their current business model relies on setting prices accurately to cover credit risk, which is assessed with very limited information. Lacking the financing to absorb pricing errors, their key focus is maintaining a balanced PGa based on a zero or positive margin on investment, complemented by an appropriate provisioning policy.

Neobanks that provide generic securities trading services are a simple business where their operating costs must be very balanced with the fees obtained from transactions, so they work with a model that scales as much as possible to find their balance.

When neobanks apply for a banking licence to expand into commercial banking—leveraging their customer experience, platform simplicity, and other advantages—they also face significant challenges, such as complying with prudential regulations when initiating deposit-taking activities.

In their business model evolution, these entities have a zero or negative margin on funding, firstly because they are new players and secondly because their proximity to customers is a plus for deposit stability and enables them to pay lower remuneration. When they consider evolving their investment model with customers, they face a highly competitive market but with one difference from commercial and universal banks: low subsidies from deposits. This means that their PGa is generally negative, but in these entities, this is caused by low margin on funding. It should be remembered that these types of institutions have not yet navigated a systemic crisis in the sector with a strong impact on financing structures. While banks experienced higher demands for remuneration and transfers to term deposits during previous banking crises, institutions with less stable deposits may face outflows that threaten their stability—an issue that must be carefully considered in their planning.

For neobanks, the adoption of the PGa methodology in their strategic planning, beyond the accounting perspective, can offer them the break-even point for profitability in their commercial deployment, both in terms of PGa and PGt, indicating how far they can go based on their financial capabilities, etc.

In conclusion, the PGa methodology is suitable for pricing purposes and for assessing business model vulnerabilities, regardless of the type of business model under consideration.

10.4 Final reflection

Through the various cases presented in the preceding chapters, the importance of implementing the Pricing Gap methodology has been highlighted. Its added value in constructing strategic plans is evident; for international banks, it can be used to assess whether to enter a specific geography. The methodology also complements existing systems for business model assessment (BMA) and the calculation of capital surcharges for P2R and P2G under the SREP framework, emphasising the need for a dynamic provisioning policy given the limitations of the IFRS 9 model for impaired assets in banking. Stress tests can be significantly enhanced through the flexibility offered by the Pricing Gap methodology. Additionally, proposed case studies demonstrate how this approach can anticipate a banking system's preparedness for various financial risks arising from economic crises, enabling the separation of economic crises from banking crises and fostering more resilient banking systems.

A cross-cutting integration of this methodology offers practical value in establishing macroprudential policies and regulations that are less capital-centric and avoid duplicative requirements. It also promotes alignment between best practices in the planning and management of financial institutions and supervisory practices based on the same methodology, enhancing the consistency of supervisory dialogue and contributing to better-managed institutions and a more stable financial system.

Selected bibliography

Adam, A. (2007). *Handbook of Asset and Liability Management: From Models to Optimal Return Strategies*. John Wiley & Sons.
Adrian, T., Boyarchenko, N., & Giannone, D. (2019). Vulnerable Growth. *American Economic Review*, 109(4), 1263–1289
Allen, F., & Gale, D. (2004). Competition and Financial Stability. *Journal of Money, Credit and Banking*, 36(3), 453–480.
Altunbas, Y., Manganelli, S., & Marques-Ibáñez, D. (2011). *Bank Risk During the Financial Crisis: Do Business Models Matter?* ECB Working Paper, No.1394.
Anderson, N., Brazier, A., Haldane, A., Nahai-Williamson, P., & Radia, A. (2022). Why Banks Failed the Stress Test: A Progress Report on Stress Testing 10 Years On. In *Handbook of Financial Stress Testing* (Farmer et al., Eds.), pp. 47–74.
Arakelyan, M., Gersl, A., & Schindler, M. (2023). *Macroprudential Policies Over Financial Cycles*. IMF Working Paper 23(171).
Basel Committee on Banking Supervision (BCBS). (2015). *Guidance on Supervisory Interaction with Financial Institutions on Risk Culture*. Bank for International Settlements.
Basel Committee on Banking Supervision. (2013). *Basel III: The Liquidity Coverage Ratio and liquidity risk monitoring tools*. Bank for International Settlements.
Basel Committee on Banking Supervision. (2014). *Basel III: The Net Stable Funding Ratio*. Bank for International Settlements.
Basel Committee on Banking Supervision. (2025). *Principles for the Management of Credit Risk*. Bank for International Settlements. https://www.bis.org/bcbs/publ/d591.htm
Bassett, W. F., & Rappoport, D. (2022). Enhancing Stress Tests by Adding Macroprudential Elements. In *Handbook of Financial Stress Testing*, pp. 455–483.
Beck, T., Demirgüç-Kunt, A., & Levine, R. (2006). Bank Concentration, Competition, and Crises: First Results. *Journal of Banking & Finance*, 30(5), 1581–1603.
Bessis, J. (2015). *Risk Management in Banking* (4th ed.). John Wiley & Sons.
Birn, M., Corrias, R., Schmieder, C., & Tarashev, N. (2023). *Banks' credit loss forecasts: Lessons from supervisory data* (BIS Working Papers No. 1125). Bank for International Settlements.
Blundell-Wignall, A., Atkinson, P., & Roulet, C. (2014). Bank Business Models and the Basel System: Complexity and Interconnectedness. OECD Journal: *Financial Market Trends*, 2013(2), 43–48.
Board of Governors of the Federal Reserve System. (2020). *Comprehensive Capital Analysis and Review 2020 – Summary Instructions*. Washington, DC.
Borio, C., Drehmann, M., & Tsatsaronis, K. (2014). Stress-testing Macro Stress Testing: Does it Live Up to Expectations? *Journal of Financial Stability*, 12, 3–15.
Bousquet, A., Henry, J., & Zochowski, D. (2022). A Comprehensive Approach to Macroprudential Stress Testing. In *Handbook of Financial Stress Testing*, pp. 557–592.
Boyd, J., & De Nicoló, G. (2005). The Theory of Bank Risk Taking and Competition Revisited. *Journal of Finance*, 60(3), 1329–1343.
Boyd, J. H., & De Nicoló, G. (2005). The Theory of Bank Risk Taking and Competition Revisited. *The Journal of Finance*, 60(3), 1329–1343. https://doi.org/10.1111/j.1540-6261.2005.00763.x
Castro, C. E., Estrada, Á., and Martínez, J. (2016). *The Countercyclical Capital Buffer in Spain: An Analysis of Key Guiding Indicators*. Bank of Spain. Working Papers. No. 1601.
Casu, B., Girardone, C., & Molyneux, P. (2015). *Introduction to Banking (2nd ed.)*. Pearson Education Limited.
Chen, S., & Svirydzenka, K. (2021). *Financial Cycles—Early Warning Indicators?*. IMF Working Paper, 21 (116).
Chorafas, D. N. (1999). *The Commercial Banking Handbook: Strategic Planning for Growth and Survival in the New Decade*. Palgrave Macmillan.
Choudhry, M. (2007). *Bank Asset and Liability Management. Strategy, Trading, Analysis*. John Wiley & Sons.

 | https://doi.org/10.1515/9783111328386-011

Choudhry, M. (2012). *The Principles of Banking*. John Wiley & Sons.

Choudhry, M. (2018). *The Moorad Choudhry Anthology. Past, Present and Future Principles of Banking and Finance*. John Wiley & Sons.

Choudhry, M. (2023). *The Principles of Banking (2nd ed.)*. John Wiley & Sons.

Clark, T. P. (2022). A Supervisory Perspective on Stress Testing – the US Experience. In *Handbook of Financial Stress Testing*, pp. 316–330.

Coelho, R., Monteil, A., Pozdyshev, V., & Svoronos, J.-P. (2022). *Supervisory Practices for Assessing the Sustainability of Banks' Business Models.* FSI Insights No. 40, Bank for International Settlements.

Cumming, C. M. (2022). Strengths and Weaknesses of Microprudential Stress Testing for Financial Institutions. In *Handbook of Financial Stress Testing*, pp. 331–350.

Dent, K., Westwood, B., & Segoviano, M. (2016). Stress Testing of Banks: An Introduction. *Bank of England Quarterly Bulletin* Q3 2016.

Deprés, M., Villegas, R., & Ayora, J. (2025). *Manual de regulación bancaria en España (4th ed.)*. Funcas.

Dermine, J. (2009). *Bank Valuation and Value-Based Management: Deposit and Loan Pricing, Performance Evaluation, and Risk Management*. McGraw-Hill.

Drehmann, M., & Tsatsaronis, K. (2014). The credit-to-GDP gap and countercyclical capital buffers. *BIS Quarterly Review*, March, pp. 55–73.

Egan, M., Hortaçsu, A., & Matvos, G. (2017). Deposit Competition and Financial Fragility: Evidence from the US Banking Sector. *American Economic Review*, 107(1), 169–216. https://doi.org/10.1257/aer.20130145

Eisenberg, L., & Noe, T. (2001). Systemic Risk in Financial Systems. *Management Science*, 47(2), 236–249.

European Banking Authority (EBA) (2018). *Guidelines on Stress Testing*. EBA/GL/2018/04.

European Banking Authority (EBA). (2025). *Draft Guidelines on Common Procedures and Methodologies for the Supervisory Review and Evaluation Process (SREP) and Supervisory Stress Testing* (Public consultation EBA/CP/2025/21, 24 October 2025).

European Banking Authority (EBA). (2020). *The EU Banking Sector: First insights into the COVID-19 impacts*. EBA/REP/2020/17. EBA Thematic Note.

European Banking Authority (EBA). (2018). *Revised Guidelines on Common Procedures and Methodologies for SREP*. EBA/GL/2018/03 (July 2018).

European Banking Authority (EBA). (2017). *Guidelines on ICAAP and ILAAP Information Collected for SREP Purposes*. EBA/GL/2016/10 (January 2017).

European Banking Authority (EBA). (2024). *2025 EU-wide Stress Test – Methodological Note*. (11 November 2024).

European Banking Authority. (2020). *Guidelines on Liquidity Cost Benefit Allocation*. EBA/GL/2020/07.

European Banking Authority. (2016). *Guidelines on the Application of the Definition of Default under Article 178 of Regulation (EU) No 575/2013*. (EBA/GL/2016/07). European Banking Authority. https://www.eba.europa.eu/regulation-and-policy/credit-risk/guidelines-on-the-application-of-the-definition-of-default

European Banking Authority. (2017). *Guidelines on Credit Institutions' Credit Risk Management Practices and Accounting for Expected Credit Losses*. EBA/GL/2017/06. https://www.eba.europa.eu/guidelines-credit-risk-management-practices-and-accounting-expected-credit-losses

European Banking Authority. (2025). *2025 EU-wide Stress Test: Methodological Note*. European Banking Authority.

European Central Bank. (2019). Recent Countercyclical Capital buffer (CCyB) Decisions. *Macroprudential Bulletin 7*.

European Systemic Risk Board. (2018). *The ESRB Handbook on Operationalising Macroprudential Policy in the Banking Sector*. ESRB.

European Systemic Risk Board. (2022). *Review of the EU Macroprudential Framework for the Banking Sector*. Section 3.1. pp. 15–27.

European Central Bank (ECB)/European Banking Authority (EBA). (2025). *Results of the 2025 Stress Tests on the European Banking Sector*. Joint ECB/EBA press release, 1 August 2025.

European Central Bank (ECB). (2020). *Macroprudential Capital Buffers—Objectives and Usability*, Macroprudential Bulletin 10.

European Central Bank (ECB). (2021). *The Role of Financial Stability Considerations in Monetary Policy and the Interaction with Macroprudential Policy in the Euro Area*. Occasional Paper No. 272.

European Central Bank (ECB). (2023). *How is the Pillar 2 Requirement Determined? Explanatory Note from ECB Banking Supervision*. ECB Banking Supervision.

European Central Bank (ECB). (2023). *Aggregate Results of the 2022 SREP*. Press release, 8 February 2023.

European Central Bank. (2021). *Guide to the Internal Liquidity Adequacy Assessment Process (ILAAP)*. ECB Banking Supervision.

European Systemic Risk Board (ESRB). (2016). *Indirect Contagion: The Policy Problem*. (Occasional Paper Series No. 9).

Dahlgren, S., Himino, R., Restoy, F., & Rogers, C. (2023). *Assessment of the European Central Bank's Supervisory Review and Evaluation Process: Report by the Expert Group to the Chair of the Supervisory Board of the ECB*. European Central Bank.

Farmer, J. D., Kleinnijenhuis, A. M., Schuermann, T., & Wetzer, T. (Eds.). (2022). *Handbook of Financial Stress Testing*. Cambridge University Press.

Federal Deposit Insurance Corporation. (2025). *2024 Annual Report*. https://www.fdic.gov/financial-reports/2024-annual-report

Fiedler, R. (2011). *Liquidity Transfer Pricing: A Guide to Better Practice*. Financial Stability Institute (FSI Paper No. 10), Bank for International Settlements.

Financial Stability Board (FSB). (2018). *Early Warning Exercises – Design and Conduct*. FSB Report, Nov 2018.

Freixas, X., Laeven, L., & Peydró, J.-L. (2015). *Systemic risk, crises, and macroprudential regulation*. The MIT Press.

Galán, J. E. (2020). *The Benefits are at the Tail: Uncovering the Impact of Macroprudential Policy on Growth-at-risk*. Bank of Spain Working Paper No. 2007.

Galán, J. E. (2021). *CREWS: A CAMELS-based Early Warning System of Systemic Risk in the Banking Sector*. Occasional Papers No. 2132, Bank of Spain.

Glasserman, P., & Young, H. (2016). Contagion in Financial Networks. *Journal of Economic Literature*, 54(3), 779–831.

Gross, M., Henry, J., & Rancoita, E. (2022). Macrofinancial Stress Test Scenario Design – for Banks and Beyond. In *Handbook of Financial Stress Testing* (Farmer et al., Eds.), pp. 77–97. Cambridge Univ. Press.

Hirtle, B., Schuermann, T., & Stiroh, K. (2009). *Macroprudential Supervision of Financial Institutions: Lessons from the SCAP*. Federal Reserve Bank of New York Staff Report No. 409.

Hull, J. C. (2015). *Risk Management and Financial Institutions (4th ed.)*. John Wiley & Sons.

Ibarrondo, J. M. (2002). *Costs in Financial Institutions*. Madrid: McGraw-Hill Interamericana de España.

Jiménez, G., & Saurina, J. (2006). *Credit Cycles, Credit Risk, and Prudential Regulation*. Bank of Spain Working Paper No. 0531.

Jiménez, G., Ongena, S., Peydró, J.-L., & Saurina, J. (2014). Hazardous Times for Monetary Policy: What do Twenty-three Million Bank Loans Say about the Effects of Monetary Policy on Credit Risk-taking? *Econometrica*, 82(2), 463–505. https://doi.org/10.3982/ECTA10104

Jiménez, G., & Saurina, J. (2006). Credit Cycles, Credit Risk, and Prudential Regulation. *International Journal of Central Banking*, 2(2), 65–98.

Kapadia, S., Drehmann, M., Elliott, J., & Sterne, G. (2012). *Liquidity Risk, Cash-Flow Constraints and Systemic Feedbacks*. Bank of England Working Paper No. 456.

Kaplan, R. S., & Norton, D. P. (2001). *The Strategy-Focused Organisation: How Balanced Scorecard Companies Thrive in the New Business Environment*. Harvard Business School Press.

Keeley, M. C. (1990). Deposit Insurance, Risk, and Market Power in Banking. *The American Economic Review*, 80(5), 1183–1200.

King, B. (2018). *Bank 4.0: Banking Everywhere, Never at a Bank*. Marshall Cavendish.

Klein, M. A. (1972). The Theory of the Banking Firm. *Journal of Money, Credit and Banking*, 3(2), 205–218. https://doi.org/10.2307/1991279

Laeven, L., & Valencia F. (2012). *Systemic Banking Crises Database: An Update*. IMF Working Paper, 12(163), 1–32. https://doi.org/10.5089/9781475505054.001

Laeven, L., & Valencia, F. (2013). Systemic Banking Crises Database. *IMF Economic Review*, 61(2), 225–270. https://doi.org/10.1057/imfer.2013.12

Laeven, L., & Valencia, F. (2018). *Systemic Banking Crises Revisited*. (IMF Working Paper, 18(206). https://doi.org/10.5089/9781484376379.001

Leitner, G., Dvořák, M., Magi, A., & Zsámboki, B. (2023). *How Usable are Capital Buffers?* ECB Occasional Paper 329.

Lo Duca, et.al. (2017). *A New Database for Financial Crises in European Countries: ECB/ESRB EU crises database*. Occasional Paper, (194). https://doi.org/10.2849/119019

Lo Duca, M., & Peltonen, T. A. (2013). Assessing Systemic Risks and Predicting Systemic Events. *Journal of Banking and Finance*, 37(7), 2183–2195. https://doi.org/10.1016/j.jbankfin.2012.06.010

Lubinska, B. (2021). *Interest Rate Risk in the Banking Book: A Best Practice Guide to Management and Hedging*. John Wiley & Sons.

Lubinska, B. (2022). *Asset-Liability Management Optimisation: A Practitioner's Guide to Balance Sheet Management and Remodelling*. John Wiley & Sons.

Matutes, C., & Vives, X. (2000). Imperfect Competition, Risk Taking, and Regulation in Banking. *European Economic Review*, 44(1), 1–34.

Matz, L., & Neu, P. (Eds.). (2012). *Liquidity risk measurement and management: A practitioner's guide to global best practices*. John Wiley & Sons.

Metrick, A., & Schmelzing, P. (2023). *The March 2023 Bank Interventions in Long-Run Context – Silicon Valley Bank and Beyond. Economics*. Working Paper No. 23107. Hoover Institution. https://www.hoover.org/sites/default/files/research/docs/23107-Metrick-Schmelzing.pdf

Monti, M. (1971). A Theoretical Model of Bank Behaviour and Monetary Policy. *L'Industria*, (2), 165–191.

Moorad Choudhry (2014). *Future Bank Strategy: Fewer Choices, Tougher Calls*. Intelligent Risk, PRMIA, Aug 2014.

Omarini, A. (2015). *Retail Banking: Business Transformation and Competitive Strategies for the Future*. Palgrave Macmillan.

Pushkina, N. (2013). *A Simple Funds Transfer Pricing Model for a Commercial Bank*. Master's Thesis. University of the Witwatersrand, February.

Repullo, R., & Suárez, J. (2013). The Procyclical Effects of Bank Capital Regulation. *Review of Financial Studies*, 26(2), 452–490.

Ritchie, C. (2016). *Liquidity Transfer Pricing: A Critique of Current Approaches and a Framework for Improvement*. Macquarie Applied Finance Centre Working Paper, Macquarie University.

Ruetschi, J. (2022). *Transforming Financial Institutions: Value Creation through Technology Innovation and Operational Change*. John Wiley & Sons.

Saunders, A., & Cornett, M. M. (2018). *Financial Institutions Management: A Risk Management Approach (9th ed.)*. McGraw-Hill Education.

Schäfer, K., Sedding, L., & Thomas, T. (2017). Funds Transfer Pricing in Banks: An Analytical and Practical Perspective. *Journal of Risk Management in Financial Institutions*, 10(2), 107–120.

Thurner, S. (2022). A Complex Systems Perspective on Macroprudential Regulation. In *Handbook of Financial Stress Testing*, pp. 593–634.

Vives, X. (2008). Competition and Regulation in Banking. In *Handbook of Financial Intermediation and Banking* (pp. 449–482). Elsevier.

Vives, X. (2016). *Competition and Stability in Banking: The Role of Regulation and Competition Policy*. Princeton University Press.

Wilson, T. (2015). *Value and Capital Management. A Handbook for the Finance and Risk Functions of Financial Institutions*. Wiley.

List of figures

 | https://doi.org/10.1515/9783111328386-012

List of tables

 | https://doi.org/10.1515/9783111328386-013

List of abbreviations

ALCO	Asset and Liability Committee
ALM	Asset and Liability Management
BBB	Credit rating category “BBB”
BCBS	Basel Committee on Banking Supervision
BMA	Business Model Analysis
CCB	Capital Conservation Buffer
CCyB	Countercyclical Capital Buffer
CDS	Credit Default Swap(s)
CET1	Common Equity Tier 1
CRD	Capital Requirements Directive
CS01	Sensitivity of the value to a 1 bp change in the credit spread
CS02	Value sensitivity to a 2 bp change in the credit spread
CSRBB	Credit Spread Risk in the Banking Book
DSR	Debt Service Ratio
DSTI	Debt Service to Income
DTI	Debt to Income
DV01	Dollar Value of 1 Basis Point
EAD	Exposure at Default
EBA	European Banking Authority
ECB	European Central Bank
ECL	Expected Credit Loss
EVE	Economic Value of Equity
EL	Expected Loss
ESG	Environmental, Social and Governance
ESRB	European Systemic Risk Board
EU	European Union
EVA	Economic Value Added
EVaR	Economic Value at Risk
FDIC	Federal Deposit Insurance Corporation
FSB	Financial Stability Board
FTP	Funds Transfer Pricing
FVOCI	Fair Value Through Other Comprehensive Income
FVTPL	Fair Value Through Profit or Loss
G-20	Group of Twenty
G-SIB	Global Systemically Important Bank
GDP	Gross Domestic Product
HQLA	High-Quality Liquid Assets
IAS 39	International Accounting Standard 39
ICAAP	Internal Capital Adequacy Assessment Process
ICT	Information and Communication Technology
IFRS	International Financial Reporting Standards
ILAAP	Internal Liquidity Adequacy Assessment Process
IMF	International Monetary Fund
IPO	Initial Public Offering
IRB	Internal Ratings-Based approach
IRRBB	Interest Rate Risk in the Banking Book
IRS	Interest Rate Swap(s)

 | https://doi.org/10.1515/9783111328386-014

KPI	Key Performance Indicator
LCR	Liquidity Coverage Ratio
LGD	Loss Given Default
LFT	Lifetime
LRE	Leverage Ratio Exposure
LTV	Loan to Value
M&A	Mergers and Acquisitions
MDA	Maximum Distributable Amount
MREL	Minimum Requirement for own funds and Eligible Liabilities
NFCI	Net Fee and Commission Income
NII	Net Interest Income
NIM	Net Interest Margin
NMD	Non-Maturity Deposits
NPL	Non-Performing Loan(s)
NSFR	Net Stable Funding Ratio
OCI	Other Comprehensive Income
P&L	Profit and Loss
P2G	Pillar 2 Guidance
P2R	Pillar 2 Requirement
PD	Probability of Default
PIT	Point in Time
PGa	Annual Pricing Gap
PGt – 1st	Total Pricing Gap – 1st line
PGt – 2nd	Total Pricing Gap – 2nd line
PV01	Price Value of a basis point
ROA	Return on Assets
RORAC	Return on Adjusted Capital
ROE	Return on Equity
RW / RWA	Risk Weight / Risk-Weighted Assets
SME	Small and Medium-Sized Enterprise
SPPI	Solely Payments of Principal and Interest
SREP	Supervisory Review and Evaluation Process
SSM	Single Supervisory Mechanism
TLAC	Total Loss-Absorbing Capacity
TREA	Total Risk Exposure Amount
TSCR	Total SREP Capital Requirement
UL	Unexpected Loss
VaR	Value at Risk

About the author

Antonio Mota Pizarro is the CFO of a Spanish financial institution within the Caja Rural Group, responsible for Asset and Liability Management, Financial Planning and Treasury. Prior to this he worked in credit risk modelling and analysis at various Spanish financial institutions. He holds a degree in Business Administration from the University of Extremadura, and obtained his PhD in Economics from the Autonomous University of Madrid, for which he was awarded the Extraordinary Doctorate Prize. He is an adjunct lecturer at the Comillas Pontifical University, where he teaches the Banking module on the Master's programme in Financial Risk Management.

 | https://doi.org/10.1515/9783111328386-015

About the series editor

Moorad Choudhry is a non-executive director and Chair of the Board Risk Committee at SBUK Ltd, in London, and Professor at Birzeit University, Palestinian Authority. He was latterly Treasurer, Corporate Banking Division at The Royal Bank of Scotland, having begun his City career at the London Stock Exchange in 1989.

He is a Fellow of the Chartered Institute for Securities & Investment, a Fellow of the London Institute of Banking and Finance, a Fellow of the Global Association of Risk Professionals, a Fellow of the Institute of Directors and a Freeman of The Worshipful Company of International Bankers. He is author of *The Principles of Banking* (John Wiley & Sons 2012, 2022).

Moorad was educated at Claremont Fan Court school, University of Westminster and University of Reading. He obtained his MBA from Henley Business School and his PhD from Birkbeck, University of London. He was born in Bangladesh and lives in Surrey, England.

 | https://doi.org/10.1515/9783111328386-016

Index

 | https://doi.org/10.1515/9783111328386-017

The moorad choudhry global banking series

Principles of Green Banking: Managing Environmental Risk and Sustainability
by Suborna Barua

Reverse Stress Testing in Banking: A Comprehensive Guide
by Michael Eichhorn, Tiziano Bellini, and Daniel Mayenberger (eds.)

Bank Asset Liability Management Best Practice: Yesterday, Today and Tomorrow
by Polina Bardaeva

Random Walks in Fixed Income and Foreign Exchange: Unexpected Discoveries in Issuance, Investment and Hedging of Yield Curve Instruments
by Jessica James, Michael Leister, and Christoph Rieger

Banking Associations: Their Role and Impact in a Time of Market Change,
by Sladjana Sredojevic and Milan Brkovic

Inflation-Linked Bonds and Derivatives: Investing, Hedging and Valuation Principles for Practitioners
by Jessica James, Michael Leister, and Christoph Rieger

Banking in the Age of the Platform Economy: Digital Acceleration Through Strategies of Interdependence
by Giorgio Bou-Daher

ALM Modeling and Balance Sheet Optimization: A Mathematical Approach to Banking
by Diogo Gobira and Lucas Processi

Climate Change Risk Management in Banks: The Next Paradigm
by Saloni P. Ramakrishna

How to Build a Bank: A Guide to Key Bank Regulations, the License Application Process and Bank Risk Management
by Ravi Takhar

Bank Treasury Management: A Practitioner's Guide to Hedging and Funding Strategy
by Beata Lubinska

Strategic Management of Profitability in Banking from Antonio Asset-Liability View
by Antonio Mota Pizarro

www.ingramcontent.com/pod-product-compliance
Lightning Source LLC
LaVergne TN
LVHW081957220926
848675LV00006B/28